STEP ASIDE & RISE

21 INSPIRATIONAL STORIES OF FEMALE BUSINESS OWNERS WHO GOT OUT OF THEIR OWN WAY AND STOPPED PLAYING SMALL IN THEIR LIVES AND BUSINESS

ANDREA CALLANAN

authors
AND CO.

Adult content and trigger warning:

These women have courageously written elements of their life experiences in the pages of this book and there may be some content that some readers may find sensitive, challenging or difficult to read. Including sexual abuse, substance abuse, challenging poor mental health and bullying.

If appropriate, please reach out to any of the women if you need support with any of the subjects they write about.

There is also occasional, infrequent explicit language.

Disclaimer:

In parts throughout this book, the authors may describe events, locales and conversations from their memories. Sometimes, in order to maintain their anonymity in some instances we have changed the names of individuals and places, we may have changed some identifying characteristics and details such as physical properties, occupations and places of residence.

Although the coauthors and publisher have made every effort to ensure that the information in this book was correct at press time, the coauthors and publisher do not assume and hereby disclaim any liability to any party for any loss, damage, or disruption caused by errors or omissions, whether such errors or omissions result from negligence, accident, or any other cause.

Copyright © 2021 by Andrea Callanan

ISBN13: 9798770035049

All rights reserved.

No part of this book may be reproduced in any form or by any electronic or mechanical means, including information storage and retrieval systems, without written permission from the author, except for the use of brief quotations in a book review.

EMPOWERING WOMEN AND GIRLS TO RISE

WONDER FOUNDATION

All proceeds from the sale of this book are being donated to

Wonder Foundation

CONTENTS

Foreword	vii
1. Anabel Morte Rodenas	1
About the Author	16
2. Beck Harrison	18
About the Author	35
3. Camilla Jakobson	37
About the Author	49
4. Ceri Gillett	51
About the Author	64
5. Claire Antill	66
About the Author	79
6. Claire White	81
About the Author	97
7. Franca Cumbo	99
About the Author	114
8. Hannah McKimm	116
About the Author	131
9. Hannah Pekary	133
About the Author	149
10. Jackie Van Baren	151
About the Author	164
11. Jane Mack	166
About the Author	180
12. Karen Marie Nicholson	182
About the Author	198
13. Katharine Gillam	200
About the Author	211
14. Kerry Jones	213
About the Author	228
15. Keryn Potts	230
About the Author	246
16. Lucy Ciaramella	248

	About the Author	263
17.	Mel Wakely	265
	About the Author	283
18.	Rachel Harvey	286
	About the Author	301
19.	Rose Brown	303
	About the Author	315
20.	Samantha Patel	317
	About the Author	332
21.	Sarah Winterflood	334
	About the Author	349
22.	Afterword	351
	About the Curator	355

FOREWORD
ANDREA CALLANAN

If you're reading this, you may be on the cusp of rising even if you don't know it yet!

If you know you're meant for more, and you can almost feel it, yet you know you're holding yourself back, this book is going to be an utter treat for you.

I've helped thousands of women step into their aligned success, and I'm convinced that we see, hear, read and experience things at precisely the point in time when we need to.

Maybe you need to read this. Perhaps it's *your* time.

Part of a coach's role is to identify the gaps. If you're not where you want to be in your life and business yet, maybe you're stuck. And here's the thing, even a tiny bit stuck is still stuck – it's like being a tiny bit pregnant! You either are, or you aren't!

So, let's explore this. As a positive psychology, mindset, business and voice coach, I introduce the concept of joy, alignment and fulfilment to women when we work together. We look at how you want to 'feel' in your day to day as much as how much money you want to earn or what business model you want to implement.

My question for you is this. Do you need to get out of your own way?

Maybe you're a familiar resident in the "trying" space. Striving for more of what you want and need. Always talking about what you want to do but never really getting there?

Maybe you're doing all the things to try and make you feel valued, accomplished and significant, both personally and professionally.

Maybe you're dodging responsibility in your business, behaving like an employee instead of a CEO, refusing to take ownership and believing the excuses you make for not progressing as truth.

How's that working out for you?

Maybe you remember a time when you were thriving? Where you remember being independent, having your own spending power, feeling confident.

Maybe life events mean you've needed to adapt and change who you are.

And maybe you're still negotiating who you are these days.

Maybe you're wondering where your adventurous, carefree spirit has gone? Perhaps you've lost your mojo and need to find it again.

I help women who are insecure and in fear, who have imposter syndrome, compare themselves to others and hold themselves back. Who might have lost themselves. They often feel guilt, shame and conflict around having a family and a business.

The overwhelm and anxiety of always hustling has taken its toll, and you might even be questioning if having your own business is right for you after all.

The women in this book have been there. Or at least, somewhere near there.

I've helped tens of thousands of people over the last few decades find their voice, purpose and confidence. I've also helped thousands of women start and grow their businesses.

And the reason I do this? There was a time not so long ago when I was broken both financially and emotionally. Waking up one day as a suicidal, self-employed single parent with a small son and a tonne of debt left me no other option but to find my voice, heal and rise. There was simply no other way to go other than up!

My personal development journey changed the course of my life and fortune. Discovering my self-worth, self-belief and courage led to me getting out of my own way so I could step into my success.

This work transformed my life and business, and I've made it my mission to pass this forward.

By empowering women to step forward into their meaning, identity and choice unapologetically, we create a legacy.

A legacy of choice. The highest form of freedom.

By helping women find their voice, they become visible. They take brave bold action that causes great ripples, and the best thing? Women do this in community. Even those lone wolves among us, we are compelled to serve, to make the best of what we have.

And then we rise.

I support women to create their own economy and step into more. As a speaker, best-selling author and entrepreneur, I am driven by helping other women access their own power, rediscover their identity, find their voice, and access more choice in their lives and businesses.

Within the pages of this book, you'll hear 21 extraordinary stories of everyday women who I've worked with over the last few years. They were all lost in their lives and stuck in their businesses in some way. And now they are triumphs. Every. Single one of them

These women courageously put pen to paper to share their experiences so they could inspire and motivate other women just like you. They bravely write about their transformations. Their business growth, their challenges, failures and learnings. They write about accepting themselves and how they've embraced their next levels.

We decided to write this book to show other female business owners, just like you, that it's genuinely possible to make lasting positive change with aligned support, transformed beliefs and strategic action-taking.

It all starts with you. If they can do it, you can too. It's all available to you. So, get excited and dive in. It's time to take that step. And as you turn the pages, remember that these amazing women are just like you.

Your transformation is waiting. It starts as you turn these pages.

As you immerse yourself into this anthology of real women finding their success, notice what's available for you and be inspired to choose higher.

Remember, your future-self five years from now needs you to take the right choices today.

Make those aligned changes in YOUR life and business, and acknowledge that today is YOUR time to Step Aside & Rise.

1

ANABEL MORTE RODENAS
PERFECTLY ALIGNED DOTS

If you had told me a while back that I'd be doing this, I would have said you'd lost your mind - not because I haven't written anything, but because I never really thought there was anything inspirational from my life... But after a great self-awareness and self-discovery journey, here I am, proudly writing my chapter, knowing I'm in the path I have chosen and hoping you'll find something here, even if it's just a tiny word, which will ignite and challenge your thoughts and self-talk.

I'm a high achiever. I have lots of personal and academic achievements including a degree in Geology, a PhD in Chemistry, and more recently, a coaching accreditation. However, I'd say my biggest achievement has been becoming a mum of two little boys. How precious they are and how they've rocked my boat! Motherhood has given, and it's still giving me, lots of wisdom and self-awareness. It has been the catalyst to rediscover my ultimate purpose, which is empowering women and supporting them to live their best life.

Throughout history, and even our own stories, we may have been told to play it small, to be modest, to keep quiet, that we are less than, that we have to be like this, look like that, be less emotional, that dreams are only dreams, etc. And even though most of the time these comments come with the best intentions, only when women realise their worth, stand in their power and follow their dreams, will the world be a fairer and better place for everybody to live.

Although labelled as a "troublemaker" at school from my early years, I was always quite a good student, so, after I graduated as a Geologist in Spain, I moved to the UK to do my PhD in Crystallography, which is the science that studies how the atoms are arranged in the matter. Afterwards, I went on and got myself an excellent position as a specialist lab manager for scientific research at a leading university. On paper, although not the usual academic career, it was a success. It was a great career progression, especially for a foreign woman... I had great colleagues, was enjoying my job, working reasonable hours, good pay, weekends free... what was not to love about it?

As a child, I don't remember knowing what I wanted to be when I grew up; did I even want to go to uni? Not even sure about that, but as I was a "good" student, that's what I was advised to do. My first choice for a degree was Psychology, so how did I end up doing Geology and being reasonably happy about it? I followed my boyfriend at the time. His first choice was Geology, and I thought it sounded cool and with lots of career options, so I went with it. Did I even know what a PhD was? Not really, but a Professor in Spain got me recommended to a Professor in the UK to do a PhD. It was too good to reject; after all, one thing is for sure, I love learning and growth and a lot of those two things came in the following years. In the last days of my PhD, trying to make some money while I finished writing my thesis, one of my friends encouraged me to apply for a part-time lab assistant role in another department, so I went for it and got the job! After a few months, they told me about a position that had just become available and I was encouraged to apply and got it! Great!! And then two more promotions! Excellent!!

I was proud of myself for all the achievements. None of those were things that I had actively chosen, but I went with all my soul for each of them. I had made the most of the opportunities that had been presented to me and adapted myself to fit in and enjoy them - it wouldn't have been nice to seem unappreciative. Looking back, I'm ever so grateful for all the people and situations I've come across; they've shaped me into the woman that I am today, proud of her journey and unapologetic about her purpose.

But what was it that I really wanted? What was it that I would find fulfilment in? It would take motherhood, adversity and outside support to push me to find out about it, or better said, to allow myself to pursue my real desires. I got to jump in the driving seat, rather than just enjoying other people's driving of my bus.

Even though it looked like I had achieved a lot, I always felt out of my depth, never felt like I knew enough, feeling like at any point they would find out how inept I was and everyone would remember me for that. It would be a shame not only for myself, but also for my family and all the people that hired me. This meant that I would continuously go the extra mile to prove my worth, to show that this "Spanish lady" deserved the position. This sounds a lot like what's called Imposter Syndrome (IS); feelings of being inadequate that continue despite evident success. This phenomenon was first defined by Psychologists Pauline Rose Clance and Suzanne Imes in 1978 as "imposter phenomenon". If you are curious about this subject, I recommend you read the original publication here.

For those of you that are not too familiar with Higher Education, academia is a hierarchical environment and tends to be male-dominated, especially in STEMM (Science, Technology, Engineering, Mathematics & Medicine). During my time in Higher Education, I was very involved in ways to promote gender equality, including being the chair of a networking group for STEMM female academics, and being part of institutional gender equality programs, hence Imposter Syndrome was very much in the discussions. So, it seems paradoxical that despite knowing exactly what Imposter Syndrome was, I still couldn't identify with it. In my view that was for the "real" academic women, and I was only a "technician".

I've always been quite outspoken and determined to reach higher. Now, I see that as a good thing, but throughout life, I've felt that I've had to reduce my volume, dim my light and lower my energy to fit in situations because I would be seen as too direct, or too ambitious, too difficult, too much. These kinds of comments, repeated over time, ended up affecting my self-belief and my confidence. That's why I honestly believe that the way to tackle gender inequality is through empowering women so they are fully confident in who they really are, have the courage to shine their true selves and have their voices heard.

Anyway, as I'm quite tenacious, I went for promotions despite the comments and got two - the second one just a few months before I went on my first maternity leave. I should have celebrated and been happy, right? Yes, I was, but it put pressure on me. Now that I had the promotion, I was going to go away and not be able to deliver... I couldn't help wonder what would everyone think of me?

After my first maternity leave, I went back to work and it was ok - well, as ok as it can be with baby brain and not much sleep, but I couldn't go the extra mile anymore because I had a little one to take care of... so my self-doubt started creeping up even more, and soon after, I went on maternity leave, again. I felt guilty for taking another maternity leave after only being back at work for a few months. I was going to be "off" again. What was meant to be a joyful and wonderful experience at a personal level felt heavy on my career.

On the outside, everything was good, and I felt grateful for having such a good position in an institution with excellent maternity policies. But inside, I was exhausted. I was tired of feeling I had to pretend. I was tired of not being able to fully enjoy and celebrate my progress and achievements. I was tired of feeling guilty when I was meant to be rejoicing the news of becoming a mum. I was tired of everything.

Why did it have to be so difficult for me? Why couldn't I be fully happy at my job like other people seemed to be? Why couldn't I be fully happy about my family life? Why couldn't I have it all? After my second little one was born, life got a bit complicated and I never went back to the job.

There I was, in a new house, in a new town, with a new baby and a 16-month-old, without family around and lots - and I mean lots - of boxes to unpack... Well, I have to admit that as blessed as I felt, life wasn't much fun then. Managing to have a shower was the win for the day and getting out of the house felt like a major victory.

It was quite a dark period of my life, probably the darkest. I thought being a mum was going to be easier, that connections would come naturally, but suddenly, it felt like I didn't exist anymore, that I didn't have needs. I have found motherhood extremely isolating. And I have to say here that I'm fortunate to have full support of my family and friends and I feel very grateful for it. But even though I knew I had all that support, I wasn't allowing myself to ask for help and at times, I felt very lonely.

Everything felt very hard. Sleep deprivation broke me, hormones all over the place, I wasn't the best person to be around of and on top of that, I had the big question of what was I going to do with my job? Now, you know what happened, but back then, the thought went back and forth in my mind for a very long time. But eventually, I took a decision, without a backup and it felt very scaryyyyy!

I wasn't well. I had feelings of resentment, that things were not fair, that I was giving up so much, that it was easier for men, that I was stuck... Have you ever felt like that? I was a Victim. I felt powerless.

You may have heard about the Karpman Drama Triangle, or the Drama Triangle. There's a lot about it and you can read lots on the net, so I won't go into much detail here. Basically, it's a model that describes dysfunctional interactions and involves three roles; Rescuer, Prosecutor, and Victim. As the Victim, you are not ready to take responsibility for what's not working, you tend to blame others and the circumstances, and you feel like there's nothing you can do to change things.

It's fair to say that at that moment, I wasn't aware of this dynamic, but something intelligent that I did, and that I'm so proud of, was reaching out for support. I was tired of not knowing what I wanted to be when I grew older... and by then I was... less young, let's say. I was determined to resolve that, so the following job would be the "right one". I invested in support for myself. I had a coach, first for a few months and then, I started working with the fantastic Andrea Callanan. Andrea helped me recognise that this was happening and guided me on ways to get out of the dreaded triangle.

How do you get out of Victim? You become a Creator. You realise you have choice, you get creative, you tune into your passions, your dreams and desires and think of small steps you can take to get there. You feel inspired, energised, resilient, and hopeful!

And I became a creator. I realised I couldn't go on like that, I was only a victim of my lack of self-worth, low self-belief and no boundaries. I had to stop allowing others to take the reins and later blame them for it. I had to take responsibility for my life. I had the choice to do something about what I wasn't happy about or to keep complaining forever after and feel that bitterness that stains all the good moments. I chose to take action and the rest is history!

There's a line in the poem "Invictus" by William Ernest Henley that describes very well how I felt from that point: "I am the master of my fate: I am the captain of my soul". A new chapter began, a chapter where I was in the driving seat.

And to be fair, it wasn't like this new chapter started on D-day. It didn't happen on a particular day, it was the accumulation of little wins; the showers, the naps, unpacking the boxes, having childcare, going for walks, taking more care of myself, learning more about myself.

I discovered what was giving me joy, what was making me happy, what fulfilment meant for me, what skills I had, and what my strengths and my desires were. And I joined all the dots, perfectly aligned dots, even those that at the time didn't seem to be in the right place, and something magical came out of it. I had found my purpose, marvellously aligned with my values and my whys, one that was "ticking all the boxes".

I wanted to help women. I wanted to tell them that they are precious, that there's nothing wrong about who they are and that they deserve everything they desire. I wanted to support women to live their best life. And that, my friend, is how I got to this moment!

Wherever you are in your journey right now, please trust that you are where you are meant to be. Everything happens at the right time. There are lessons to be learnt from everything that we go through, from the good and the not so good, and if I hadn't gone through what I have, in the order that I have, I wouldn't be here right now writing this chapter, so TRUST.

Being honest (and I don't do it any other way), at some points throughout my journey I've felt lost, directionless, unhappy, overwhelmed, confused, exhausted physically and emotionally, that I didn't matter and that I didn't know who I was any more...

And I'm ever so grateful about it because I now can help other women, who feel similarly, transform their lives too!

I help these women thrive in their lives and businesses with clarity, choice and confidence. And I do it from a place of full understanding; in a safe, supportive and fun space, to encourage and motivate them to have the life they desire and that I surely believe they can have!

There are seven main areas we work on during the sessions with my clients, they are the ones I have found most transformational in my journey. I would like to share them with you in this chapter, to spark thinking and see what comes up for you.

It's quite an exhaustive list and by no means feel you need to be a master in all of them or all the time, just be curious and explore. There are lots of tools and tips that you can use, or not use, as you see fit. I think the key is to adapt them to yourself and your lifestyle and take what works for YOU, whatever serves you and makes you feel good, and do those as consistently as you can.

And please don't beat yourself up if you don't do them consistently! I have found willpower and discipline don't sit too well with me (I tend to rebel), what works for me is reflecting on my thoughts, feelings and behaviours and how they are different when I follow those practices as opposed to when I don't.

Sooo, let's get down to business:

YOU come first!!

You may have heard this phrase before "You can't pour from an empty cup", it may sound cliché but it's true. Think of a car for a moment. You wouldn't expect a car to take you to places without filling the tank, or charging the battery if it's electric, right?

Nothing else will work if we don't top ourselves up first. Many of us know that very well, but why is it then, that it is what tends to drop first? It's very common to feel guilty, selfish or unproductive... Acknowledge and explore those feelings, but keep your self-care going. The feelings will quiet down the more you practise putting yourself first.

Self-care is about your physical, emotional and spiritual well-being. Tune into your body, listen to what it may be asking you for: rest, sleep, relaxation, walk, fresh air? Be kind, patient and gentle with yourself. Consciously schedule "YOU" time - think of it as a doctor's appointment or an important meeting, after all, what meeting is more important than one with yourself?

The most magical thing you can do, not only for yourself but also for others, is to prioritise your self-care. Only then you can show up as your best self!

Be in the NOW

Be in the present moment, find ways to tune into yourself. You may find this hard because it's not always a comfortable feeling when everything stops and it's just you... you may feel restless, like you want to start doing all the things, but it's very important that we are patient with ourselves, take this time and learn to be in our own company and what's more, enjoy our company! Or maybe you are with your family, friends or other people but you're not really there...

Breathe, meditate, practise spirituality, be grateful, show appreciation, give thanks, dance, sing, do a brain dump or journal to quiet your mind, focus on one thing at a time or do other things that you enjoy. What do you think will make you connect with yourself?

Know your WHY

What's your purpose, your calling? What are your dreams? What's the most important thing for you?

Sometimes, to move forward we first need to pause and look around to choose the right direction. Take some time to grow your self-awareness and to dig deep into your desires and the reasons behind them. This, for me, was the hardest bit because I had just been going with the flow and never really allowed myself to dream bigger at other levels.

Knowing your why will help you when you're feeling stuck and procrastination and perfectionism are knocking on your door.

Plan, Plan, Plan

Have you heard of Benjamin Franklin's quote "If you fail to plan, you are planning to fail"? I encourage you to plan, but plan in a way that allows you to achieve your dreams!

Think about how you'd like your day or week to look and plan backwards. Plan time for yourself first, and then fill the gaps with other important activities. Make sure it's balanced and follows what's most important for you.

When thinking about all the things that "need" doing, keep in mind the 4Ds: Drop, Delegate, Delay and Do it Smarter.

Drop: What tasks can you stop doing? What would happen if a particular task doesn't get done? First time I asked myself this question, my mind blew, suddenly that task wasn't as critical or urgent as I had thought...

Delegate: Can you ask someone else to do it for you? Delegating is a fine art, you can learn so much about yourself if you lean fully into it! Clear communication and trust are key.

Delay: Can you do it another time? If you delay a task, make sure you arrange a particular time to do it. If something keeps getting rearranged, ask yourself why that may be, does it belong to the drop category instead?

Do it Smarter: What systems can you come up with that will allow you do to do something more effectively and efficiently?

There are a few tools that you may want to test to see if they make planning easier: planners, calendars, reminders, break tasks down, find systems, create routines, batch tasks, time block (assign chunks of time for specific tasks), stack habits...

Having a road map for your week will give you peace of mind and will improve your productivity! Focus on one thing at a time - multitasking is not productive... And keep your planning realistic, specific but flexible so it doesn't become something you end up using to beat yourself up!

Make the most of YOU

Get to know, accept and love yourself! And leverage it!!

So much can improve when you tune into yourself and learn when your energy levels are the highest, when you focus better, whether you are an early bird or a night owl, how hormonal cycles affect you, when you show up your best, whether deadlines motivate you or make you anxious, how long things take you - not your friend, not someone else, YOU!

There will be moments when you'll feel overwhelmed with your emotions and that's completely ok, but it may mean that we don't show up as our best selves. In these moments, being able to change your state of mind is a game-changer!! Get present, breathe, meditate, move, walk, dance, listen to music, do something you enjoy... What are the things that will get you into the right state?

Let GO!

Do less! I know... how can you do less if you're still not doing everything you've set yourself up to do?? Letting go! Let go of control, learn to trust others and delegate or outsource tasks, set boundaries and communicate them effectively. Find systems that will allow things to happen without your direct input.

Let go of everything that doesn't serve you! Declutter items, thoughts, limiting beliefs, toxic relationships, expectations...

Letting go has a huge impact on our mental load, suddenly there's room to think! What can you let go of?

Find your VILLAGE

And finally, but not for that less important: find your village! This was, and still is, a tipping point for me. Having a support network is a must, and for me, it's another way to fill my cup. Belonging to a community, getting help, guidance, advice, and knowing that I can also offer the same to others, is so nourishing. Who is in your village? Think creatively: family, friends, success sisters, your team, someone else's team, neighbours, favourite barista, trust me, they all have a role in your village!

If you think of me as a coach, putting all the above into practice, you may think my life is perfect. Well, let me tell you, it is far from it! But what is perfection anyway? I'm a work in progress, as we all are. Louise Hay says "The work I do on myself is not a goal, it is a process – a lifetime process and I choose to enjoy the process."

I am committed to growth, to be my best self every day. I am committed to not giving up on my dreams, however tough life gets. I am committed to serving through my purpose.

I can't put into words how grateful I am that I get to work with amazing women. I learn so much from each of them. I get to share space, celebrations and encouragement with my "success" sisters. I get to touch people's lives. I get to live life on my terms; paraphrasing the loved Frank Sinatra: I do it, I do it My Way!!

And I'm no more special than you are!

You have the power, the power to choose!! You may not be fully happy with your life, and that's ok, but you can choose to complain about it and change nothing or to take action, a little step, one aligned with your vision.

You don't have to wait for anyone to change, or to get a new job, or for the kids to go to school or whatever "excuses" you're giving yourself, you can take action today. In fact, you've already taken that action because you're reading this book, so what's your next step?

"If you can't fly then run, if you can't run then walk, if you can't walk then crawl, but whatever you do, you have to keep moving forward." Martin Luther King Jr.

The best measure of success for me, is the feeling of internal peace, of knowing that I'm on the right path, of trusting that whatever life has for me, it's all part of the journey and that I'll embrace it and learn from it. The feeling that I'm aligned with my values, the feeling that I'm finally in the square hole!

It's knowing that I offer possibility to my clients, I help them live their best life!

To support this big statement, I'd like to share with you the case of two of my clients. The first one was feeling like she couldn't keep on top of things; she was working long hours and at home, things were out of control. She'd had a challenging time coming out of lockdown and grieving as her dad had passed away. She felt the relationships with her husband and kids were very tense and that she was carrying all the weight on her shoulders.

We worked for a few weeks through her challenges and blocks and the transformation was impressive. Not only did she get back on track and got everyone else on board, but also found the confidence to start applying for promotions, looking at other jobs and allowing herself to dream bigger!

> *"I feel more in control of everything. I look at potential issues and have the tools to work through what needs to be done. I am more confident and feel happier in myself and know that I can tackle anything if I plan my course of action and stick to it."*

> "I have found it really easy to open up about how things made me feel and how I have been able to acknowledge my achievements, I'm usually very uncomfortable acknowledging my achievements and abilities and general keep my feelings closely guarded. Your coaching is caring, supportive and gentle."
>
> "The benefits from talking through the issues is immense. The way you guide people, asking questions that probe but are not intrusive, getting people to think differently. The discussions are great, as you really do work together to come up with a plan that is manageable and most importantly, achievable. It's great having someone to talk and guide you, unpicking blockages along the way."

Another of my clients wanted to get on top of various areas of her life. She felt like she was constantly on catch up and never in control of where she was in her home and work life. She was very overwhelmed, especially with the mental load of being a working mother. After working for a few weeks on her mindset and strategies to be more organised she said this:

> "I feel so much more in control and calmer. I also am aware of patterns of getting into overwhelm and how to see the signs. Generally, I am more relaxed and have a sense of moving forward."
>
> "Anyone who feels like they're overwhelmed and has too much on their plate should work with you. You have a great understanding of what a working mother is dealing with. You give me great insight into my patterns and any self-sabotaging behaviour, which means I can start to address behaviour that's not helping me and change it for the better. You are also amazingly good at telling me how to be more organised without being at all judgemental or patronising. Your tips and knowledge are so, so useful. Your coaching has impacted both my home and working life in a fantastic way. I now get so much more done and feel calmer and less stressed. I was at the point where I felt like I couldn't cope but now I feel like I'm winning!"

Maybe all this or some of it has spoken to you. I'd like to encourage you to challenge your thoughts. I'd like to remind you that you have choice. I dare you to become more self-aware, and practise self-compassion, self-care and gratitude regularly.

I'd like you to know and believe that you are perfect as you are, that as my wonderful coach, Andrea Callanan says: You Are a Pearl! That you're becoming wiser, more beautiful and more precious the more life throws at you, that the world needs YOU.

I'd like to ask you to dream. I'm going to ask you to allow those dreams to wake up, to fly, to come alive. Tell me, what can you hear? How does it smell like? What are you feeling? What does your desired life look like? And what can you do today, however small may seem, that will get you closer to that dream life?

Now write that vision down, or draw it, and every time you feel a bit down or a bit off, or you're having one of those days (because it's completely normal to have those days), reach out for it and refill yourself with excitement and belief!

And very importantly, as I mentioned earlier, reach out for support. You're not alone; find your village, surround yourself with like-minded people, find the people that will build you up, that will nurture you, that will celebrate you and that will inspire you!

I'd like to thank you deeply for your time. I would really love to know how you've found this chapter helpful and what has been your biggest takeaway? Please get in touch, I'd love to connect with you!!

You can reach me at:

Email - hello@anabelmorterodenas.com

Facebook - /anabelmorterodenas

Instagram - @anabelmorterodenas

Linkedin - anabelmorterodenas

ABOUT THE AUTHOR
ANABEL MORTE RODENAS

Anabel is The Easier Life Coach, a mindset coach who helps professional women and female entrepreneurs find clarity, choice and confidence so they can thrive in their lives and businesses.

Before starting her coaching business, Anabel was awarded a PhD in Chemistry and worked for over 10 years at Cardiff University as a manager in a cutting-edge scientific research laboratory. After a successful career as a scientist and an advocate for gender equality in STEMM (Science, Technology, Engineering, Mathematics and Medicine), Anabel became a mum to two little boys.

Determined to bring together her passions, experience and knowledge, Anabel gained a coaching accreditation and now coaches and empowers women to live their best life, helping them boost their self-worth, take ownership and lean into joy.

Anabel is a graduate coach of the fully accredited Aligned Coaching Academy and a Member of the Institute of Leadership and Management (ACA MInstLM), she is also a certified Story Work Coach with Andrea Callanan (ACSWC).

Anabel enjoys spending time in nature and with her family and friends, especially if there's music and dancing on the menu.

Anabel is available for 121 coaching, group coaching, workshops and speaking events.

You can reach Anabel at:

Email - hello@anabelmorterodenas.com
Website www.anabelmorterodenas.com

facebook.com/anabelmorterodenas
instagram.com/anabelmorterodenas
linkedin.com/in/anabelmorterodenas

2

BECK HARRISON

STAND ON YOUR STORY AND RISE

I have a story to tell. One of grit, courage, resilience, trust, compassion, forgiveness and triumph.

I have learnt how to stand ON my story, rather than being stuck IN it. I am now the victor, not the victim. Going back through my life story I now recognise that I get to choose how I feel about the things that happened. I recognise when things happened through no fault of my own, or when they were down to the choices I made. I celebrate those times when I was brave, when I chose courage over comfort, when I came back fighting and I've learned how to no longer feel the shame, the blame and the judgement.

> *"Owning our story and loving ourselves through that process is the bravest thing that we will ever do."*
>
> — BRENÉ BROWN.

There are usually two parts to our stories; the ones we tell the world and the ones we tell ourselves. Self-awareness is key. The fun comes with recognising I'm a work in progress, working at bringing all the parts of me back together to be a whole me, a version of me who stands in her honesty and integrity.

I am a Positive Psychology and Resilience Coach and it's been one hell of a journey to get here, one that I am now so incredibly proud of.

I help women to build their resilience by exploring where they are experiencing a fixed mindset, and supporting them to develop a growth one, to enable them to reframe their story and discover their self-worth.

Perception is everything when it comes to one's story. My narrative these days is dramatically different. I'm on a mission to help other women just like me to change their perception, and to stop letting who they thought they were define who they are going to be.

When I was 27, I moved to Australia, leaving behind a catalogue of catastrophic fuck-ups. That's when I developed my own understanding of the phrase *'No matter where you go, there you are'*. I was running away... with bells on!

Becoming the queen of reinvention throughout my life had served me well so far. I'd never had a 'proper job'. I'd arrived on the other side of the world where no one knew me, and blagging was one of the things I did best! I had contacts in the music industry back in the UK, so that helped me to get 'creative' with my CV and I landed my first job in the music biz, working for a concert promoter (first gig the Ricky Martin's Livin' La Vida Loca Tour!)

Next, I got a job at a Foxtel music TV channel. This was one of the best periods of my life. I met so many amazing people. I felt truly accepted, being surrounded by young, fun, talented, creative people, living and working in a holiday destination. It was like a celebrity lifestyle without the troublesome fame part; getting tickets to any gigs and festivals I wanted, travelling around the country, meeting all the musicians I admired... and this was work!?

I never felt like I truly deserved any of it, the incredible lifestyle. I didn't deserve the amazing people in my life that I called friends and the feeling of something being missing was always there, lurking in the background. The imposter syndrome was real and as a result, I never dared to truly be me, as the true me wasn't anywhere good enough to deserve this life.

So, in full self-sabotage fashion, I gave up my wonderful life and returned to the UK after 5 years. I continued to work in the music industry in various roles and, despite working on some fantastic and fun projects, I always felt that I never really achieved any great success in my career. I met my now husband in 2006, and in 2011, I became a mum. With the incredibly rewarding and fulfilling experience of becoming a mum also came the widely recognised feelings of loss of identity, inadequacy and guilt. If it wasn't before, it most certainly wasn't safe to be me now! I had to be a responsible, decent human being now that I was a mum.

After four years of feeling like 'just a mum', I wanted something more, so I set out on my journey to become self-employed. Other mums were becoming successful entrepreneurs left, right, and centre, but they were something special, so, so different from me. I could never be anyone like them. I wasn't as amazing as them. I wasn't even 'cool' or edgy anymore; that part of me was dead.

I slogged away, for almost three years, at being a social media manager, working really hard for very little reward, both financially and professionally. Feeling extremely disillusioned with that career path, I jumped at the opportunity to become a Facebook Ads specialist, and this is when life started to become more promising.

When it came to work, I'd always felt that I needed to work for other people, be an employee. I had to have someone more experienced, 'better than me', to tell me or show me how to do something. I felt I needed permission, for someone else to give me a work title.

If I could go back and give advice to myself, there is so much I would say, but the big one would be to stop comparing yourself to everyone else, stop being so hard on yourself, celebrate your achievements, no matter how big or small, because YOU made them happen!

I used to believe I was fundamentally a bad person and that's why bad things happened to me.

Success and happiness, that was for other people. You name it, I covered the whole A-Z of self-limiting beliefs. I'd spent my life hiding the real me, I was an expert at it, and with my ego always running the show, it came easy to me to create whoever I wanted to be, to please other people. The massive highs and crushing lows, the drama of it all was so addictive and all part of the story of who I thought I was.

Every time I moved on to a new chapter in my life, I rejected and abandoned a part of me, a part of my story, too ashamed to own it. Afraid of the judgement. With friends, I used to wonder why they wanted to be friends with me, what was in it for them?!

Growing up, I was good at some stuff but never 'the best'. If someone else was praised for something, that immediately meant that I was rubbish at it. If someone commented on how good looking someone was, it meant I wasn't. I never felt good enough. The huge rejection and abandonment I experienced had always been the proof to me that it was true.

As I got older, I created a totally shameless persona for myself; I was reckless and completely lacked a moral compass. I had to be tough as no-one else had my back. I had zero integrity or self-respect. I was so judgmental of others, looking for things that were wrong with them or their lives that would somehow make me feel superior. I hid traumatic events from my family, the people that actually did care about me, despite me never believing it.

In 2018, I wrote my life story for the first time for Andrea Callanan's Self Mastery course. It was a pivotal moment, to see how broken in pieces I was. I'd come from a broken home, broken parental relationships, broken leg, broken heart and broken relationships, friendships and career, due to my fear of commitment to myself and others. I had zero self-worth.

During some family constellation work, which is performed by a Shaman, I identified the feeling of having a huge void inside me. It made me feel unsteady on my feet, like there was nothing supporting me. I went on to recognise the parts of me that I had cut away over the years, the parts I didn't want to identify with. I knew I had to work on accepting all of me, welcoming back the rejected little girl, the wild child, the criminal, the underachiever.

I'd suffered chronic, debilitating comparisonitis for so many years (something I still have to work really hard at!). Being fascinated and naturally perceptive about other people is a gift and yet I used it as a weapon against myself, to beat myself up for not being as good as other people. Them being amazing meant I was worthless. I always assumed other people's lives were better than mine, that they were at a better party than the one I was at! I never really stopped to enjoy the present and appreciate where I was at and how far I'd come. The easiest way to prove to myself and others that I have never been successful was to never acknowledge my accomplishments, to constantly put myself down, both outwardly and with my own self-talk.

I was stuck in my victim state, focusing on all the negative stuff from my past, never celebrating how far I'd come, never truly recognising how resilient I was. I just put it down to needing to survive, as anyone would. I didn't feel particularly strong, I just put my head down and got through it.

Through doing story work in the Self Mastery course, I was able to work through my life story and clearly see the pivotal experiences and events which led me to feel such rejection, blame, shame and judgement towards myself.

Me and my older brother were both born in Melbourne, Australia. My mum was desperately unhappy there as my dad worked a lot and she was lonely having no family there, so she came back to the UK when I was about six months old.

We never went without. I was well looked after and felt safe, but didn't always have a sense of stability, or feel fully supported or loved. I sometimes felt a void in my stomach and chest, like there was a part missing.

In my normal, everyday home life as a young child (living with my mum, Les (stepdad) and three brothers), I can only seem to recall the shit stuff and just longing to be with my dad. It seemed as though my mum was always shouting and in a bad mood and Les used to treat me quite badly - he was extremely strict with me and I was petrified of him.

I hero-worshipped my dad as a young child. He spoilt me and my brother massively when we were kids. He worked off-shore in the Middle East and always had plenty of money to show off; taking us on holidays and buying us anything we desired and more, being full of exciting promises for the future and so much fun to be with. To me, he was the life and soul of everything. We only saw him every other month. I just couldn't wait to see him and we'd keep in touch via letter and sometimes talk on the phone. My dad always went on about how wonderful it would be for us to live with him and always promised that one day we would.

When I was 12, that dream did come true. I moved to live with my dad and his new wife (when mum was changing husbands again). Me and my brother were there for 18 months and it was a total disaster. We felt mistreated and were finally, catastrophically rejected by my dad. My brother left home at 16 years old and my dad drove me to my mum's and literally dumped me on the doorstep and drove away. It was just before I turned 14. I felt like a massive burden to my mum and her third husband. I'd overheard a heated discussion about how they couldn't afford to look after me.

Enter the wild child! I did everything too young: smoked, boozed, had sex, took drugs. I don't think at this time I had people in my life who were true friends. I confused sex with feelings of love, so I was promiscuous, which also led to a devastating episode of sexual coercion. It felt like rape at the time. I never told anyone about it.

Ten days before my 16th birthday, one of the most life-changing things happened. I was hit by a car when attempting to cross the road. I was very badly injured and lost a lot of blood as my right lower leg was smashed up big time. I spent 8 months in hospital altogether, and had over 45 operations to try and save my leg. The decision had just been made to amputate it when a surgeon from the US happened to be visiting the hospital and he took over. I will be forever grateful, as he managed to save it.

I'd become institutionalised, so it was difficult to return to 'normal life'. It had been a huge ordeal and despite being a survivor, I always felt that people were judging me and thinking that it had all been my fault. In fact, my mum even told me it was one day!

Having missed a whole year of school set me on a new path, with a different friendship group and I started A levels (I probably would have left school after GSCEs if the accident hadn't happened). I had magazine articles written about me, was invited onto TV shows to be interviewed as 'The Miracle Walker', started seeing my first 'proper boyfriend'. Life was kind of good apart from one thing... the whole time I was in hospital, my dad never came to see me, never even contacted me. I saw him at my Grandad's (his dad's) funeral. He didn't acknowledge me. He came into a room where I was sitting to retrieve a beautiful, blonde-haired toddler, who had burst into the room like a little ray of sunshine. That was my baby half-sister... I'd been rejected, abandoned, and now replaced.

Writing this now still gives me that crushing feeling when I think about how totally destroyed that 17-year-old me felt.

When I came out of hospital, I made up for lost time. I lived life to the full, well, in terms of partying hard I certainly did! I was swept up by the rave scene, big time. Despite all the raving I was doing, I did well in my exams and of course, at that time (1990), there was only one place I wanted to go to university... 'Mad-chester', here I come!

My time in Manchester was legendary; so many good times. The clubbing and music scene was incredible and I was right in the thick of it. My life at that time was like a plot from a Tarantino movie, I kid you not... but that's for another book. There were bad times, very bad. The truth was, I'd gone down a very dark path and believed I was tough enough to handle it. I made some seriously bad choices, one of which was to stay in a physically and mentally abusive relationship for five years, the other was getting deeply involved with criminals. My moral compass was non-existent. I had no self-worth or self-respect.

I was completely broken when I left Manchester and ran away to Australia. That was easy with my dual nationality. It's when happier times and my career in the music industry began. I knew I deserved a second chance.

> *"You may not control all the events that happen to you, but you can decide not to be reduced by them."*

Those words, and these...

> *"If you don't like something, change it. If you can't change it, change your attitude."*

— Maya Angelou

sums up the best advice I can give to start work on re-framing your past and no-one says it better than Maya.

You have the freedom to choose, just like choosing vanilla or chocolate ice-cream. To fully understanding that you are in control of how you feel about your story, the good, the bad and the ugly, is where the transformation begins.

The F word -Forgiveness - was the key for me and it could be for you too. It's what I needed to embrace, to start to pull the pieces of me together to become a whole me, the all present and correct, perfectly imperfect, wonky me. The forgiveness letter is a powerful exercise...

Dear Beck,

Thank you so, so much for trusting in this process we call life. You need to believe and trust that you are exactly where you need to be right now and I'm so incredibly proud of you!

You have shown such strength and incredible resilience throughout this crazy journey and just look at where you are now... could you have ever imagined, all those years ago, you'd be where you are now?!

Thank you for finding the courage to forgive. What a game-changer, right?! I'm so grateful to you for all the lessons and all the work you've done on YOU to get to this point, and it's only going to get better, more powerful, because here's the thing, it's now time to work on something bigger than just you.

I feel that you are now ready to understand more about your bigger purpose in this world and I know there is so much more gratitude heading your way, as I know you will be helping thousands of women, just like you, on their journeys to change their mindset and reframe the past.

In discovering your path to true forgiveness, self-love and self-belief, you have created the freedom you 100% deserve. I believe in you and your ability to help others do the same.

With forgiveness, love and gratitude,

Beck x

I am a work in progress, and this is the fun part. This is where I get my dopamine hit from these days, as there is always so much more to experience and learn on this journey. I believe there is still a lot of healing work to be done. Life is constantly throwing curve balls at us, right? And I have the choice to continue with the work or not. I am free to choose and so are you!

Writing your story and identifying a time in your life where you first felt like you weren't good enough, weren't worthy of love, is key to discovering where you have a fixed mindset, which is where you can dig into your self-limiting beliefs.

A growth mindset focuses on the journey of experiencing, giving things a go, failing and learning until you succeed, viewing life events as opportunities to grow. Failures are only setbacks and opportunities for improvement and learning.

People with a growth mindset take charge of their success and the process of attaining it and maintaining it. People with a growth mindset also recognize that all judgements are just assumptions, not reality!

Here are some questions for you to ponder on, to recognise where you have blind spots and where you might be experiencing a fixed mindset:

- When do you feel overly defensive?
- What language do you use with yourself when you make a mistake?
- How do you typically react to life's difficulties?
- How do you treat yourself when you run into challenges in your life? Do you stop to give yourself care and comfort? Or focus exclusively on fixing the problem?
- Do you tend to get carried away by the drama of difficult situations, so that you make a bigger deal out of them than you need to? Or do you tend to keep things in a balanced perspective?
- Do you tend to feel cut off from others when things go wrong, with the irrational feeling that everyone else is having a better time of it than you are? Or do you try to

remember that all people experience hardship in their lives?

A mindset shift happens when you start to become more self-aware, more mindful, more intentional with your thoughts and therefore, your actions. When you can begin to re-frame your past, you can start to learn how to stand on your story and not be stuck in it. When you're stuck in the past, you feel that your story defines you. You subconsciously and constantly search for and find evidence to support your self-limiting beliefs.

Digging into the most uncomfortable emotions is where the magic happens. The thoughts that trigger you, the places that feel too painful to go...

> *"I want to be in the arena. I want to be brave with my life. And when we make the choice to dare greatly, we sign up to get our asses kicked. We can choose courage, or we can choose comfort, but we can't have both. Not at the same time."*
>
> — BRENÉ BROWN.

To live the life you desire, you must get in the arena.

It starts with you. Put your own oxygen mask on first. Getting your head around putting yourself first is such a hard thing to do for most people (especially if you are a mum!). You may worry that you are being selfish (or perceived as such by others), or self-indulgent... fixed mindset alert right there! I've had moments of feeling self-indulgent, writing this chapter, thinking who in their right mind is going to want to read about me and my life?! The amazing Inspirational Speaker, Jermaine Harris, said to me once that I could save lives with my story. Well, that's one hell of a responsibility I can't turn my back on!

It's important to recognise where you have support and stop thinking you must do everything yourself. One of the best ways to get out of your own way is to focus on where others can help you.

Reflect on your accomplishments. Us humans are negatively biased, which means that we are prone to only think about the negative stuff that's happened. One great quick exercise to help with positive reflection is to make yourself draw out a timeline of the last year and to plot the ups and downs. You'll recognise that it wasn't all bad, and that can set you off on an upward spiral of positive emotion. I always make sure that I take time to celebrate my accomplishments these days. Doing this as a weekly practice is hugely powerful. I also practice gratitude every day, a real life-changing habit!

Life is made up of ups and downs. No one is immune from negative emotion and positive psychology is far from about ignoring the bad stuff. It's about building on the good; your strengths, your resilience, providing you with the tools for life to keep you flourishing in the face of adversity. And sometimes, you just need to 'sit in the shit'. And that's ok, just don't do it for too long!

You can stop hiding. It's totally possible, and quite frankly, you just should. Some of the biggest hurdles to get over are believing that you don't have to be perfect, you don't have to do things the same way everyone else has. It's totally safe to be you. Decide what it is that makes you unique and embrace it with all your heart. You will notice how compassionate you will start to become, not only towards yourself, but others too.

Always remember that YOU create the opportunities. You do deserve them. You don't need wait for permission. Stop comparing, stay present and intentional.

Becoming the queen of reinvention throughout my life served me well. I am still alive, and this latest incarnation is one I'm particularly proud of as it encompasses ALL of me. Now, in my late 40s,

I'm ready to step into the real me, warts and all. My life has renewed meaning and purpose and it's really exciting to be here!

We all love a great story; our brains are hardwired for narrative. It's how we make sense of the world; we think in stories, remember in stories and turn just about everything we experience into a story, often adjusting or omitting facts to make it fit. It can get pretty messy, right?

Here lies the problem, as we sometimes get stuck in the story of who we think we are, as it's who we think we 'should' be. Most of that story is formed early in childhood, with new chapters added in adolescence and adulthood. To put it simply, our understanding of who we think we are is a mishmash of other people's perceptions of us, our parent's stories, dreams and expectations, our experience of the world, with a bit of cultural influence chucked in there. The ridiculous thing is, the stories we tell ourselves about who we are, are mostly other people's stories!

I'm now proud to think of myself as a role model for resilience. Looking back at my story, whenever there was trauma, when I felt like a lost cause, I always pulled myself out the other side by trying to better myself. I might not have identified it at the time, but it was me knowing, deep down, that I had choice. I now see the silver-linings. All of it made me who I am today and actually, the universe does have my back.

"And just as the Phoenix rose from the ashes, she too will rise. Returning from the flames clothed in nothing but her strength, more beautiful than ever before".

— SHANNEN HEARTZ.

Recognising those pivotal moments in my life showed me a pattern of resilience. Then something amazing happened. I started to trust myself more. I started to trust in the journey, fully understanding that happiness is not a destination and that it's already here if I choose to embrace it.

I am now the creator, not the victim. I'm not the 'fundamentally bad person' I believed I was. I take full responsibility for who I am and who I was. I made a choice to invest in myself, big time. I chose to get out of my own way. I am now hugely grateful for my story.

I am recognising my breakthroughs and the positive impact me doing the work on myself has had on my family and others close to me. Something incredible happened quite recently.

After 16 years of silence between my dad and me, in 2000 when I living in Australia, I found the courage to track him down and contact him. It wasn't an easy conversation, as you can imagine. And I found myself left with the feelings of utter disappointment because, surprise, surprise, he didn't have all the answers! What had I created in my head for all these years?! A person that I thought could fix me with one simple conversation - three words: 'I love you', two more words: 'I'm sorry'. What the hell was I thinking?! Over the years, I concluded that I was never truly going to be able to forgive him and I accepted that and made my peace with it.

What I discovered recently is that it's never too late. It took me another 20 years from that conversation and a lot more investment in myself to finally be able to authentically and wholeheartedly forgive him.

The transformation happened when I was about halfway through the PPCA (Positive Psychology Coaching Certification). Me and my brother decided to visit him. It had been a few years since we'd seen him and we hadn't been good at keeping in touch as neither of us felt a duty to do so, but we thought it might be one of, if not the last time, we'd see him. The few times I had seen him over the years, there had always been an elephant in the room, with him not really knowing whether he should talk about the past and if he still needed to make excuses for his actions.

This time, I didn't feel that elephant. It was like a superpower came from nowhere when I told him that I was there purely out of love for him. I can't describe the energy I felt. I know how much I impacted everyone in that room at that moment because I truly meant it. Years of heartache and pain for all of us was just gone. My dad had recently suffered a minor stroke and was struggling with his comprehension and speech, which was apparent when we'd first arrived. After I said what I did, his words flowed more easily and he understood what I was saying to him. We had a great time together, just like old times.

Fear is what had stopped me from making the most of the opportunities that the universe has presented to me. Did I hide to avoid the drama? To avoid being knocked down again? To avoid the judgement? "Where does the fear come from?" is such a powerful exploration, which coaching can help you to find those answers for yourself.

It's my strong belief that taking that leap of faith, investing in myself and connecting with the incredible women I met from then is fundamental to where I am now. Through meeting the amazing Emma Van Heusen at that pivotal moment when I joined her Facebook ADcelerator programme in 2018, I met the incredible Andrea Callanan, and that's what started me on my journey to becoming a coach. It took me some time and a lot of work on myself to realise this is where I was destined to be, and since I did, I've never doubted this is my purpose in life.

I invested in coaching for myself over three years ago now. I now tune into the meaning and purpose of my life. I finally feel completely aligned with my work and how it's so much bigger than just me. I'm not only committed to myself and my family, but also to the many people I can help with my Positive Psychology and Resilience Coaching practice.

Through working with me clients can:

- Identify what is going right in their life and build on the positives;
- Explore their values and their purpose;
- Elevate their strengths and understand their relationship with their weaknesses;
- Become more resilient and resourceful;
- Establish and maintain connection in their relationships;
- Accomplish their goals and define what success looks like to them individually;
- The possibilities are endless...

Life will continue to throw curve balls at us, it's how we bounce back that's important. I help women to create their 'tool-kit for resilience' with the power of Positive Psychology.

You too can learn how to stand on your story and rise!

"Whether we remain the ash or become the Phoenix is up to us."

— MING-DAO DENG.

ABOUT THE AUTHOR
BECK HARRISON

Beck Harrison is a Positive Psychology and Resilience Coach with a difference. With her journey from wild child to wise woman, she brings an undisputable wealth of expertise and life experience.

Since discovering her life's purpose, Beck is on a mission to show women who feel stuck in their stories, how to create their 'tool-kit for resilience' with the power of Positive Psychology. Helping them to re-frame their story and to discover their self-worth, so they can step out of their own way and rise.

In a previous life, Beck worked for 18 years in the music and entertainment industry. Before becoming a coach, she was a digital marketer, and a Facebook and Instagram ads strategist for five years.

Beck has been on a journey of self-discovery and transformation in recent years. Her own personal story is one of true grit, courage, resilience, trust, compassion, forgiveness and triumph. She is passionate about helping other women to explore, discover and embrace their true selves, warts and all, so they too can feel triumphant.

Her passion for music still strong. She loves singing (Karaoke anyone?!) and especially the live music experience of gigs and festivals. Beck loves a great party and the beach, in any kind of weather. She lives with her husband and two kids in Kingston Upon Thames.

Beck has a BSc (Hons) in Psychology and is a graduate of the fully accredited Aligned Coaching Academy, (ACA MInstLM). She's also a certified Positive Psychology Coach (PPCA), certified Story Work Coach, with Andrea Callanan, and a Resilience Quotient Inventory (RQi) Practitioner and Coach.

Beck is available for 1:1 coaching and you can reach her by emailing Beck@beckharrisoncoaching.com or by connecting with her on LinkedIn or Instagram.

instagram.com/original_becks
linkedin.com/in/beck-harrison

3

CAMILLA JAKOBSON
RECLAIM MY LIFE - FROM BROKEN TO BRILLIANT

If you had told me five years ago, three years ago, or even as little as only one year ago, that I would create a life and business that not only gives me joy and fulfillment, but that also comes with the flexibility that I so desperately need, I wouldn't have believed you. And sometimes, when I wake up, I almost don't believe it myself. You see, except for being an entrepreneur, I am also a full-time single mum of three beautiful and very energetic kids. And I am also a person who desperately needs to keep that fire in my belly burning by having space to be creative and work on my constantly new ideas and projects. The life that I've created doesn't just come with the perks of flexibility, fulfillment, and freedom; it also comes with an essential ingredient to have a sustainable life, especially if you're a single parent: it comes with income.

I love that I today, have the "time freedom" to tailor my days according to what fits around running the "empire" called house and family. And to be able to take a moment to myself every morning after a busy, sometimes borderline chaotic, start of the day, culminating in a school run. To have a walk in nature with only me, myself, and I; a time of peace and serenity that is something I know many mums out there find as precious as I do. I also love and sometimes find it a necessity as a single mum that I can decide to take a couple of hours off in the middle of the day when the kids are in school to run some errands or, from time to time, focus on self-care. And have that flexibility to catch up on those lost hours in the evening, if needed.

But it wasn't always this way, and my story of getting to where I am now will probably be a bit different from many of the other authors of this book. I didn't have a blooming career or a well-paid corporate job before embarking on the path of entrepreneurialism. Being an entrepreneur has always been my dream, and the constant idea popping pot that I carry on my shoulders has probably always known that that was the only way for me to stay true to myself. Even if, most of the time over the last decade and a half, I doubted my capabilities to make it happen. But life has thrown me some curveballs, which got me derailed from my track for nearly two decades. And it has been a long and hard inner pilgrimage of therapy and personal development to reclaim my power and, with that, be in the position to reclaim my life and create the life and business that I now have.

When I was seventeen, the first big traumatic event that threw me of the rails happened. Afterward, I desperately tried to withhold the image of still being a normal and functioning person by going along with the idea of what was expected from me. For example, carrying on with my higher levels studies, even though I felt that I was *doing life* instead of *living it,* all while at the same time, I seemed to be slowly crumbling inside.

But my constant hunger for knowledge made me continually seek refuge in the academic world and made me consume more and more courses, which has left me with only one semester left from my second bachelor's degree and this one in Psychology - the first one is in Social anthropology. And alongside that, I tried to launch my first business.

But even all that knowledge of human behaviors didn't save me from my inner demons and lack of self-worth, which led me straight into the arms of a narcissistic, abusive man. A man I didn't have the courage to leave for a little over five years and who, at the same time as he made my life and home living hell on earth, also facilitated the blessings I got in my three beautiful children.

So, life before setting out on the path of entrepreneurship this second time around was focused on recovering from years of traumas and abuse. I was juggling pressing charges and fighting for custody, going through trauma therapy, and meeting other women from similar situations as myself. All this while, at the same time being the full-time single mum I still am today. Which, to be honest, was a heck of a lot easier than being a full-time single mum while still living with my abusive ex-boyfriend, as he was definitely causing more stress and problems and rarely was of any help in the raising of the children.

During this time of my life, my idea popping brain became like a lighthouse in the dark and stormy sea, shining its light of infinite possibilities that I still somehow believed were out there. That hope was a big part of what kept me going. Dreaming about what kind of business I wanted to start and how I wanted my life to change offered a safe haven to escape to amid the chaotic life I was leading. Even though I didn't realize all of the many ideas I had over the years, my brain had found another place to seek refuge in; alternative education. High on business courses and personal development, my brain was buzzing and occupied with possibilities of the future, letting me escape the depressing reality I was caught up in.

But if I had known back then what I know now, I would tell myself that there is no escape from your reality. My desperate chase of tomorrow was just a repetitive dissociate pattern that I had played on repeat for years and years, trying to avoid the pains of the traumas in my life. But that stressful hunt of trying to find the "key," the answer to my problems, turned my search of therapies and self-help methods into what felt like a game of quidditch in life, trying to catch the uncatchable "golden snitch" like Harry Potter. I hadn't yet realized that what I needed was to make a complete stop, take a breath, and learn to be okay with me where I was right there and then. And, much like you have to pull the string back in the slingshot to make your object catapult forward; sometimes you need to pull back, identify what is blocking you, really dare to see it, and then honor it and release it; so that you can finally soar.

But at the time, I was stuck in my trauma responses to the extent that I wasn't even fully here, present, living my life. I kept my dissociative pattern and sought refuge in the self-actualization part of Maslow's Hierarchy of needs. Even though all the rest of my needs weren't yet met, leaving me living in a trauma response, with an extreme lack of self-worth, fear of rejection, judgment, and abandonment, sprinkled with massive imposter syndrome. My lack of confidence, limiting beliefs, and fear of failure kept me from trying, which was a brilliant self-defense mechanism. Because as we all know, it's impossible to actually "make it" if we don't even try. But unfortunately, the pattern of not fully trying, which led me not to make it, fed my belief of not being worthy of success, which became a self-fulfilling prophecy playing on repeat.

So, I kept playing small, worked with the few clients that had sought me out, and worst of all, I wasn't even charging for it. And when I finally did charge, I charged a fifth or less of what the work I did was worth, and still, I felt that I wasn't even worthy of that. And to be honest, working for my clients for scraps wasn't the real problem. The fact that I didn't even feel that I was worthy of scraps was the real issue.

At the time, I couldn't see a way out of the maze of self-limiting beliefs that I had gotten myself into, and I didn't dare to share my lack of trust in my abilities with anyone. So, what was going on inside me wasn't congruent with most people's image of me. I've always hidden behind my smile, and, as the outspoken social extrovert I am, I love connection and being of service to others. Therefore, I freely shared my creative ideas and strategies for either business or tools for healing your inner wounds with anyone that needed it. Which left most people shocked when they found out that I was, and to some extent still am, crippled by imposter syndrome and filled to the brim with fears of judgment and limiting beliefs. The only vision I shared with the world was one of my hopes and dreams and what I wanted to achieve, meanwhile secretly thinking that I would never be able to get out of my own way enough to ever pulling it off.

And living in a family with wildly successful siblings and father, the fact that I feared I would never be able to crawl out of the dark pit I had been digging for myself over the years, created a massive barrier between myself and my family, making me feel that I didn't genuinely belong, not there nor anywhere. A feeling I most probably had carried with me from growing up due to a series of minor events, but that got multiplied by millions when the carpet was pulled from underneath my feet, and my whole world got turned upside down when I was seventeen. For this part of the story, I want to warn anyone that might be triggered by certain events and might, like me, also suffer from PTSD. But my story is one of overcoming adversity, and in my case, adversity is one of sexual assault, rape, and abuse.

So, when I was seventeen, I was brutally raped by someone that I considered a friend. And that day, everything in my life changed. I became a mere shell of who I once was; a ghost, feeling that I had lost the most significant part of myself, my soul. It took me more than thirteen and a half years and sixteen different therapists and multiple alternative healing methods to be able to, for the first time in detail, own my story and share what had happened with my brother first and then with my father. And a couple of months later, at a stage in front of thousands of people and five major news channels in Sweden. All thanks to the #MeToo movement and a manifestation that was arranged when that storm swept around the world.

The #MeToo movement was so liberating for me, and I was so grateful for being able to get on that stage where I could rip off the bandage and tell the whole world what had happened to me. I had spent the last decade and a half lying to everyone and constantly trying to save face, but all the lies and pretending to be someone I wasn't was absolutely exhausting. So getting that chance to go up on that stage and share my story was nothing less than a feeling of liberation from the imprisonment of a life of lies that I had tangled myself up in.

The only problem was that I only shared half of the story. I only shared the part of the story that I had overcome. The story of how I had had to fight off what I thought was a friend and not manage to withstand his attack fourteen years earlier, even though I knew that the adrenaline I felt pumping through my veins would have made me capable of lifting a car, but the exact second, his body pumped the same super strength into his veins; I no longer stood a chance against him.

That part of the story I got to own and share on that particular crisp fall morning on a stage in front of thousands of people. But no one that attended that manifestation, nor my family, got to hear about how, that very morning at five o'clock, I woke up by the sound of the door to the room I was sleeping in sliding up. And before I even realized that I was awake, I heard myself pleading to my ex not to rape me, not that morning, not just hours before I was going up on stage talking about precisely *this*. And even though this was the only time throughout our five-plus years together that he heard my pleas, I know for a fact that it wasn't because I was pleading or because he felt any form of empathy towards me, it was simply because we luckily had company staying over that night.

And the fact that they were sleeping right next door to me; became my salvation.

But even when my ex left the room, and I double-checked that he wasn't still there, lurking in the corner, I couldn't believe that he had listened to me. I spent the next two hours with a racing heartbeat and the adrenaline pumping through my veins, making it impossible to fall back asleep.

I always tell people that when I envisioned breaking free from the chains of that first trauma, it would be like opening a door and stepping out on a green open field and finally feel free. But that wasn't the reality. Instead, when I finally had done enough work with that first trauma and opened that door, I couldn't feel the grass underneath my feet, and I didn't end up on a green open field. Instead, I walked straight into my living room, then, for the first time, realizing that I was living in an abusive relationship where I was reliving my first trauma on repeat. When that realization hit, it was as if someone had just cut off the curtains. And for the first time, I had gotten my head enough over the surface to see what was going on in my life. Including seeing all the abuse, I was living through. Mentally, economically and sexually. And seeing that was the first step of a series of events that finally led to me gathering enough courage to be able to leave him, although that didn't happen overnight.

He had taken advantage of the fact that I was already broken when we met, and he made sure to break my spirit even further so that he could pressure me to get what he wanted. Already, just a mere month into our relationship, he had had me convinced that I wasn't going to make it out of that relationship alive. And that the only option I had was to learn to live with this beast of a man and constantly navigate what could potentially set him off.

Living all those years with him, I felt like I was walking on a minefield. Always trying to remove any potential triggers so that I wouldn't have to live through the pain that I would have to endure when I didn't manage to remove all potential stressors, which wasn't easy, seeing as we were also living with three small children in the same house.

But when I finally had managed to get that helicopter perspective over our relationship and realized what happened, it was as if he could sense that he was about to lose me. In response, he desperately tried to tighten his grip on me by escalating the abuse, especially the threats and death threats in the months leading up to the breakup.

All of the time we were together, he was gaslighting me and making me question my reality, telling me how ugly I was and that I would never find anyone that could ever love me. Telling me how he was so kind to me and that I would never find anyone that could be so kind to me, all while I was wiping off the tears rolling down my cheeks after he had raped me. All of this left me with a significantly damaged self-image, and I was, throughout these years being a self-hate addict, constantly hitting myself and finding those proofs of how much of a screw-up I was.

When I finally managed to break free from my ex, I was juggling pressing charges and fighting for custody, all while going through trauma therapy, coaching, diving deep into personal development and spirituality, being a full-time single mum, and launching a consultancy business. And even though I felt that I was doing everything I possibly could to "deal" with my traumas, I wasn't healing. I was tackling life the same way I always had, like a marathon of "to-do's," hoping that I would find salvation when I reached the end of that list. The only problem was the problems of to-do lists in general; they are never-ending. So I came to a point where I felt that there wasn't anything else I could *do*, and I found myself at a new low.

After having had a couple of weeks of self-pity and licking the wounds caused by my feelings of defeat, I came across a challenge hosted by the very person responsible for this book collaboration, the lovely Andrea Callanan. And doing what I always do, I tackled my feelings of despair by engaging in self-actualization and personal development. And I signed up for her signature program, Unapologetic Self Mastery Accelerator, which came at a time in my life when I desperately needed it.

And even though this program, in many ways, is filled to the brim with brilliant self-help practices like affirmations and great tools and tricks to flip your mindset, it's so much more than that which genuinely sets this course apart from the rest. It offered a safe space and a community of women holding each other up while pulling back the string in the slingshot and examining what it is that is truly holding you back. And I needed that community. I still lacked that sense of belonging in so many areas of my life, and funnily enough, it felt provided by a tribe of women in the digital sphere — a place where it felt safe to be heard and seen. And have a place to heal, all while sharing our journeys with one another.

Brene Brown says that shame can only survive on the illusion that you are all alone. And my brilliant coach here in Sweden adds that shame is like a vampire, growing strong in the darkness and shadows but can't withstand the sunlight. So, finding a safe space to be able to be your whole self, traumas or no traumas, and to be held in that space is truly important to be able to make it in any of the endeavors you might take on in your life.

When deciding that I would join that course, it felt like the universe started to conspire to help me get what I needed from it. Certain events that proved to be of the utmost importance in my self-mastery journey started coming up in my sessions with my coach here in Sweden during the weeks just leading up to the start of the course. Throughout the course, I was parallel working on my self-esteem and letting go of my past with my Swedish coach and my self-mastery and sense of belonging with this fantastic cohort of women online, and things started to truly change for me. I saw how my lack of self-worth was reflected in my business and with my clients and how I let my imposter syndrome drag me down. Within just a couple of weeks of the course, I made a huge and scary, but also very empowering decision to increase my rates with my clients drastically. I was determined to start seeing my worth and to let go of badmouthing myself.

What I have come to realize during this year of inner pilgrimage of personal development is that to move forward, it's important to sometimes make a complete stop. And that as long as you have turmoil within, there are no affirmations or mantras in the world that will make that magically disappear. That there are no shortcuts or "golden snitches" out there, even though I've spent so many years desperately trying to find them. And that the only way to truly reclaim your life is to actually dare to see the events and your life for what they truly were and to know that salvation lies in the awareness and understanding of the events in themselves. And, as much as I hate to say it, we have to be our own saviors; no one else can do the healing work for us. Still, they can help facilitate the suitable space and provide the right tools for you to let go of what is holding you back and then finally catapult forward and soar.

And know that it's okay to need help and have a community that supports you and a safe space to guide you and help you up, if and when you stumble and fall along the way. Being strong doesn't mean having to fight our inner battles all by ourselves. Sometimes, the most courageous and badass thing we can do is acknowledge that we need support and dare to reach out to get it. And also, know that whatever you're going through, you're not alone and no matter how bad it might seem, know that there is always a way forward, even if the smog is so thick that you can't make out the whole path ahead or maybe even the very next step. Just remember that sometimes, the most significant healing occurs when you can see, dare to truly lift the veil, and work on accepting where you are at in right this very moment, warts and all. Because if we can't find a way to be empathetic with ourselves and accept ourselves at the moment when we need it the most, we will never find the strength we need to see the circumstances for what they are and let go of the limiting beliefs, fears, and judgment that are holding us back.

So, this is what I managed to do. I managed to truly see and accept where I was, crumbled by traumas and adversity, owning my story and then working on making things better from there by cautiously putting one foot in front of the other. And taking control over what I actually could control and letting go of the need to control things that I couldn't. I had to work hard on my self-worth and limiting beliefs and pull back the string to see where the self-sabotaging patterns first began. I had to be empathetic with that part of myself, understand it, love it, honor it, respect it, and then finally release it to be able to give myself permission to eventually soar. All of this finally helped me, after years and years of constantly searching for the answer out there, find the right coaches and communities to facilitate the healing that had to take place within so that I could finally get out of my own way.

Or, to be fully transparent and honest, I got enough out of my own way to start making some vital pieces of the puzzle fall into place. I'm not going to pretend that my life is filled with rainbows and unicorns today, but I've come to a place that has allowed me to move from surviving to *living*. You thought I was going to say thriving, didn't you? And in many ways, that's true; I am thriving. But I consciously chose to leave that as the next step on the ladder because even if I've made it to the place that I've long dreamt about, my mission is far more significant than where I am today, even though today, I can finally say that I've made it. I've created a business that I love and that supports my life. I get to use my creativity to help coaches and educational businesses shine online as an online biz strategist. And I also get to help business owners and women heal their inner wounds and get out of their own way as a transformational coach.

And by having done the work myself, I can now not only support my clients in their businesses as an online business strategy consultant, I can also add that additional layer of support to them by having added another string to the bow as a transformational coach, which is a work that I find deeply rewarding.

But had I not made this journey of healing and inner work to get out of my own way, I wouldn't have been able to get to where I am today professionally. I am sure that my inner limiting beliefs would have made me stumble and fall. And therefore, I still make it my utmost priority to continuously work on myself and keep the healing and growing as a vital part of my life because I know that my life, my kids, and my business is dependent on that. Because I wouldn't be the brilliant badass entrepreneur I am today if I was still emotionally broken. And, of course, I still stumble and fall. Still, the difference is that I can now stand back up, dust myself off, and be the brilliant full-time single mum and entrepreneur that I am, despite the many hurdles I had to go through and the hoops I've had to jump, and the pain I had to overcome to finally feel that way.

So, if you would have told me a year ago that I would, in one year, reach my first stepping stone of a target income in my business, become an accredited coach through the aligned coaching academy, become certified in the coaching method that for me was life-changing, already starting my second coaching accreditation (with a focus on trauma) and that I would also soon be a published author in this very same book you're reading right now, I wouldn't have believed you. And sometimes, when I wake up, I don't believe it myself.

So, my mission now is to expand the part of my business where I can help women overcome adversity, go from broken to brilliant and reclaim their life. Because no matter what crap you've been through in your life, the truth is, as the mighty Tony Robbins says: *your past doesn't equal your future*. And, as cliché, as it might sound, I know for a fact that if I can do it, so can anyone.

ABOUT THE AUTHOR
CAMILLA JAKOBSON

Camilla Jakobson is an Online Biz Strategist and a transformational coach who helps educational businesses and coaches shine online with her solution-oriented, idea-popping creative mind that comes up with ideas that are not just aligned with her client's brand, but that are also authentic with the person's running the show. As a transformational coach, she also helps women overcome adversity and heal their inner wounds so that they can reclaim their life and finally soar.

Before setting out on this endeavor of entrepreneurship, Camilla spent a decade studying human behavior as well as taking multiple courses in digital marketing, business strategies, and personal development. Camilla is also an accredited coach by the Institute of Leadership through the Aligned Coaching Academy, and is also certified in Andrea Callanan's Storywork, a modality that proved to be of utmost importance in her own healing journey. Camilla is also adding another string to her bow with a trauma informed coaching certification so that she can better help women who have experiences all sorts of adversity in life.

Camilla loves dancing (anyone up for an online dance party?), spending time with family and friends, and loves creating new projects and popping new business ideas.

Camilla is available for courses and one-to-one support in online strategies and personal transformation. You can follow her in the channels below to see what she has currently going on.

You can reach Camilla at:

instagram.com/reclaimmylifenow

4

CERI GILLETT

It's a breezy, early September evening. The play park is filled with kids in September-pristine uniforms. The mums sit on the stone wall that lines the park, they reach into their bags for snacks and pass them into the chubby, grass-stained fingers of zooming children. They chat easily about whether they will treat themselves to a takeaway because they can't be arsed to cook, or will drag something out of the freezer. They trade stories about the summer break and the teacher that got married recently. A woman at the left of the park stands on her own. She wears the accepted mum uniform of striped tee and dungarees and she has remembered the snack. She watches her small person zoom between the slide and the swings with a phone pressed firmly to her ear. Her partner is cooking dinner tonight, he always does. It's easier if you stick to the things you are good at, she says and *'things on toast'* is not the cookbook anyone needs. She celebrates. You can tell by the way she triumphantly raises her hand while talking, she touches her neck, looks up to the clouds. She ends the call. Starts another. She motions to the child to follow her and begins to walk to the small, new, blue and silver car parked nearby.

I am her; she is me.

I grabbed the school run snack from a garage en route, pleased I had not forgotten on the first week back. The call was with a board of investors who had been analysing my business. I was successful. It took weeks of work, late nights, spreadsheets, meticulous planning, and a whole heap of dreaming big. Taking any business for investment is hard work; taking a social business where no one can legally profit from it for investment is one of the hardest things I've done for the business this far.

Like many women, I'm not just focused on my businesses. This week, I've ironed all the school uniforms, made all the packed lunches, done every morning drop off, and been there for 3:15 pick up. I've worked on the social business, navigating the financials of this investment with the demands of welcoming new students to our accelerator course. I've spent two days working with 1-1 clients in my coaching business - one of my clients got insanely visible and another has had a brilliant idea for a corporate offer. This week I was nominated for a 'best social leader in Wales award and I skipped the celebration dinner because of football practice. My biggest celebration was that I actually remembered my son's reading book and spellings! My house is a bit messy, but I've loved being back at my desk after the summer break. My days have regained some order and I feel at home, not just in my house. I feel at home in me.

I am a girl from a tiny town in Mid Wales.

I am a girl from a working-class family who never really knew where she fit in.

I am an award-winning businesswoman who started a non-profit that has helped women all over the UK to start and grow businesses. From the box bedroom in my home in South Wales, I have partnered with banks, technology, and software companies to deliver the business accelerator I created and reach the women who need it most. I am a certified coach. I have helped hundreds of women to get visible and create growth strategies for their businesses. I've been on the radio, in magazines, in the paper. I have collated data, published research, and pushed for what I believe. I have worked with the government on a local and national level. I am a teacher, I am a speaker, I love what I do. Most of all, I love to do it my way, but it hasn't always felt this easy for me.

I had been waiting to turn thirty for most of my twenties. I thought my thirties would be a magical time where everything finally made sense. I longed to feel more comfortable in my body. I wanted to connect to people on deeper levels and do work that I loved.

Like many women, I chased in all areas of my life. I grew up in an age where women like me could '*have it all*', so I ran after it without stopping to ask myself if I actually wanted it all. Surely it was pretty ungrateful to have all of this opportunity and then opt out, right? So, I chased.

There were certain areas of my life where chasing meant I excelled. I have always been a person who has fallen forward. I am a person who can quit quickly and I'm a person who can make shit happen. These are great traits to have in the world of work. Growing up in a working-class family, 'hard work' was something to be celebrated and I learned early that if I worked harder, scored higher, did more and generally out performed, I was celebrated. I was celebrated at home, at school and when I found myself working a corporate job, I really found my groove.

It was like someone gave me a ladder that was created just for me; I knew how to climb it with no instructions needed and nothing was going to get in my way.

There were a few problems though. These ladders, in my experience, were pretty short, so I'd get to the top of mine quickly and then I'd realise the view from the top wasn't quite right. I got the thing I thought I wanted, but nothing happened. I was still exactly the same. I grabbed another ladder and continued the climb.

When you are busy climbing, it can be pretty dangerous to get distracted. It's hard to have a social life, it's hard to maintain deep and meaningful friendships and don't get me started on the difficulties of starting, let alone maintaining, any kind of love life.

I told myself and my friends that I wanted what they had: a settled life, a lovely partner, a wedding dress. But I didn't. I had, deep inside me, a burning ambition that was never, ever, satisfied. An ambition I didn't dare tell anyone about for fear of being judged, singled out and feeling different. I kept that version of me in the place it fit in, at work. Outside of work, I played the game I needed to in order to survive. I kept all my relationships at surface level. I never let anyone get too close.

On the night of my 30th birthday, I stayed at London's famous Savoy Hotel. I drank Red Wine with some friends - a wine that cost more per bottle than my current mortgage payment. When my meetings had finished the next day, I had strolled off to Sloane Street to buy myself a Chanel handbag as my 30th birthday present. I sauntered out of that shop and off towards the train. My boyfriend was at my house cooking dinner as a not-so-secret surprise. It sounds blissful, right? Except because I'd not booked annual leave for my birthday, I was late, as usual. "The dinner was ruined" he said. I threw my perfectly wrapped gift to myself on the spare bed upstairs. He said that gifting myself stuff like that made his effort, his gift, pale into insignificance, so he faked the night away and broke up with me when the 30th celebrations had settled. I knew it was coming. I always did. The message I told myself was that I had to be less ambitious to be loved.

Friendships were also a casualty in my life. I just couldn't do them like other people seemed able to. I struggled to find an effortless, easy flow. I feel bad saying this because let me tell you, I have some of the best friends, I truly do, but I have also had my share of extremely toxic friendships that really left their mark on me. I had friendships where I could not be myself. I had female friendships with women who behaved and spoke in ways that led me to question if they had ever really liked me.

The struggles with friendships and relationships rumbled through my twenties but it was my thirties when it really hit me. The realisation that something was wrong was like a freight train ploughing through me. I was shaken. The same thoughts ran through my mind on a constant loop. I had wanted to be here. This was the place I had strived to be; this was the place I was going to get acceptance but what I got was a question. Why aren't you happy?

I couldn't find the answer. With my mind working overtime, my physical body suffered. I burned out. Lost and unsure what to do next, I booked and boarded a flight to Malta and it was there, on the tiny sister island of Gozo, that I started the most important job of my life. Finding my way back to me. There on that island, alone, I had no choice but to sit with my thoughts, to sit with myself and in just a few months, I learned some valuable life lessons about me that I'd love to share with you.

I discovered that my self-worth was directly linked to my work. If I wasn't working, I didn't see how I could be of value to anyone.

There was a reason for all that ambition and striving. Working made me feel like I was worthy of praise and love. I had to learn who I was without work. I had to learn what it was I really wanted to do with my life and I had to leave the industry I loved when I realised it wasn't really what I wanted to do with my life. A year after I started the journey back to myself, I met someone. An easy, laughter-filled relationship began. In the year that followed, I became a mother. Sleepless nights and a new business became my new normal. I started to recognise many of my old patterns and programming started to reappear. In those early motherhood years, I felt isolated. I was the mother of a very small baby, my work 'output' was low and, though I was working hard raising this beautiful baby, I never felt like I was doing enough.

Ambition is something I have always possessed but it's also something I felt like I need to hide, the thing that would make people dislike me. I became secretly ambitious in the early motherhood stage. I stood firmly behind my partner as we created a strategy for his successful business. I campaigned for a change in enterprise support in Wales. I excelled in going just far enough to give me a taste of success, but never pushing myself into the spotlight. I didn't want anyone to look at me.

It's really hard to feel a burning ambition inside of you and not know what to do with it. I remember as a child, expressing these huge desires for what I wanted to do with my life and them being met head-on with practicality. Here I was, this girl from a tiny town in Mid Wales; who was I to think I'd make it as a singer in the West End? (Actually, I couldn't sing, but ambitious girls do not let that stop them.) I never seemed to fit in anywhere so I excelled at being a chameleon. I got really good at assessing what other people needed me to be and becoming that version for them. I got used to quietening my inner voice, keeping it a thing for only me and firmly, firmly standing in my own way, petrified of what might happen if I let myself run wild and free.

The result of this was conflict. Internal conflict.

I never trusted myself. I ignored my gut. I opted to take a well-trodden path and not the one I wanted. I chose to put myself and my desires in a box and lock it up tight.

It was easier for people on the outside to understand this version of me. I made friends easier, people seemed to liked me more. It was easier to navigate my life when I ignored the ambition. There were fewer questions, all I had to do was follow what everyone else was doing, like what they liked, listen to a collective group external voice instead of my own.

Can I tell you? It was really lonely. I felt like no one knew the real me. I wondered how on earth I would ever get the connection I craved when I couldn't show people who I was? How could I be loved when I didn't love myself? And how could I allow that ambition to be free, free to take me to all the places I longed to go, when I was petrified that someone might find out I even had it? Nice girls didn't feel like I did. I was sure of that.

Despite all this inner turmoil, a small voice inside of me refused to accept that this was all I could have in my life, and I continued to work on my mindset as well as my business. It was hard with a small child, but I plodded on steadily. I dragged my feet through the mud. I let that ambition out and not just in work. I let it out in all areas of my life. I started, in tiny ways, to own the fact that I was a woman who always wanted more in my life. I craved deeper connections, bigger love, I wanted more from the relationship I have with myself. I am a seeker, of sorts, and over time, that became ok.

I got up close and personal with my self-worth woes and, my friend, there was work to be done there. I found I had to get to know myself again. I had to learn to trust myself again and I had to learn to love myself - all of myself, the light and the dark.

In this process, I found out that connection is vitally important for me. I realised I could be liked, loved, held and cherished. I realised I could just be myself. When I got out of my own way in life and in business, slowly things started to fly off in the direction I had hoped.

As a business coach and strategist, most people come to me about their business problems, mostly that they aren't earning as they would like. Most of these clients, much like myself, want to focus on the business and not the person fronting that business. I know from my own experience, that working on myself first was the key to unlocking all the success I have had and will continue to have within my businesses. Working on yourself first is the key to the door you want to open, I assure you. What did I do to kick-start it?

I started with two simple things and these are two of the things that inform all my work with clients.

Permission and a Plan. That's all you need.

I've had many people challenge me on the word permission.

You don't need to give yourself permission they'd say. It's your right. Permission makes it seem like you have to ask someone else before you start, but I have to tell you, I needed to give myself permission.

I needed to give that small town girl the permission to say out loud that she was a girl with huge dreams. I needed to give that shy teenage me the permission to go out there and be seen and not judged by everyone around me. I had to give myself permission to ditch the years of imposter syndrome I had felt and allow myself to stand in the powerful truth that I was really good at my job, the thing I have chosen to do.

As a mother, I had to give myself permission to be something outside of my role as Fred's mum. You may not have to do that but equally, this may really resonate. I usually find it does. I've struggled with what I feel a mother should be. It's tough at times, to balance the ambition and desire to be an ever present and in the moment mother.

Permission.

You need to start by thinking about the thing you really want to achieve. Why did you seek out this book? What is the thing you so desperately want for yourself that you can't imagine not being it? Doing it? Having it?

Define it.

Write it out in detail and get crystal clear on what it is you are hoping to do... and then, give yourself permission to chase it. Give yourself permission to stick with it when it's tough. Give yourself permission to have it, to have exactly what you want and nothing else. For my work, that looks a little something like this:

I want to work across my businesses with ease and flow. I want to do work that lights me up with people I love to work with, who understand me and my vision. I want to employ a female team of mums with school age children. I want to earn in excess of £7,000 every month with consistency and overflow. My work is highly praised by my clients. I retain clients and gain new clients with ease and alignment. I am a trusted and valued voice in my industry and people turn to me for comment, interviews and collaboration. Overflow is my consistent state of being.

Write it down.

Like me, you may have read many books and skipped the exercises. I always did that. Promise me you will do this one. There is magic in getting crystal clear on what you want. There is magic in claiming your numbers and there is so much to be gleaned from writing down the core feelings that you desire to feel. It gives the statement a sense of life that really allows you to anchor yourself to it. It feels like a living, breathing thing. A statement that has possibility. A statement that can be.

Then, I ask you to give yourself permission. Move through that statement you have just produced and give yourself permission to go for each part. You can do it in writing, you can tell yourself in the mirror, you can talk it into life while you walk the dog or drive your car. Whatever you do, do not write it and forget it.

I give myself permission to work across multiple businesses with ease and flow. I give myself permission to only do the work that lights me up. I give myself permission to only do the work with people who understand me and my vision. I give myself permission to reach this level of success so that I can employ an all-female team. I give myself permission to set an energetic minimum of income in my business at £7,000 each month. It is safe for me to always earn in excess of £7,000 each month and for there to be consistent financial overflow.

You will see overflow a lot in my work. I don't mind admitting that, as a woman who has battled with imposter syndrome and a whole heap of money mindset blocks, overflow, that feeling of consistent replenishment is the thing I love most in my work and the feeling I always strive for.

Do this. State it and claim what you want. Give yourself permission and do it as often as you need.

The plan.

As a business strategist, you knew I'd be all about the plan, right? But honestly, the plan is actually the easiest part. How many times have you planned something for your business but: a) never actually executed the plan or b) gave up when it got hard, you got bored or you thought no one would notice? Yeah, I've been there at times too, don't panic.

Thing is though, friend, I want you to have everything you have listed out in your desires. I want you to be the most wildly successful woman I have ever spent time with and if you are going to get there, it will be a whole lot less painful if you create a plan that will help you.

It's always harder to get to a destination with no map, and I'm guessing that you've never managed to get to most of the places you listed in your desires list?

I want you to create a plan for it, my friend.

Go through your desires list and, just like you gave yourself permission for each, also start to break down each item. What needs to happen in order for you to achieve it?

I desire to work across my business with ease and flow – what does that actually look like?

- I'll have to plan my calendar in advance so that each of the

businesses gets time and I've factored in important things like programme launches and new products for each.
- I'll need systems to ensure both of the businesses are streamlined and take the pressure off me – how can I do that?
- I want to always earn more than £7,000 per month – what does that look like though? How can I create a strategy so that financial flow is consistent and systemised where possible?

A good strategy will encompass all of your core desires for your business and allow you to breakdown a blueprint or roadmap to get there.

When I work with my clients, we usually go deeper in our strategy but for the purposes of this book, if you do nothing else, do these two things and I promise you, you will see a change in how you feel, how you work and hopefully the impact you will be able to have in moving towards where you desire to be.

I couldn't have got to the destination I am at today, writing to you, had I not given myself permission. I got pretty far by ignoring all the messy mindset, money, self-worth and imposter syndrome stuff, but I never got to a place where I could enjoy any of it. I never felt like what I had done was enough. I never quite got to where I wanted to be. When I released some of that stuff, I won't trivialise it, I got a lot of coaching and some therapy, it all started to move forward. It took a year for me to really see a shift in my circumstances but when I gave myself permission to grow because I wanted to, when I gave myself permission to really believe in myself and what I could achieve, that's when things started to shift. That's when I found it easy to strategize for myself in the way I was be able to for clients. That's when I started to move closer to the destination I desired and most importantly, throw the financial target out of the window. When I did that, THAT'S when I could finally feel the way I wanted to feel. Ease, overflow, satisfaction. Enough.

When I give myself permission and create a plan, I am able to divide my work. I own that variety is the spice of my life. I feel fulfilled by working on my non-profit. I feel challenged as I come up with new products for the mum-in-business market. I love the chase of getting new financial backers and I feel proud that I created something that helps hundreds of lower-income women each and every year. When I gave myself permission, I allowed myself to push the boundaries of what I could have in my work life and I started my coaching business. I help women get rid of their fears around being visible for their business. I help them own their superpowers and create authentic social media content that their customers love. Many of those women carry on working with me for growth strategies and believe me, there is nothing I love more than empowering those women to do this work for themselves. Set the goals, create the plans, sprint at them, rest up, move the goal, go again. I believe that having more brilliant women in business will change the world and I am showing up every day to play my part in it.

In my non-profit, I've seen women with no business idea, turn up, do the work and start something so right for them, that they were able to stop claiming government benefits for the first time in eight years. I've seen highly skilled women gain employment at their local supermarket and then realise that the online business world would allow them to leverage their skills in a business, for more money, more flexibility, from their homes. I have watched women come alive in their businesses, no longer scared of what 'someone' might say about it, free of judgment, full of purpose and happy to share their beautiful, imperfect and oh-so-needed selves. In my coaching, I have looked into the eyes of women who tell me I have handed them the missing puzzle piece. There is no shame in needing to get help at any stage in your business. I would not be writing this without it. One of the biggest common myths we feed ourselves as female entrepreneurs is that we should know it all. I have lost count of the number of conversations I have had where a woman says something along the lines of: shouldn't we know more/ learn more/ get more qualifications/ be more perfect before we put ourselves out there?

Let me help you. You don't know it all now. You won't know it all in a year. Stop waiting. Just start.

All of us can get lost in the doing part of our businesses. It can happen at many stages, the beginning and at all moments of growth. It's at these moments when you may need to reach out for help to navigate, be that a great strategy, a coach, a group of friends who know what you are going through... get whatever you can. Do not hold yourself back because you feel can't access this part. You can. Ask for it, pay for it, volunteer it, just make a pledge to yourself that you will do what you can to get it. If you are seeking that space, if you are on a mission for more, seek out my free Facebook group and I will be glad to hold that space for you, friend.

ABOUT THE AUTHOR
CERI GILLETT

Ceri Gillett is a business coach and mentor who helps women to start and grow a business where authenticity leads to authority.

Ceri believes in failing fast and forward. She trained as a nurse, worked as airline cabin crew and read the travel news for national radio stations before finding herself working in business development for some well-known financial institutions.

Ceri is the founder of a non-profit that works across the UK, helping mums to start a business. She has partnered with banks and tech companies to provide free entrepreneurial support to hundreds of women in the UK every year. She is a mentor for a variety of start-up programmes and a coach for women looking for visibility and growth strategies.

Ceri runs multiple businesses, both on and offline, and outside of work she loves wild swimming, walking the countryside of Wales and enjoying time with her family.

Ceri is available for coaching and consulting. She is a regular speaker on a variety of topics related to motherhood and start-up/growth for female entrepreneurs.

You can reach Ceri at:

Email – ceri@cerigillettcoaching.com
Website – www.cerigillettcoaching.com
Download my free resource 'A Simple Content Solution' as my free gift to you.

facebook.com/cerigillettcoaching
instagram.com/cerigillettcoaching

5

CLAIRE ANTILL
CREATING A BUSINESS AROUND YOUR SELF

It all starts with a morning routine they say. My three mini alarm clocks (twins Grace and Sam and their little sister Olivia) usually wake me. There is a brief moment for reflection, to set my intentions for the day and to be grateful, before the whirlwind of getting ready for school and drop-offs, before my 'work' day begins.

But I have an overwhelming feeling of contentment. I'm grounded, and I'm exactly where I need to be. I have bravely stepped off the corporate ladder and into the unknown. This is my proudest achievement and it's been quite the journey to get here.

Gone is the feeling in the pit of my stomach: the nerves and the constant adrenaline rush of what is next? And, what have I missed? Or, who have I let down? Now, I can set the course and the pace. I have the space to create, to think and to do.

As someone who has always viewed success in status and monetary terms, in who I work for, in being respected for being the hard worker, the dependable one, the expert, the shift to redefining my professional life has been huge. I've set out my stall based on what others think of me and looked for their validation. I've grappled with feelings of guilt for wanting more: to create a life that celebrates my family and all that I am, while meeting the deep need within me to learn, grow and achieve. And to make money.

Let me tell you, it's not an easy journey, but we only get one shot at this life so it's time to get going.

You are never really prepared for how much you change after having children. It is an identity shift like no other and hits you like a train. Suddenly, your world is full of responsibilities and looking after others. You can immerse your whole self in this and, quite frankly, can become lost.

Don't get me wrong, there is joy and unconditional love and wonder, but you can feel like the space for you - your desires, your ambitions - is somehow now taken up and has limits. And you don't want to express this because: "what will other people think of me? I should be grateful for what I have."

I felt like a square peg in a round hole: at first, I didn't feel like I took to motherhood like a natural (whatever that means) and equally, I wasn't the same 'self' at work anymore. No longer could I stretch to meet every demand by working harder or longer hours, and the weight of expectation didn't diminish.

Challenging dynamics, office politics and stepping through the daily minefield eventually eroded my confidence and self-worth. But, I'm forever grateful for this experience, because it was the catalyst for change. I had always made rational decisions and taken the sensible route in my career, but now I felt I'd reached a dead end. It was the push I needed.

What if I could go it alone? I had re-trained and upskilled in digital marketing whilst on maternity leave. I'd seen others make a success of it and there was no shortage of businesses looking for help. Could my years of experience be put to use elsewhere? Could I do this in a way that would allow me to be a mum in my own way and be there for the kids and spend precious time with them?

Then the questions and the fear started: was I enough? Who would pay me to work with them? What if I failed? There was also the minor issue of a global pandemic to navigate.

It has taken me time and a lot of work to get here, but I've realised that your worth has to be defined by you and all that your life is. It's not what you do professionally, or how much you are paid, it's what YOU stand for: your values and your beliefs, that gives you purpose. If I could go back to my younger self, I'd reassure her that she should believe that opportunities are truly limitless - change makes them happen and it's uncomfortable, but so worth it. This is how the magic happens, and it can for you, too!

I've always been a 'study', a grafter. If I want to know how to do something, I set about learning all there is to know about it. From a young age, I recognised the freedom that came with doing well in school. I enjoyed the challenge, particularly if someone told me I couldn't do something; I liked to show them they were wrong.

Coming from a working-class background, in a small seaside town, where school was seen as a necessity rather than a priority, there wasn't the expectation of going on to do great things. University was not something that was familiar to our family. When I discovered I could succeed, I knuckled under and these were the first signs of me working to create a life for myself, the first little spark of an entrepreneur. I had love and support and the only pressure came from me. I knew I wanted more, but I didn't know what was available to me or how to get there.

Despite success with learning - I would go on to complete a degree and postgraduate qualification in different languages even - I always felt that there was a limit to what I could do: some form of invisible barrier. Whilst working for different companies and sectors (public, private, not for profit, at home and abroad), I couldn't shake the feeling that I wasn't achieving my potential. I didn't know how to define what that was, and so, became stuck.

I would describe myself as being an introvert at heart, and someone who has learnt how to be seen to be confident, because if you don't speak up for yourself, then you don't get anywhere, right? I can remember being terrified, sitting on the train with a single suitcase, when I moved to Brussels on my own at the age of 22. I gave myself a talking to: "I know it's scary, but what are you going to do, sit at home and never do anything?" I often think back to that moment whenever a new change or transition seems too big or overwhelming and it comforts me.

I have spent large parts of my career having to learn quickly and talk about subjects as an expert, even if I've not always felt it inside. This, at times, gave me the feeling that I was always waiting to be found out, and that my value would be questioned. My knowledge and ability to learn facts has always been my strength and so I look to it to feel reassured about who I am.

Working in very traditional and male dominated industries (politics and energy), I tried to mould myself to be more like men to succeed. You have to be good at numbers and finance and putting yourself forward, grease the wheels by making the right connections. Communication skills and diplomacy are 'soft skills', useful around the edges, but will never help you be the main event. It was all about covering up perceived weaknesses and not realising how to celebrate the strengths or being unique.

Instead, I was happy to be the reliable and trusted lieutenant that made things happen behind the scenes, with the fundamental belief that if you work hard, you will do well and that you have to work hard to earn 'good' money. And by working hard, that meant devoting everything to work, all the hours, all the extracurricular activities, to get noticed and make a mark.

But the trouble with that is, if you pour all of your perception of your self-worth into work and how you are viewed through the lens of others, you will always be chasing an unachievable version of success. You can't please everyone all the time. When you become a mum, your priorities and responsibilities shift even more. It's like walking a tightrope, that feeling of constantly living on the edge, with people ready for you to fall.

And when you don't meet the expectations of others, your 'self' takes a knock. Maybe it wasn't meant for me, maybe I'm not one of the people who succeeds? Why do others have it in them and I don't? Perhaps I'm just not cut out for the business world and I'd be safer doing something less ambitious. Sound familiar?

Like many women at work, I felt, in my early career, that I needed to behave in a certain way to succeed: don't be too assertive or 'pushy', be modest when talking about your achievements. I was told by one male manager that "Not everything you say always makes sense." Your voice can be undermined by people who speak louder than you, or those who go on and on so that there is no gap for you to say anything, or by those who repeat your point to the applause of all.

As I said above, I have shaped myself to impress people. I have worked for companies and organisations with status (I was a political assistant in the European Parliament in Brussels, I ran a campaign group on sustainable energy in the Houses of Parliament in Westminster, and managed marketing teams for a large energy company).

Why did I do this? Firstly, because they provided incredible and fulfilling opportunities to be able to make a difference. But I know that a large part of it was to go back to that search for validation. If she works for them, she must be good, right?

Having been blessed with a happy personal life, and once I settled down to have a family with my husband John, there was a new sense of ease. But with it, a fear of what came next for my career after children? Perhaps I had already reached my peak and now it was my role to step back. Would my skills still be valid and valued? Could I get back on the wheel?

Going back to work after maternity leave is a huge transition (if you've done it, you'll know). You feel like the whole world has moved on and coped without you and you're from a different time. I took two full stints of maternity leave and a career break. On my first time back, there was massive change, with many people, including myself, facing redundancy. I rolled the dice and in the shake up, I saw the potential to shape something new and reinvent myself. I took my subject expertise and content skills and put them into practice in a new direction: marketing, building a new team and reputation in the process. I could have made a safe choice. I didn't. I was brave.

I chose to cement this new direction and to upskill whilst off for the second time (back to my learning) in strategic social media marketing, with the fabulous Digital Mums, and then later with Emma Van Heusen for Advanced Facebook Ads. I saw all this as an investment in my future to have in-demand skills and to give myself choice. Importantly, skills that could be used anytime from anywhere. We'd now relocated as a family from London to the South Coast to have a support network.

With learning comes freedom. These new skills also reignited my passion for learning and opened my eyes to the fact that careers are no longer static with one direction. It was possible to have a new story. I learnt that it was ok to not know all the answers and that it was a process of exploration. The world of digital constantly adapts and evolves, and this is your most important asset: to be open to the possibilities and go with it.

I didn't know it at the time, but this was the start of the end for my corporate career.

By this time the twins were starting school, with the littlest one in nursery. I made the long daily commute on the train, always arriving an hour late and leaving an hour early. Enough was enough. I missed out on their school meetings or mornings where parents could come in to see their children play and learn in the classroom.

I made the important bits, the school plays and parent evenings. Those were non-negotiable for me. I felt sad that I couldn't drop them off and pick them up every day.

The constant rush, the struggle and trying not to give in to feelings of resentment, were too much. It was only when I came to a breaking point that I had the strength to walk away from my job. I invested in a business coach and I levelled up. What could I do with my skills and could I go it alone?

As high achieving women, when we want to start something new, we tend to judge ourselves: what will other people think? What if I fail? But a mentor once told me: what if you succeed? What if it goes really well? I realised that I had more to gain. I had the chance to create a business from scratch and to be the wife and mum I wanted to be.

I'm not telling everyone to leave their jobs! But you must look at what it is in life that really drives and motivates you.

To find this, rather than looking to others for validation, concentrate on recognising your own self-worth. You are more than what you do for a living. What are all the elements of your life that you're really proud of? It could be that you are a loyal friend or passionate supporter of a certain cause, or that you have an obscure skill. You are truly unique, so lean into this as it is what people will be drawn to.

Another key part of the preparation is to set out healthy habits and clear boundaries for yourself. You've no doubt heard the expression 'filling up your cup' - making sure that you are looked after so you can look after all those around you who rely on you. As women who want to rise, this is so important. We often want to do all the things and put our own selves and needs after those of everyone else. This is when burnout can happen. Nothing good or creative can come from this space.

Once you have the healthy mindset foundations in place, you can consider your next steps: How do I want to feel? And, how do I want to get there? The trick is to find the sweet spot between what you enjoy doing (your purpose) and where there is a need for your products and services.

How can you find your purpose? It doesn't have to be big and ground-breaking, although it could be. It can be something as simple as discovering appreciation for the life that you have already, for your family and friends, your health, that you are safe and well, that you have freedom and choice (even if it doesn't always feel like it).

This sense of appreciation can bring an amazing sense of satisfaction and calm - the total opposite to a life in the corporate world, where you are dancing to someone else's tune. Having that freedom and control to work with who you want and in the way you thrive is incredible.

From there, you have space to access your creativity and allow the ideas to come through. You can nurture that little gem of a business idea or product that you've always wanted to develop. Put yourself in a mindset of service: the world needs you and your ideas. How can you help others and make their lives easier, more joyful, more fulfilled?

But how will you get people to take notice of you and find your business? It's no good putting all your time and effort into creating the perfect solution, only for it never to be discovered. The times they are a changing, so how can you adapt with them? Let me share some thoughts with you.

We've come out of a difficult 18 months with COVID (at the time of writing). Who could have predicted what life would be like and the major shift that has happened? Remote and flexible working, once deemed impossible for many women, was the norm overnight. This has transformed opportunities and families, with new avenues into work that would have been unthinkable before the virus struck.

It's also been a catalyst for change for those who have decided that the life of working as an employee no longer feels right. Out of the most challenging circumstances, and adversity, there are often also great flights of creativity. People have started businesses and are carving out new lives for themselves and their families. The digital economy means that we can create and run global operations from our homes.

I never used to think of myself as artistic and creative. Probably because these are not skills that we are encouraged to develop. I focused on 'doing' and was the person who got things done, did the planning and the strategy, the 'important bits'. My appreciation of all things creative changed when I pivoted into my new role in marketing and when I started studying social media. Here, I saw that everyone has the power of endless creativity at their fingertips, and to reach masses in an instant. What a gift!

Digital is all about changing and adapting, it continuously evolves. The old rules of academic learning do not apply. You learn by doing, trying things out, testing and then always improving. It was a huge thing for me to be out of my comfort zone and not know all the answers, but instead discovering that you learn through experience. This is empowering, because it puts you in the driving seat: you can learn and grow at a pace that suits you and there is no limit to your potential.

With this new lightbulb moment on learning, all my past experience has come together in what I do now: the fact that I can use my words, my love of books and language (writing in this book is a dream!), my planning skills, attention to detail and analysing facts, branding, marketing and strategy. I have worked with all different kinds of people and with businesses, large and small. Looking back on my journey to get here, it all makes sense. I know my self-worth.

Importantly, those 'soft' skills in communication are what sets me apart. I care about building relationships and I thrive when working with others. I love the buzz of bouncing ideas off a team and seeing people's different expertise and experiences come together to create something phenomenal. Now, as a business owner, I can work in partnership with other businesses and be an extended part of their team/(s).

Understanding how to build relationships with people and make meaningful connections in the digital world is crucial. There are many automations and technical solutions to talk to people, but there are areas where the human touch cannot be replicated. Telling your story is one. Yes, an AI machine can probably put some text together, but could it make it sing with meaning and evoke emotion in the reader? You should always bring a personalised approach to your marketing and be human. This is what brings results and your purpose.

My purpose is to help ecommerce businesses, those who have sustainability at heart, to create, grow and thrive, all built around the life that they want. I understand the way that digital marketing and advertising works on a technical and human level. It is rewarding to see how people can become empowered by creating wealth through growing their businesses. And by this, I don't just mean financial wealth. It can mean being able to spend more time with their families or by enriching their lives through creativity and bringing solutions to the lives of others.

I love what I do. It's so rewarding to build something of your very own. I can help you be found for what you stand for and be known for what you do, creating strong online brands in a busy digital world. It's so exciting.

My life now is very different than it was yesterday, the week before, or even a year ago. I feel that I'm growing every day in what I'm learning, how I'm feeling and in my relationships. There is abundance in all things. I have found a new sense of purpose and direction, one that comes from within. I'm building a life around what matters most to me, my family.

I am creating a business that lifts others up and I love seeing other people grow and thrive on their own terms. And, I am fulfilled with creating my own wealth. Yes, I can make money myself! Not bits around the edges, but money that can support a family. It can be scary to step away from the security of a monthly pay cheque, but nothing is so satisfying as money that you have earned from your own creativity and in your own time.

Most importantly, I have learnt to value what I do and what I bring to the world in all parts of me. I'm a loving wife and mum, a supportive family member, loyal friend and someone who cares for others. Everything from the past, the experiences, good and bad, have moulded and strengthened me and I'm very grateful.

This sense of contentment and appreciation has opened me up to new opportunities that I never thought would be possible. I have worked as part of a creative team for a global media agency for a household nappy brand (who would have thought that changing nappies for 3 small humans would be a defining factor in my creative insight??), I have run campaigns for scaling ecommerce businesses for fashion and baby brands. Everything has come together at the right time.

I feel strongly that my children should have an example of what they can achieve and that it starts with them being sure of their self-worth and values. They see a mum who takes care of herself and is able to be at her best for herself and those around her. I no longer feel guilty for going out for a restorative walk in nature or a swim. It's essential and not an indulgence. They are proud of who I am and I should be too.

I have a voice. Others no longer speak for me or over me. I can step into my power as a strong and determined woman and use my communication skills to forge successful relationships in my community and in business.

I work well with others and like to build meaningful connections. I've found that in business, for it to be successful, you have to be on the same wavelength. You usually get a sense of whether you're going to be a good fit at the beginning, or if it doesn't feel quite right. If you try and force things, or bend yourself to be someone you're not, it doesn't work. It's all about alignment.

This is one of the great benefits of running a business rather than working for one, you get to choose how you work and above all, with whom. Say goodbye to office politics!

One of the things I have always loved in the different places I've worked is to train and coach people, having been a mentor to others throughout my career. Put simply, I like to see others do well. I firmly believe there is room for all of us to succeed and grow.

I like to share the experience and knowledge that I have built up in a specialist area, such as marketing and online advertising (along with 15 years of working for a variety of roles in the public and private sector) and in turn, learn from others about their business and what matters to them. You learn and grow together.

One of my superpowers is to explain complicated things in a simple way. I've done it my whole career in briefs and speeches for politicians or senior managers, or presenting to groups. It gives me tremendous pleasure to see the 'a-ha' moments when it all clicks into place and people are adding knowledge or a new skill to their toolkit.

I have worked with business owners who have no particular joy for marketing but see it as a necessary evil. I enjoy sharing how it can simply be couched in terms of telling your story and thinking about who it is you want to reach and what you'd like to say to them. It is so rewarding to see business owners turn their dream into reality and watch their monthly sales grow as more people discover their products and services. It's incredible.

I have helped multiple business owners to learn how to create adverts themselves and even if I'm running the strategy and management myself, I like to work with integrity to show them how the process works. In this way, they get to see under the bonnet and have a clear understanding of where and how their money is being spent - no hiding behind the technical side or the numbers, complete transparency, so they can be empowered and make informed decisions on the direction of their business. And when the time is right, they can take over the reins and run their own campaigns. It's creating growth for everyone and is very inspiring.

If you have been reading this and parts have resonated with you, I'd love for you to reflect on your own journey. If you are working in a role or an environment that doesn't bring you purpose or meaning or if you want to create a new way of doing things, rest assured that it is possible.

You can have a family life and a business one that fulfils you. Balance is an outdated term, but for me it's about finding work that brings me purpose and allows me to connect with others, but doesn't take over. It's part of me but doesn't define me.

I'll leave you with some final tips. Start with yourself. Think about why you are so special and unique. If you are clear and confident in your own worth and value, nothing can shake that. It will be your rock. Find your purpose that combines doing what you love and that brings reward and share it with others who are waiting for you to help them.

You don't have to do it alone. If you'd like guidance from someone who has walked the path, then get in touch with me to see how I can support you with creating and growing your business. I can't wait to get started.

ABOUT THE AUTHOR
CLAIRE ANTILL

Claire Antill is a marketing consultant and specialist in Facebook and Instagram ads. She helps businesses sell sustainable products and tell their brand's story to grow and scale through paid social media.

Before starting her own business, Claire worked for 15+ years in the energy and sustainability sector in a range of roles, including leading big brand marketing teams.

As well as working with her own clients (she has worked with businesses in sustainable clothing, gifting and lifestyle), Claire has been a consultant for household brands, creating social media ads for Kimberly-Clark (Huggies UK) at VaynerMedia.

Claire enjoys living by the sea in her hometown of Bognor Regis, with her husband and 3 children. Probably part fish, she loves being in and around water and completing charity swims.

Claire is available to provide specialist coaching and training to you or your marketing team or done for you strategy and management in paid social advertising.

You can reach Claire at:

Email: claire@littleolivesocial.com
Website: https://littleolivesocial.com/

facebook.com/littleolivesocial
instagram.com/littleolivesocial
linkedin.com/in/claire-antill-33831a50

CLAIRE WHITE
THE SUCCESSFUL WALLFLOWER

Kintsugi – *the Japanese art of putting broken pottery pieces back together with gold. Treating breakage and repair as part of the history of an object, rather than something to disguise.*

Seven months into a global pandemic, I embarked on a course with my coach that would alter me both personally and professionally.

I now have more alignment than I ever have done before. I feel at ease, I feel like I can finally inhale and exhale deeply, rather than holding my breath.

I now know who I am and finally know what I want to be as a 'grown-up'!

I now have purpose and know my potential, and that it is limitless.

I now help introverted women through transformational coaching in mindset, consistency, visibility and infusing the real essence of who they truly are into their business.

I now see my introversion as my superpower rather than something that holds me back. Things about myself that I always took for granted or assumed that everyone did are now shining as my purpose.

I now start my day with a routine that nourishes me and, although still a work in progress, it shapes my days.

I now have a circle of women that know me better than anyone else and that I can go to with anything, both on a personal and business topic.

I now see myself as a piece of *kintsugi* pottery; the cracks are there for the world to see and I am stronger and more beautiful for them.

> *"A good rule of thumb is that any environment that consistently leaves you feeling bad about who you are is the wrong environment."*
>
> Laurie Helgoe

When I left school, I felt small and not quite enough for a long time, which led me to play small and not be enough.

I didn't go to university and instead trained as a beauty therapist and fitness instructor, and, after working in these roles for a time, I took a year out to travel around South East Asia, Australia and New Zealand with my then boyfriend, now husband. Travel and adventure are in my nature and were in my upbringing. My family travelled with my dad's work and by the time I was 12, I had lived in four different countries.

Coming back and working in admin roles, I never really took the 'career' path. I set up some kitchen table businesses so that I could work around my two daughters, but a change in work for my husband meant that I once again entered the workplace.

Being an introvert, and not really knowing enough about it, meant that I played to the myths and stereotypes: I wouldn't be successful, I was too quiet, you had to be outgoing in order to progress, I wouldn't be able to get my message across, I felt more comfortable in the background.

I'd had kitchen table businesses since 2011, but January 2019 saw my turning point. Having lost my Mum six months before, I was no longer willing to waste my one and only precious life living a fraction of my full potential. So, I embarked on a path of self-employment and self-discovery and I was determined to do it 'properly'.

I invested in myself and trained firstly as a Social Media Manager, and then a Facebook Ads Strategist, and it was on that course that I first received personal coaching. It opened my eyes to the potential that was in me and a whole new chapter of my journey began.

By investing in myself and training in digital skills, I was able to set myself up with my own businesses. It still wasn't filling my heart with joy though and the pandemic gave me an opportunity to really delve into why I was feeling that it wasn't working. I was stuck. I had no identity; no self-care routines and I was stuck in a cycle of self-sabotage. I used to get a physical reaction when I had to meet or think about my clients whilst not at my laptop.

I woke up and took action, just small steps to start with, but action none the less. I found a mindset coach and a circle of women who got it, who got me. I found where I belonged and it all changed. That sense of belonging is the key to stepping out as who you truly are; find your circle and you'll find yourself. I gave myself permission to embrace who I was as an introvert and I then worked really hard on my self- awareness. I got to know who I really was and that I could shine as an introvert because I understood and celebrated those wonderful qualities.

> *"Be regular and orderly in your life, so that you may be violent and original in your work."*
>
> — GUSTAV FLAUBERT

Regular and orderly I'd got down to a tee. And that was where the problem lay; boldness and creativity had eluded me. Action had eluded me.

I felt small and therefore, played small. My beliefs were that life is a struggle sometimes, being a 'grown-up' is not easy. I had very little ambition as I just didn't feel I deserved it. My hopes, dreams and expectations were small; I had shrunk inside myself. If I kept myself small then I wouldn't fail, right? Yes, I probably wouldn't fail, but I certainly wouldn't succeed.

The job roles I applied for were a make do.

Did it fit around the school holidays? Mostly, but we'd make do.

Was there going to be enough money? If not, we'd make do.

Was it going to be fulfilling? If not, I'd make do.

Was there any progression for me? If not, I'd make do.

As an introvert and empath, I very quickly and keenly become aware of levels and states in the energy around me. At the time, I believed that there was nothing particularly 'special' about little old me and assumed that everyone felt this way too. I even investigated what vitamins or minerals I might be lacking in as I was so exhausted by certain situations.

Working in open plan offices, and using my own energy to raise the vibration of the room, led me to self-isolate and shrink. I would often eat my lunch alone and would always volunteer to walk over to the other site if needed. Even in friendly meetings, I would stay quiet as I was so afraid of being shut down or talked over and not listened to. This had happened to me too many times before and I didn't want to put myself through it.

Of course, this did not serve me in any way, shape, or form, and I truly believed that this was it; this is what I deserved and I should be grateful for it. The choice I made to be able to take the school holidays off was the flexible life I'd wanted. So why did it feel so exhausting? Because I was making do. All. The. Time.

"Not all those who wander are lost"

— J.R.R. Tolkien

As a result of my dad's work, we moved around more than the average family, and this meant that at age 11, I went to boarding school whilst my parents and younger brother moved to Cyprus. It took a while for me to settle, but I formed friendships quickly and one, in particular, remains dear to me today. Being an introverted child in an environment that required you to be with others 24 hours a day was a lot to take in, and my pattern of self-isolation started. I remember that in one particular boarding house, there was a bathroom that had a radiator and a pile of old magazines, and this became my place to sit and just be when I needed it.

My school reports always mentioned that "Claire seems a little lost" and I carried that for a long, long time. I listened to opinions of others and believed them to be true. I felt that I was not enough and when I didn't take the expected path of 'do well at GCSE, do well at A level, go to University', and fell down after step one, I felt a huge failure: I would forever be behind all my classmates. I've let my family down. I'm not good enough. I'll never be successful (whatever that means). This all stayed with me in the back of my mind until very recently.

The amount of travelling I had done as a child meant that I had a yearning to keep the fire of adventure stoked and by meeting Rob, who also had the same spirit of adventure, meant we donned our backpacks and set off for the best part of a year and travelled around South East Asia, Australia, New Zealand, coming home via Fiji and LA. Being among like-minded people from all different kinds of backgrounds was so enriching, and landing back in the UK just before Christmas was hard, despite the fairy lights. We had so many stories, but no one was interested in hearing them as they couldn't relate, and why would they? So, without me really noticing as I was a people pleaser, I shrank a little in order to fit in.

When I re-entered the workplace, it was as a temp to start with. I classified myself as 'just' the temp and this was a pattern that repeated for me for a long time: Just a mum. Just a little business. Just me. After the birth of my first daughter, and not really managing to be enough at either work or home, I made the choice to start my first home business. This wasn't a massive success, due to my lack of funding and knowledge, if I'm honest and after the birth of my second daughter, a new business followed. This one also went the same way as the first – I loved it though and it was in the snow sports industry, which was exciting, vibrant, and fun. With two entrepreneurs in the family (Rob ran his own business, too), it was cycle of feast or famine and when the proverbial hit the fan due to something out of our control, it was time for us both to return to an office environment.

Working with people, who I now realise were quietly suffering as a result of being out of alignment or dissatisfied in some area of their lives, was not serving me. I couldn't understand why they weren't making a change. Having seen ads on social media for a social media course especially for mums looking to retrain and upskill in the digital space. I took a deep breath, borrowed some money (thanks Dad!) and signed up. This was a breath of fresh air for me for a while; I was learning again and connecting with other women just like me - those who had felt lost in what they were doing and wanted a change. Upon graduating the course, I soon got some work via friends and I was off on my new journey. It was a slow start though. I didn't want to be seen, even as a business owner. I was terrified of being judged, both by those who knew me but most often, by those who didn't. I joined in-person networking groups but always felt the odd-one out and never really pushed the value I could bring to their businesses – I now know that although I had loved the course and the new knowledge, it wasn't really what I wanted to do. It didn't make my heart full or my soul sing. I was still out of alignment.

So, I took action again. I invested in myself once more and upskilled into Facebook ads. The learning fired me up again and gave me another skill to offer out to the world. As part of the course, we received a monthly mindset call with a coach, Andrea Callanan - my first experience of anything like it. Andrea guided our mindset shifts during the course and supported in the membership group afterwards. I stayed on the side-lines and compared, a LOT. I realise now that I was using my introversion as an excuse to stay quiet, stay small, not be noticed. I didn't realise my true potential came about BECAUSE I was an introvert, not in spite of it.

I graduated as an ads strategist in January 2020, and via some previous contacts, got my first clients. I decided to niche into the private school sector as it was an area familiar to me, both as a pupil and through previous job roles. Then March 2020 happened, and my work potential and confidence took a nosedive. Being gifted the time to reflect as the world shifted made me realise that my heart was not filled, and my soul was not singing. This was my wake-up call as I knew that something, or as I now know, somebody (that would be me then) had to change. I took the opportunity to work with Andrea once again in a group setting, and set about self-mastery and the coaching accreditation with her via the Aligned Coaching Academy.

Through these courses, I really got to know myself as I had never done before. I embraced myself as an introvert and can now bring my purpose into the light without compromise.

> *"The privilege of a lifetime is to become who you truly are."*
>
> — CARL JUNG

OK, let's have a chat.

Get comfortable, unclench your jaw, take a deep breath in, and out, drop your shoulders and roll your head from side to side.

Let me tell you about what I do for introverted women who are ready to tackle all of those limiting beliefs, whilst embracing all those wonderful introvert qualities and work with them not against them.

So, let's start with getting to know yourself. What is an introvert? A very simple way to look at it is how do you respond to external stimulation? If you gain your energy from it, then you are extrovert and if you are drained by it (could be straight away or after a time), then you are introvert.

Now, just like the number of shades of green in a garden, there are lots of different types of introverts and you may not have all the traits that are typically shown in the personality tests you can take online. So, I encourage you to use the tests as a guide but build up your own self-awareness - what fuels you, what drains you, who fuels you and who drains you.

I urge you to look deep inside yourself and get to really know who you are as a person, not as a parent, partner, daughter, sister, aunt, not as a job title, but the truest you.

I want to start with what introverts are NOT.

We are not all shy and socially inept.

We are not all rude and aloof.

We are not all boring.

We don't hate all people.

We don't want to be 'fixed' and become extrovert.

Shyness can affect both introverts and extroverts alike and social skills are not reserved just for the extroverts amongst us! If we seem aloof, then we are probably processing and reflecting. We are not ones for small talk, in general.

Just because we might prefer a cosy night in rather than a huge gathering does not make us boring. I love a night out as much as the next extrovert, but they drain me, rather than replenish me so, when I have to leave, I have to leave. I'm convinced that the Fairy Godmother in Cinderella is an introvert because of the midnight curfew!

Do you find that you become more extrovert when around certain people? When we find someone to connect with, we hold them dear, and our true selves come to the forefront. These are the people we can chat for hours with about anything and everything.

Our primary brain pathway is longer and more complex so we, as introverts, might need a little longer to process and respond. We're not slow thinkers but instead, are deep thinkers. I could not be a stand-up comedian, for many reasons... but the main one is that I would not be able to give the witty comebacks to hecklers in the moment. In the car on the way home, I'm all over it!

I recently ventured out to an in-person networking event, subbing in for a friend of mine and when we were waiting to be seated and I was introducing myself to others and told them what I did, one lady exclaimed "but you don't look like an introvert". This got me thinking (of course it did!) about misconceptions about introverts. Do we hide ourselves in plain sight by dressing like extroverts? Is there a uniform or badge that I'm not aware of that will identify me as introvert?

I get it though. A search on an online design app for images of an introvert brings up images of sad, lonely looking people, and this seems to be the view on it, despite nearly half the population being introvert. No wonder we can be misunderstood.

There is a lot of science behind this, and I still have a lot to learn on this, but by understanding that we were born this way and that our brain pathways, nervous system and neurotransmitters are wired differently, makes total sense.

I've listed what introverts are not so what are we?

We are deep thinkers.

We are creative.

We think before we speak.

We are listeners and we don't just hear words. We are aware of body language and subtleties that go unnoticed by most.

We are observers – I love being able to people watch; I find it fascinating and one of the reasons I love going to gigs and festivals. I get to observe a lot of people but don't have to interact with them – win, win!

We are often a calming influence.

When we go quiet, we are not withdrawing but contemplating. That special inner world that we create for ourselves is where all the breakthroughs and solutions come from.

Don't withdraw for too long though. Be aware of when you slip into the shadows and make sure you step into the light. We need the light to bloom and so that those that need us can see us. By hiding, you are not serving the people who need you, whether that be friends and family or your clients who haven't come across you yet, but you are the perfect person for them. I know that you have so much to offer.

Where are you being small? Why? These are huge questions, especially the second one and you will need to dig deep.

Take action.

Because we are blessed with the power of deep thinking, we may be quiet but our minds can be loud and this can send us into over-thinking. My advice? Reflect but don't ruminate. Keep things positive and proactive, keep moving forward and find solutions.

Do the work. Get intentional and organised and take action. It doesn't need to be huge steps, but one tiny step daily.

Ponder on the following questions.

What do you want? What drives you? Is it money, recognition or more of a feeling? What and how do you want to feel, every day?

Where are you now? Do you feel aligned and at ease? If not, what needs to change? How can you move forward?

What makes you happy? I mean really, heart burstingly happy? How can you bring joy into your everyday?

What do you need? Perhaps more importantly, what do you not need?

Where are you in your cycle? Lunar or menstrual. This makes a huge difference, and it is often in hindsight that the penny drops, having trouble sleeping, concentrating, focusing, (checks cycle) ah, that would be it then. Part of getting to know yourself is getting to know how you function at your best. When is your energy high and when is it lower throughout the day, week, month, and year? Then, plan accordingly.

I have a little energy slump at around 3pm, so all my tasks that need me at my energetic best are done before lunch. I am now also very aware of how my energy is during the month. I know of female entrepreneurs that have a quiet week every month; they slow down and don't have client calls that week, they go inwards and focus on themselves and their business. That might not work in your life and business, but take note of how you feel throughout the month.

Get support. You could do this alone, but it takes time and effort and support. I truly believe in the village mentality and it's much better to surround yourself with people who get it, who resonate with you and where you are on your journey.

Imagine two mountain peaks with a valley in-between them. You are standing on the first peak, and you'd like to get to the second one. You can go the solo route down the mountain, across the valley and up to the other peak or you can take the coaching support route and use the bridge that runs between the two peaks.

You'll also need some non-coaching support along the way; this might be family, friends, your significant other, people who you have met online in groups, courses or memberships who you have never met in human form, but you feel the pull. Seek them out and hold them tight. These are the people who will cry happy and sad tears with you, celebrate you and lift you when you need it.

"In a gentle way, you can shake the world."

— MAHATMA GANDHI

My path has not been special, there is nothing special about me at all in fact, because we are all special. I'll say that again in case you missed it. We. Are. All. Special.

By becoming the true version of me and sitting comfortably with her, I have embraced myself as the piece of *kintsugi* pottery - absolutely one of a kind, stronger and more precious now than before.

I feel incredibly fortunate to have met Rob my husband when I was just 18, and to have grown together on our journeys ever since. This has given me the great gift of a true understanding of what secure attachment feels like. That sense of core stability has positively impacted every area of my life and business including my work with my clients. We have two incredible daughters and have created a loving family together, for which I am grateful for every single day.

By going on my path of self-mastery, I now realise that the path I followed was the one that has led me here, and that I needed to go through the steps in order to arrive here. It's been hard and, I hesitate to use the word, painful at times.

Coaching has always been in me, since I was a young girl, I have been known for my empathy and being aware of the emotional state of others, often instinctively offering counselling sessions and energy work to adults starting when I was a young teenager. When travelling solo to Cyprus to my family, I had a middle-aged lady open up to me on a four-hour flight and share details of her marriage, impending divorce and what that might mean for her. Reader, I was 12.

I am the person that strangers are drawn to and will share with. When I worked in office environments, I would ask colleagues "How are you?" and then ask again "No really, how are you?" sometimes bringing them to tears (in a healthy, emotional release kind of way), and I discovered that I inherently had the ability of seeing behind the mask that we all sometimes wear.

I am now creating impact by working with women who are where I used to be. I am showing my daughters that, as an introvert, you can make an impact and have purpose. My eldest daughter is extrovert and my youngest an introvert, so the knowledge I can give to both of them will serve them well.

I cherish the space that I give myself to recharge and because I am able to communicate my need for space or support, my relationships are healthy and successful.

By finding my true purpose and being aligned at last, I feel lighter. I feel like I have arrived and that I can help women step into their true being and shine as they were meant to.

It takes a village

The reason I was able to do the work on myself (and continue to do so) is because I was held. By working with Andrea, my coach, I had a safe container in which I could dig deep, then go deeper, and a bit deeper still, fall apart and build myself back up again. A breakdown to breakthrough initiation if you like. This is not something to embark on alone and be able to move forward quickly, it takes courage and there were times I wanted to quit - many, many times - but my coaches and success sisters gave me the support of which I had not known before, and I am forever grateful.

My clients have wonderfully illuminating lightbulb moments, both during our sessions and whilst reflecting on things in between them.

'A' came to me as she was finding it hard to be consistently visible. She knew she should get visible, yet it was the judgemental thoughts that were affecting her 'showing up'. She was looking to master her introverted personality to its highest potential, to stop the feelings of being judged, overwhelmed or not being good enough. She was also aware of not giving herself any time for personal or business owner time and therefore, was slipping into unhealthy habits.

She showed up and did the work, both in and in between our sessions together, and she is now able to reframe discussions that support her introverted personality which has led her to reignite her lust for her business. She also now feels at absolute peace with who she is, and no longer feels the need to change or fit the mould.

'N' came to me with a few beliefs that she had held on to for a long time and she knew she wanted to change her perspective on them. She found that a lot of perspectives shifted for her in just a couple of sessions.

'J' found that things were foggy in her head and she didn't seem to have clarity of purpose. There was a lot of overwhelm. Now, by giving herself permission to park some of the things and working daily routines into her life, she feels happier, more productive, and now has purpose. She also felt heard for the first time in a long time. I was able to give her the clarity that she needed.

'C' found that our sessions allowed her to learn to let go of feelings, to be at peace with certain situations out of her control and to develop a genuine surrender and acceptance mindset over things she cannot influence or change - in both her personal and professional life. She has allowed herself to find a dose of self-love, self-belief and acceptance that had been missing for a long time.

"Everyone shines, given the right lighting."

— SUSAN CAIN

Imagine how it would feel to feel at ease with who you are, connect in with your dreams and have the freedom and choices that you have always wanted. To do what makes your heart sing with total alignment. And, when things go pear-shaped - which they will - have the toolkit and support to get you back on track. To have the self-awareness that recognises you and how you operate, what you need, what boundaries need to be in place.

There is room for everyone. I truly believe this with my whole heart.

Introversion is nothing to be ashamed of or something that needs to be fixed – we can shine so brightly and share our talent and our gifts with those who need them. It's why I set up my fb group, The Successful Wallflower. I want to create a community of wonderful women who can celebrate their introversion with those who get it.

Once you feel comfortable with who you truly are and choose alignment, then everything shifts. Yes, it can be painful and you will wonder if it is worth it (spoiler alert: it really is, far far more than worth it!)

What is it that you want? Actually truly desire? Who do you want to be? How do you want to feel?

What is stopping you?

How can you embrace the true essence of you to step aside and rise as you are meant to?

Is the process a quick one? Sometimes yes, but more often, no, and you will always have things to keep working on. This is the reason that coaches have coaches who have coaches who have coaches. We stand on the shoulders of others.

Whilst writing this, one of my daily affirmations popped into my head and I'm getting goosebumps, which I'm taking as a sign that I need to share it with you.

I am enough.

Say it with me, out loud.

I am enough.

Because you are enough. You are more than enough.

So, keep the blinkers on, stay on your own path, stop comparing, invest in the right help for you with someone who you feel comfortable in talking to and working with. Trust your instincts on this one. Your success is not only possible but inevitable, it's your time to step aside and rise just as you are meant to.

I'm here cheering you on xx

ABOUT THE AUTHOR
CLAIRE WHITE

Claire White is a mindset and consistency coach who supports introverted women entrepreneurs to discover their hidden 'superhero powers' so that they can tackle their limiting beliefs, embrace their introvert qualities and work with them, not against them, allowing them to move forward with their life and business.

Before starting her coaching business, Claire worked as a social media manager and Facebook ads strategist. Claire now coaches female introverted entrepreneurs on how to identify their dreams and desires, their limiting beliefs, and then moving on to celebrate their introvert qualities and move forward with new habits that enrich both their personal and business lives.

Claire enjoys going to gigs and festivals and music in general, and can often be found singing enthusiastically out of tune in her car. She lives in the Buckinghamshire countryside with her husband and two daughters.

Claire is a graduate coach of the fully accredited Aligned Coaching Academy (ACA MInstLM), and a certified Story Work Coach with Andrea Callanan (ACSWC) and is available for 1:1 coaching.

You can reach Claire at:

Email – claire@claire-white.com
Facebook –
The Successful Wallflower - Mindset & consistency for female introverts
Website – www.claire-white.com

instagram.com/claire_white_coach
linkedin.com/in/clairewhitecoaching

7

FRANCA CUMBO
A JOURNEY OF REDISCOVERY

I am a British-Italian working mother of two, living in Amsterdam, who after many years of searching has finally found a career that works for my life and that I can be proud of. Today, I'm a business owner, growing a team of paid social specialists to help good brands make a bigger impact using social media. This wasn't an overnight achievement. I spent many years unsure of how to contribute to the workforce again after having children. I also spent many years working without boundaries and feeling fraught with self-doubt.

Today, I know myself better than I ever have done. I value myself and am less afraid to face uncomfortable situations. I am proud of the business I am creating and of how I am designing the life that I want. I have built up more resilience to everyday challenges that, in the past, would make me doubt myself and my chosen path. I am not afraid to fail or show vulnerability. I don't feel I have to hide certain parts of myself. I place the same value on my work relationships as I do on my personal ones and show up with integrity and sincerity.

I can work from anywhere. I can work with anyone. And if I don't have the answer, I can figure it out. Today, I'm ok with not knowing it all.

I've always worked from home and enjoy peace and solitude when no one is there. I prioritise early morning workouts to give me the physical and mental boost I need to start my day. Daily habits, such as gratitude lists and morning walks, have helped me manage the overwhelm that's so easy to feel when you're managing a family and a business.

Before children, I was a highly ambitious and 'successful' digital marketer. I write 'successful' in inverted commas because my success then was defined by others. I was successful on paper, but deep inside, I felt misaligned and unfulfilled in my career. I never felt comfortable in my own skin. I frequently felt anxious and stressed and believed this was how it was meant to be - that this is what came with the next promotion and more responsibility. The more 'successful' I became, the more stressed and anxious I felt. I felt incompetent in some areas of my work and awesome in others. Deep down, I knew I was good at what I did but I sometimes doubted myself and didn't feel good enough. I compared myself to others and strove for perfection. And when I wasn't perfect, I felt like a failure - and failure was a very bad thing. It was not ok to show vulnerability - this was considered a weakness. You kept going and worked long hours and worked whenever and however in order to get it done.

I climbed the ladder in the traditional sense. I worked hard and looked for more responsibility and challenges. This led to promotions and pay rises - more income to buy nice things and go out with my friends. But that did not make me feel more confident or happy. I was going after what I thought came next to progress and be successful. My outlook was external.

After marriage and in my late thirties, I knew I wanted children. Conceiving wasn't easy for me and I obsessed over this every day until it finally happened. Motherhood came with a big identity shift and the old 'career-focused/high-achieving' me was slowly disappearing. I was very happy to throw myself into motherhood. I was good at it and, after all the self-doubt I had felt in my career, I was grateful that another path opened up to me.

Many years later, I wanted to get back to work but I didn't know how. I didn't know how to reconcile the old me and the new me. I didn't want to go back to working like I used to. I didn't want to go back to feeling how I used to. I felt stuck. I didn't know I could choose how to work and how to feel at work. I wasn't ready to seek the support I needed and I didn't even know what that support was.

After many years of inaction, I finally took steps to address the limiting beliefs that were getting in my way. I invested in myself by working with a mindset coach. And I continue to invest in myself and my business with no regrets and a multitude of rewards.

> Today, I know what I am capable of. I know I can learn new skills and that growth doesn't ever stop. I know nobody is perfect and nobody knows it all.

I wish I had understood this then and had not relied on external validation for my self-worth. I now know I have the power to change situations and myself. I now can listen to my gut, or intuition as some call it, and be the guide for my life and my business. I now know that perfection is a trap and that failure is a good thing because that's how we learn. I now know when situations, connections or work opportunities don't feel right, then they probably aren't.

In my thirties, the environment I worked in was very masculine. The women were few and far between in senior-level roles. It was a boy's club but I didn't see it that way at the time. I accepted the inequality and didn't even consider more senior positions than an

Account Director as, in my mind, that wasn't a realistic or achievable goal. I worked with some amazingly talented people and learnt a lot. I was presented with incredible opportunities to work with some of the best global brands. We were given the freedom to be entrepreneurial within the agency itself and were encouraged to create opportunities for ourselves. And this is what I did. I was one of the first employees to request an overseas transfer after a global merger. This allowed me to work in San Francisco in 2005 for a few months - a city I fell in love with and also moved to on a more permanent basis - and the city in which I met my husband.

My work in the agency world was very full-on. It was all or nothing - or that's what I believed was normal. I found it difficult to put boundaries in place and I gave it my all. It was the old cliché: work hard, play hard. But after a while, I was tired of working and playing so hard. It was draining. I wanted more 'balance' but I didn't know what that meant or how to do it without giving something up, and I saw that as being less ambitious. I knew I didn't want my entire life to be taken over by my work. Deadlines were imposed by clients and we all had to bend over backwards to fulfil them. We weren't saving lives, was the old industry joke, yet we behaved as though we were.

Looking back, I recognise that I was close to burnout on more than one occasion. I remember spending weekends in a daze, unable to function, but I thought this was all normal and part of having a successful career.

I sometimes faced challenges with senior male colleagues and these conflicts would consume me. I felt belittled, undermined and undervalued. I did not know how to deal with these feelings or situations so I would vent to anyone who would listen.

I often didn't feel good enough or feel that I knew enough. This created a lot of anxiety for me - especially when it came to presenting. Being in the spotlight and presenting to clients made me very, very nervous. I still feel traumatised by some of those past situations. I felt nervous but didn't realise that nerves were normal and a good thing. I thought it was a sign of incompetence.

I felt like an imposter before I had even heard the term imposter syndrome.

I thought there was something wrong with me or my chosen career.

Today, I understand that I simply need to practice - as many people do before presenting. The illusion that people can wing it is just that. I also understand that a lot of my insecurities were my inner voices being allowed to dominate and influence me. In times of conflict, I would fall into a victim role rather than stepping outside the situation to find a solution. I now understand that imposter syndrome is felt by many high-achievers and that with growth comes fear and discomfort. And this is all ok.

This incongruent way of working is what spurred me to abandon my career when I had kids. I couldn't see how working in an agency would allow me to also be the kind of mother I wanted to be. Long working hours and stressful deadlines would not work for me anymore. My priorities had changed. But I felt stuck. I knew I didn't want that but then, what did I want? How could I use all the experience and skills I'd accrued over the years? How could I work with more meaning and harmony? How could I deal with my insecurities and stand in my worth? What I didn't know then is that to do this, I had to prioritise myself and invest time and money to create the life and business that I wanted and deserved.

I was raised by very hard-working immigrant parents. The work ethic was very strong in my family, as well as the idea of sacrifice. My point of reference for success was my entrepreneurial parents who gave up a lot to build a life and business in a foreign country. Their purpose was to provide their children and other family members with better opportunities than they had had themselves.

With very little and minimal education, they left their home and moved to a country where they couldn't speak the language and didn't know anyone. They started with very low paying jobs and worked long hours. Sacrifice was an accepted and expected part of life. When I was ten years old, my mother stopped working and became a full-time, stay-at-home mum. I never asked her if she was happy with that choice or if she was encouraged to do so because it was the 'right' thing to do. She no longer needed to graft alongside my dad as the business grew. But did she *want* to give all that up and stay home to cook and clean and play carer to her two younger children and my grandparents? I never got the chance to ask her.

I was the first to go to university in my family. I did not have a lot of career guidance from my parents as they weren't familiar with the education system and did not have a formal education themselves. I chose my degree based on a false idea of what I thought I wanted. I knew after the first few months that it wasn't right for me but I didn't change it. Do I have regrets? Yes. I wish I had followed a path of learning because of what I enjoyed and not based on external factors. This was one of those early pivotal moments where I did not tune into my gut. It resulted in me struggling with my degree and thinking I wasn't good enough or smart enough.

My first job after university was at Christie's, the auction house. I eventually worked my way into a marketing position but again, I didn't quite fit in. The world of fine art was unrelatable. I learnt a lot as I progressed and was rewarded with more responsibility, but I was consumed with work in a negative way. It did not fill me up - I felt drained and anxious.

The next move to the digital agency felt closer to what I was looking for. I loved the energy and enjoyed being surrounded by creative, innovative young people, doing ground-breaking work for big brands. I felt honoured to be learning from them. I was inspired by the drive and vision of the founders and I was learning about a whole new world of marketing called 'new media'. It was cutting-edge and cool. I had fun at work and it also became my social life. The people were smart and overall, it was accepted to be yourself. We were pushed to be above average and avoid mistakes at all costs. The standards were high and this worked well for a perfectionist like me. I did not have female role models there. The founders were all male and anyone who moved into a management position was also male. There were female Account Directors and I became one of them. In my mind, that was my limit because I didn't see it happening there or in other agencies at the time. We would eventually leave to have babies, right?

I grew up with working parents as role models, but my mum was home with us from a young age and before then, I was cared for by my grandparents, which was acceptable childcare in our Italian culture. My mother's caregiver role was as a traditional one and one that is greatly undervalued by society, government and businesses. It's unpaid and relentless. My dad would work long hours and expect dinner on the table. Paying for childcare wasn't an option at the time. We kept it in the family.

When I became a mother, I chose to quit my job and throw myself into my new role, motherhood. I gave up one for the other. That's what I believed I was supposed to do to be a good mum. How could you have both? I didn't really enjoy my job anyway, so why would I leave my children to be raised by strangers? I was also in a privileged situation where my husband's income could support us. And then there was the guilt. I had worked so long and hard to become a mum, so why would I choose to work instead? My inner voice was saying 'good' mums were with their children all the time. You didn't abandon your children to go and earn money when you didn't need to. I now know what a falsehood this is. All mothers parent, live and work in different ways and do what's best for their children and families.

Judgement amongst women (and mothers) is holding us back. Respect, compassion and empathy toward each other are what we should be focused on instead.

Living in Amsterdam, a small city with simple living, afforded us a great quality of life with a single income. I had mum friends who were working mothers and some who weren't. The working mums I knew were mainly in corporate roles and their lives felt stressed and busy in ways that my stay-at-home life wasn't. I felt completely disconnected from the old me, my old career, that person who worked at a desk and earned a salary. I became obsessed with everything baby-related. It was my new 'job'. Breastfeeding strategies, how to carry your baby in a wrap, what food to cook them, how they 'should' play, what stimulates their brain development. I was in a mummy bubble. A mummy fog. I didn't keep up with current affairs, I wasn't passionate about social injustice or the damage we're doing to our environment. I didn't listen to podcasts about topics that I could learn from or open my mind to. At dinner parties, I felt flat. I didn't have much to say if the topic wasn't about babies. I felt lost.

On a physical level, I didn't like my body and I didn't know how what to do about it. Any form of exercise was so alien to me. How do I even start to exercise after all these years?

Almost eight years had passed since leaving my last job to have my first child. I knew I wanted more. I wanted to feel more significant. I wanted to contribute more to the household and to society. I wanted to be seen, I wanted to be heard and I knew I deserved more. I stopped the inner voice that being a stay-at-home was better for my family and that it was the right thing to do. Instead, I started to ask - what is right for me? I gave myself permission to consider other possibilities. I broke free of the invisible shackles that I imposed on myself. I stopped believing that I could only work the way I did before children.

I stepped outside of the mummy fog to see the reality of working mothers - that they were human - like me, like you. Everyone was figuring it out. Everyone was winging it.

And everyone loved their children and families - regardless of the paid or unpaid role they were in.

While I was neck high in nappy changing, the working world had changed and so had the digital landscape. Social media was blowing up to be the predominant way for people to communicate, connect, share and do business. The gig economy happened and there was a rise in independent contractors, freelancers and more flexible opportunities, thanks to online platforms and new technologies.

The catalyst for me getting past my mummy fog was a referral from a friend. She had reskilled in social media and this piqued my interest. I began to consider new possibilities, new areas of work and study. I began to look forward and not let my past experience limit me.

I decided to sign up for the same social media course. This allowed me to take *action* and stop second-guessing myself. It was the *doing something* that gave me the confidence to keep going and to keep growing. The course was tailored to working mums and perfectly suited my circumstances. The course organisers, Digital Mums, campaigned for more flexible working in the workforce and I felt immediately drawn to their mission. Going back to studying and retraining my brain for deep thinking stimulated me in so many ways. I was so used to multitasking, my brain couldn't concentrate for long periods of time. It was hard to retain information, but this also got easier over time. I made genuine connections with other mums in the training and even though it was all virtual, I felt a new sense of belonging - of being part of something. I had a real-life client again and this time, it felt like a partnership. It didn't feel like work and I loved it. Every little step I took, made me feel more confident. I was finding myself again.

However, I hadn't yet addressed the limiting beliefs I still carried with me. I was still experiencing imposter syndrome in a way that would paralyse me. I didn't feel confident in my abilities. Any criticism would send me spiralling into self-doubt about my entire career and self-worth. Old patterns were with me and my inner voice was still a doubtful and negative one.

I decided to take another course - this time learning about social media advertising. This was much more aligned with my background and what I had enjoyed in my past life. I was learning how to run social media advertising campaigns for clients and could see immediate results. This, combined with creativity and strategy, was beginning to light me on fire.

In this course, I met the mindset and business coach, Andrea Callahan. Andrea led monthly calls on how to take steps to improve your mindset and this, coupled with the new skills I was learning, was a game-changer. Yes, I can do this!

> It's not just about what I *know*, it's also about how I *think* and how my *attitude* can affect my situation.

Andrea addressed how we wanted to feel in our business and how to manage those negative inner voices. We worked on our story to help us identify patterns that hold us back. We became aware of triggers and were given tools on how to manage them. With these new skills and habits, I have been the conductor of my own orchestra.

> I have discovered a new awareness and understanding of myself as well as acceptance and compassion. Compassion towards others and most importantly, towards myself.

I joined Andrea's Unapologetic Self-Mastery programme and embarked on a journey of rediscovery and reconnection. The pilot light was lit again. It brought about a new perspective on what I could achieve - in work and in life. I got clearer on what I wanted - and what I didn't want. I gave myself permission to get out of my own way and go for what I deserved. I learnt how to tune into my true self and feel what's right - and what's not right. I learnt to be in a place of receiving and to open myself to what I want. I stopped needing clients, and instead started assessing if they were aligned with my values. I began to focus on how I wanted to feel on a daily basis: free, fulfilled, passionate, purposeful, connected and significant. And I stopped stressing about my work/life balance and instead saw it as a choice. I choose to work in a more meaningful and aligned way.

Today, I'm not only working again, I'm working in a way that makes me happy. I'm running and building a business that I believe in. I'm clearer on my purpose of using my social media skills for good. I'm helping ethical small business owners make a bigger impact in the world. These businesses are working hard to do business in a new way so we can minimise our impact on our fragile planet and I want to do the same. I want to use my experience from working with big, global brands to help emerging brands cut through, find their ideal customers and grow their business so we can have more good brands to shop from. I have amazing clients that I get a lot of energy from and am really proud to be part of their team and their growth.

My children may have been the trigger for me to find a career that would work around family but now, I'm focused on building a career that works for ME. I'm putting my needs first.

> My children will hopefully see me as a positive role model. Someone who wasn't afraid to change course later in life, someone who figured out what they wanted when things didn't feel right,

someone who didn't let age or skillset get in the way of a new career.

Do I believe you can have it all? I don't think having it all should be our measure or our goal. And what does 'all' even mean? Do I believe you can keep learning about yourself so your life evolves with you? Absolutely. Do I believe we are forever students and learning new skills keeps us stimulated and growing? Definitely. Do I believe relationships need to evolve as we and our children grow older and our needs change? For sure!

When I look back at those pivotal moments that gave me the inspiration to keep doing what I was doing, there is one particular organization I think of fondly - SheSays Amsterdam. SheSays is a global creative network for women that organise events to inspire, engage and educate. As a newly skilled social media professional, I attended many networking events but I felt uncomfortable in all of them except SheSays. SheSays is run by smart, relatable women who show a human side of themselves and I always leave an event feeling energised and inspired. During one of my freelance engagements, I was honoured to work with the SheSays Amsterdam team and help manage its socials. Now working for myself, I have volunteered some of my time to be part of the leadership committee to promote and support the events. My goal for next year is to be able to dedicate more time to specific programs that help women get back to work after a long break, or those women that are looking to change careers.

> I understand how hard it is to propel yourself forward when you don't know where you are going. I will pay it forward by helping those women - like those amazing women helped me.

Being part of Andrea's Unapologetic Self-Mastery and now, Unapologetic Success Accelerator, I've met many wonderful, smart women on a similar journey to me. We are not all the same, but we share many of the same challenges that have held us back from realising our true potential. I've witnessed the transformation in all these women who have learnt how to not let their story define who they are today. They have worked hard on breaking apart those limiting beliefs and getting comfortable with the uncomfortable. We are not broken, so there is nothing to fix, but we are all a work in progress. The learning and discovery never ends. This is what makes life rich and interesting. We are not fixed, but pliable beings that can flex this way and that, depending on where we find ourselves.

I've learnt how important aligned relationships are for me. When my values are in line with my clients and my co-workers, everything makes sense. Work is not a grind. I feel part of their team; I am working to help them realise their goals and I am making a difference. It was only through Self-Mastery that I realised how much I enjoy working with other people and how much I enjoy their energy. I had worked in teams before but they were sometimes filled with anxiety, competitiveness and negativity. I discovered that it's the aligned relationships that would bring about the difference to feeling more positive about my work today.

I want to help my clients create success in their businesses. I care about their business, their brand, their products and services and their customers. I consult with integrity and passion and treat their budgets as though it was my own money. Many small business owners have nurtured their businesses with blood, sweat and tears, and it's not an easy feat for them to delegate and put their trust in partners.

> The clients that I work with are ambitious and brave. Like me, they're stepping out of their comfort zone to create something they believe in.

And some, like me, are getting out of their own way to go to the next level. Some want to stay small and national; some have global ambitions. I'm their cheerleader and will work hard to help them realise their goals.

This journey has also positively impacted my relationship with my life partner and husband. I was independent when we met but over the course of our relationship as a stay-at-home mum, I grew insecure and a little resentful. I felt like I was standing in his shadow and in simple terms, just wasn't that interesting. He has never criticised me for who I am or my decision to stay home. Having grown up with a stay-at-home mum, I think he also hung to the traditional roles of motherhood. However, he has been nothing but supportive of my decisions throughout and I've always felt completely seen by him. The inner voice was all mine and it was the realisation that I was depending on him for reassurance, release and validation that made me turn to therapy as well as Andrea's program. I want to be able to work through issues and challenges on my own. I want to trust in myself. I want to stand next to him as an equal.

Today, I understand myself better than ever before. I like who I am but don't expect everyone to like me. I accept that not all clients are going to be the ideal clients for me. And I'm ok with that. As a paid social marketer, I accept that I don't know it all, but I have the expertise to figure it out to help my clients be successful.

> Motherhood changes us in different ways. Our identity changes and keeps changing as our children grow and their demands on us evolve.

Even for those who did not take a career break, it can be difficult to understand who you are after taking on the biggest new role of your life. Maybe motherhood has been extremely rewarding and fulfilling for you, maybe it's made you feel constrained and lonely, or maybe it's been all of these, as it was for me.

As I approach my half a century birthday, I am grateful to my children whose love inspires me to be the best version of myself. And I am grateful for this journey of rediscovery. But I did not do it alone. I gave myself permission to invest in myself and get the support I needed. Yes, it's a privilege to be able to afford this type of coaching but you will reap the rewards in so many areas of your life - your family, your relationships, your career. It's time to put yourself first so you can fill yourself up and look after others from a place of giving, and not from a place of lack and resentment. Learning to listen and trust yourself, to love yourself, to prioritise yourself, to reignite the passion inside of you, to find your place in a world that gives you purpose beyond your family - is the best gift you can give yourself. Your family and friends will thank you for it.

ABOUT THE AUTHOR
FRANCA CUMBO

Franca Cumbo is a paid social marketer specialising in Facebook, Instagram and Google ads, who helps smaller good brands make bigger impacts on social media.

After years in the digital agency world, working with some of the best-known global brands (Target, Gap, Microsoft, Xbox, P&G, Philips to name a few), Franca launched Lionstar Social so she could work with brands who fill her up and give her energy. She focuses on using social media and Search ads to spread the word for brands that make a positive impact on our planet. Franca has experience in the food and beverage, skincare, beauty, fashion, publishing and ecommerce sectors.

She is passionate about living a more conscious lifestyle and wants to use her experience to introduce good brands to more people. She is also actively involved in SheSays Amsterdam, a non-profit organisation that runs free events to help more women get to the top.

Franca grew up in London, in a big Italian family, with hard-working entrepreneurial parents. Seeking adventure, she moved to San Francisco to expand her worldview across the pond. She was drawn back to Europe and now lives in Amsterdam with her husband, two children and an adorable French bulldog.

If you're a good, ambitious brand and would social media advertising support, Franca offers bespoke packages to suit different types of business.

You can reach Franca Cumbo at:

Email - franca@lionstarsocial.co
Website - www.lionstarsocial.co

instagram.com/franca_lionstarsocial.co
linkedin.com/in/francacumbo

8

HANNAH MCKIMM
THE WAY OUT IS TO REACH OUT

Just as a cell in the body contains everything it needs; I believe we have everything we need inside us to become the people we want to become. The cell, however, only sustains itself by being part of the whole. My journey of connecting to the whole has been about learning to reach out to myself and connect vulnerably with others.

To connect, I had to reach. For me, this was about accepting, trusting, releasing, surrendering to and following a deeper knowing. Accepting this support, love and kindness has been the scariest, most uncertain, but also most rewarding thing I have done. Not only for myself, but for those I love, for my clients and anyone I connect with.

This chapter marks a milestone of transition into a life I have dreamt of and now believe I deserve. I feel more vulnerable but more boundaried, more passionate but more peaceful, freer but more connected, stronger but more at ease and most of all, more balanced in who I am.

This equilibrium has connected me to a part of myself that shows love for herself rather than criticism and harm. I now trust myself and my intuition and accept all parts of me. I follow my passion. I own a business aligned with who I am. I work with clients I love supporting and know I can support as we have walked similar paths.

I support women who have experienced sexual trauma step into the lives they desire and deserve. I bring an academic understanding but also a bodily knowing, as I myself am a sexual abuse survivor. From this place of rounded knowing, I support others to bring to consciousness what was once unconscious and form an authentic connection to themselves.

I am no longer the victim I once was. I have become the creator of my life. Learning to embrace this connection with myself and the world around me has been my journey and is the essence of this chapter.

For much of my life, I focused on being the supportive daughter, sister, friend, partner or friendly colleague. I wanted others to feel included because I knew the pain of not feeling heard or seen. I was that nice, outgoing, friendly person everyone could talk to and I made friends easily.

Behind the mask, I didn't know who I was without seeing myself through the lens of supporting others. I wasn't including my own needs in any decisions until it became overwhelming and I retreated. As I was driven by my sense of belonging, my boundaries were undefined. I didn't dare do anything to jeopardise this need for belonging, even when it meant compromising my values.

I was a chameleon, trying to be everything to everybody. I served the needs of others, telling them to be kind to themselves while neglecting my own needs and fostering self-criticism in my mind. I didn't rock the boat by voicing my opinion or asking for my needs to be met, for fear of rejection. I said what I knew people wanted to hear; if it was the "right" answer or helped fix something for them. I believed what I was saying, but it was coming from a place of fear rather than authenticity, courage and vulnerability, the place from which I now strive to speak.

Eventually, this made me feel lonely, confused and resentful but not knowing why. I knew I didn't want to be the person I was showing up as, feeling and reacting this way, but I couldn't see a way out. I wasn't aware of the core beliefs I developed when I was younger that led me to this place, to putting up these walls.

I felt putting in place boundaries, saying no, or putting forward my point of view would bring more pain, abandonment and disappointment and I didn't want any more of that. Ultimately, by being nice to others, I wasn't being kind to myself or them. I felt my worth was in what I could DO for others and couldn't understand they valued me for who I was and wanted to be with ME.

To me, my needs were irrelevant, I was irrelevant if I couldn't BE something to someone else. My value was having a purpose to others and in my mind, this equalled acceptance. If I was accepted, I was safe. I now know that any child who feels they must choose between their own self-expression and a sense of belonging, will always choose belonging. My inner child chose to belong.

There were many times in my life I wasn't the person I wanted to be. I was in survival mode. My go-to reaction to a perceived threat was avoidance. I thought I was protecting myself but really, I was digging myself deeper into shame, guilt and rejection. I walked away from difficult conversations because I felt unable to contain the physical sensations they conjured up. This lost me many friendships along the way.

My need to be perceived as nice and supportive attracted people who I thought I could rescue. However, it was preventing the true connection to others and myself I deeply desired. If I sensed we were past the honeymoon or small-talk phase and you were getting close to the "real me", the walls and defences went up. Then came the excuses. I would withdraw, feeling unable to contact anyone, particularly when there was conflict involved.

When I felt overwhelmed, I found it hard to ask for support because I feared letting go of control and letting the independent identity slip. If I let people in, they might see the hurt, pain, shame and guilt. They might judge me as I judged myself, abandon me like I felt I abandoned myself and hurt me, like I was hurt in the past and hurting myself now, emotionally and, at times, physically.

The intolerance of these uncomfortable feelings drew me to leave my home country as soon as possible. Travelling and living in other countries gave me a connection to others, it gave me a reason for being different. It also gave me an escape, allowing me to identify with something other than the pain, disconnection and at times, numbness, inside.

Unconsciously, I wanted to find the untouched places of beauty. If I could find those, then maybe I could create them within me. I thought this would be enough to stop the thoughts and emotions but soon realised I would never get away from myself. What I was resisting was most definitely persisting and I was aware of the illusion of bliss that came from ignoring it.

If you tried giving me a positive affirmation, I would look at you like you had two heads and dismiss it for some wishy-washy unrealistic thinking. I couldn't see how they worked or how I would ever believe these things about myself. I wanted to release this heavy weight of emotion and feel the freedom I saw in others, but didn't know how to achieve this for myself.

My lack of self-worth and people-pleasing tendencies were causing me to make decisions that in the long run rarely made me happy. My choice of career in the film industry enabled me to live this life and hide large parts of myself. I was hiding in plain sight.

Due to being in constant survival mode, I wasn't present. I struggled to remember the events and occasions others recounted with intricate detail. Most of the events I recounted were traumatic. My mind needed to remember these to protect me from similar events in the future. Survival was my number one driver.

At this point, my relationship with myself was fractured. I was used to feeling low; sadness and crying were my comfort blankets; drinking to relax or feel at ease or to connect better with others was my norm. Shifting this and making the unconscious conscious was not going to be easy, but I wanted to try.

When I was younger, I learnt from those around me that anger was destructive and my emotions were best hidden. I had learnt I should place the needs of others before my own. I was taught how the direction of my life was in God's hands, not my own. I felt powerless.

I felt things were happening to me, not for me and I was being pulled along with little choice. Feeling I had no voice, I turned much of my emotion inward and sought the answers for my life from external sources.

In school, I felt unable to connect and had different friend groups almost every year. All I wanted was to hide away in the art room. It was my happy place and would turn out to be my safe haven in years to come.

One night, when I was 16, me and a friend went out to a bar. I knew we shouldn't have been going but my need to seem normal at school overrode this thought. Little did I know, this marked another turning point in my relationship with myself.

I remember being watched by a man, talking to him and then leaving - without my friend. My drink had been spiked. That night I was raped. I was sent home the next day with a deep sense of shame, guilt, hurt, rejection and confusion. I felt sinful and wanted to hide even more now.

I didn't speak about it for several years. When I did, I didn't get the support I needed, so kept quiet for several more years. Again, not feeling heard or valued, I did what I learnt to do earlier in life, I turned my emotions inward.

It was a strange time. Everyone at school was exploring their identity and sexuality. I remember my sister taking her boyfriend up to our shared bedroom. Being stubborn, I sat on my bed as "it was my room too". Unconsciously, I was trying to protect her from what had happened to me.

The years that followed were filled with self-harm and self-judgement. This was my way of controlling emotions and thoughts and relieving the inner pain. Even when the physical self-harming stopped, I self-harmed through self-sabotaging behaviours. These reinforced the views I had about myself.

My high expectations meant I inevitably failed. My binge eating and drinking gave me the false impression I was supporting myself emotionally. Over-giving in relationships meant I wasn't meeting my own needs.

At times, these relationships became emotionally abusive. I was drawn to these situations because they reflected my own inner turmoil. The frequency allowed me to believe it was normal and that I deserved it. Rather than being the main character of my life, I was the victim of my life and the rescuer of others.

Albert Einstein famously said "We can't solve problems by using the same kind of thinking we used to create them." Ultimately, it wasn't my intellectual knowing that saved me, it was my embodied knowledge and I was starting to listen to its whisper. The more I listened, the stronger the voice got. I knew I was meant for more and this is what pushed me into action.

The first whisper I remember came while still working in the film industry. A colleague told me to never let the industry change who I was. These words stopped me from continuing down a path where I was not just changing myself, but losing myself more and more. I was unaware that how I was showing up was directly shaped by my past traumas, and these were becoming harder to escape.

The next whisper came through my interest in what made people tick and a yearning to be creative again, so I enrolled on a Masters in Art Psychotherapy. I thought the intellectual route would teach me to fix and shift the part of me that felt out of place.

Crippling shame and fear of abandonment prevented me from celebrating the news of my new course with my colleagues. What would they think about me and my choices? Was I good enough? What would they think it meant about how I saw them? Keeping secrets was something I was getting very used to.

When I finally told them, I was surprised - they were pleased. Some even admitted feeling jealous, as they wanted a way out too. This affirmed that I was on the right path by beginning to say yes to myself and trusting I knew what was right for me. This caused a few bricks from my defence wall to crumble.

The next whisper came with the climax of a toxic relationship. A relationship based on co-dependency, as were many of my relationships to this point. I sensed it wasn't right but felt unable to walk away. Unhealthy communication and unconscious coping techniques were at play, but to me, it felt comfortable, familiar and safe. I knew my place in relationships like this, I had a purpose. I was seeking the validation I so desperately craved. Despite being hurt emotionally numerous times, it was when I feared I'd be physically hurt that I left.

The safe space of the therapy I received while on my masters supported me to set these boundaries. I also learnt to talk about the rape and accept it as part of my reality but that it was not my fault. A few more bricks of my wall were crumbling.

A few years after graduating, I felt everything was going well. I lived in a beautiful place by the sea, with great friends and a job I found rewarding. Then one day, while talking with someone, I suddenly felt like I was underwater. I didn't know what I was saying and or what was being said to me. I was experiencing burnout.

While I loved my job and my colleagues, I was finding recent changes difficult and felt I wasn't getting the support I needed. A few days off led to a few weeks and then a few months. Initially, I was barely functioning. I started with small tasks I hardly noticed before, but now being on my to-do list gave me a sense of achievement.

Gradually I realised to recover fully, I needed to move home. This was a place I never thought I would return to live but was now my sanctuary. By gifting myself this time, space and attention, I gradually started the journey back to myself.

The next, much louder, whisper came from clicking on a post asking if I wanted to get out of my own way and create the success I wanted in my life. The week that followed was full of lightbulb moments and tears. The pivotal point was a slide saying, "I am enough". I remember sitting in my car, mascara running down my face and for the first time in a long time, feeling an empowering fire in my belly - I was coming back.

On a sunny Friday evening in September, I sent a voice note saying, "I just needed to go, and you have given me the push I needed. So looking forward to everything in my life from this point".

I finally felt able to get curious about what was next. Over the following months, with support from my coach, Andrea Callanan, and the Self-Mastery ladies, I started giving myself permission to release and let go of the shame and judgment I was holding on to.

I was stepping into a life I desired and now believed I deserved, simply because I was worthy and enough as I was and not for anything I had done. The internal battle was dissipating and massive holes were being knocked out of my wall. Things were starting to align and I was starting to feel at ease.

I was feeling the benefits of reaching out to myself and others.

Things were starting to shift. I was facing myself and taking responsibility for who I was and who I wanted to be. Before this, I was unaware I had the choice to change how I treated myself, and had no idea of the impact it would have when I finally did. My trauma, and my response to it, was not my choice. Moving my life forward could be. My way out was to reach out. Reach out and connect to myself and others.

If you have resonated with my story, you are likely struggling to trust yourself, your views, your instincts, that niggle in your gut you always wondered why you didn't trust. If you have a desire for change and to break free of the effects of trauma, I invite you to lean into trust.

Start by trusting yourself, for this is the longest relationship you will have. Long after you read this book, after each life event or decision you make, you are left with you. Unless you learn to face it, no matter where you go, the struggle with who you are will always remain.

Trust you know what is right for you, trust you have all you need within you to take this next step, trust that your younger self did the best she could have with what she had available to her. Trust that healing is possible for you, trust you will look back one day and say, THAT was the day I said yes to me.

Reach out to yourself, connect with yourself, observe what is coming up and allow yourself to feel it in its wholeness. Once we feel it, we can see it for what it is. No emotion we have is bad - each one has its strength. Only when our emotions aren't given healthy modes of expression, do we react in ways that negatively impact our lives.

Once you give permission for the difficult emotions to surface, you can then start to understand why it is there and what you need to help you move through it. This self-awareness is our superpower and will be our guiding light if we can learn to listen to it. The more you listen, the more you will hear.

You can also learn to accept the part of you that feels these emotions. This part is likely hurting, confused, lost or angry. Ask yourself how you feel towards her. Do you judge her? Do you feel sorry for her? Do you want to erase her and pretend she was never there?

Instead of self-judgment – my go-to reaction for a long time – try self-compassion. This helps with the acceptance and understanding that each part was doing the best it could with the information it had. There was a need being fulfilled by their actions and this part helped you through difficult times and to survive.

See it like driving a car with each passenger being a part of you. You have a younger self, a teenage self, a young adult self, and each one may be feeling emotions like shame, hurt or trauma or have unmet needs. Each part has its own satnav. Each one programmed in relation to its experiences, memories or needs. None of them has the full picture or can see the possibilities ahead. They only see where they have been and each one is doing the best it can with the information it has.

You have a choice here; you can listen to them and maybe still get where you want to go. It could get noisy and overwhelming; you might shout or lash out at each part for their contribution and you probably won't enjoy the experience.

Alternatively, you can thank them for their guidance and decide to go a different way. Going a different way requires a different way of thinking, a different way of being and a different approach to how you listen to yourself and make choices that best serve you.

This acceptance for what is, creates a space for compassion to grow and an understanding that we are more than our pain and more than our experiences. You can take back control. You can be in the driver's seat of your life.

Throughout this process, be curious about what comes up and support your body in knowing you are safe. You are not where you once were. Hug yourself, smile at yourself in the mirror, date yourself and learn what makes YOU glow. Show compassion for what has been and give permission for what is to come. You CAN feel seen and heard but first, you need to see and hear yourself.

As a society, we can place more value on what we know logically over what our bodies, our instincts, the whisper is telling us. Whether it's saying no to an invite or yes to an opportunity, nourishing yourself or seeing your worth - it's all about listening. Our bodies are very intelligent, so it's time we started listening to them.

This is the natural flow and balance of life and is something I'm still learning. Unlike walls, boundaries are not meant to be solid, they let things in and out, there is a flow. Like a tree, whose roots connect to the earth and leaves connect with the air, the sun, wildlife and the elements. There is a movement ensuring what is inside is sustained and what is outside is also supported. One can't exist without the other - too much holding on and the tree couldn't survive, too much given out and it would also perish.

The second part of trust I invite you to lean into is connecting to others. This was the gamechanger for me, the thing that allowed me to finally surrender to the unfolding of the life I desired. How could others accept me if I didn't show them my authentic self? How could I show them if I didn't know myself what she looked like?

Remember the flow of the boundary. Embracing this natural exchange teaches us that we can let go or give while also receiving. Embracing your wholeness and becoming aware of your needs, allows you to ask for them to be met. In turn, you can give more authentically from a place of overflow, rather than depletion.

People want to see the authentic us, flaws and all. Find your tribe, those who resonate with you, that bring out your true self and allow her to shine. In doing so you will find how connection to others opens you to a deeper connection to yourself.

In the past, being open to this may have meant being hurt or disappointed. Our minds work to protect us from this pain by pointing out potentially similar situations. This can be helpful but can also stop us from doing and being who we want to be. Reaching out to ourselves is where it begins and reaching out to others is where it can be sustained.

I always knew the kind of person I wanted to be. When I was twelve, I put a picture of Halle Berry and an Oscar up on my noticeboard. I was unaware of it but I was starting to manifest the person I wanted to become.

The Oscar signified achievement, what I thought would make me happy, worthy and make me ME. Halle Berry signified who I wanted to be - a person who achieved her goals, exuded strength and power and used her voice for good. She stood out for the right reasons, showing me what was possible.

I now know these things have always been available to me, I just needed to trust and believe in myself. No Oscar yet, but I have won at connecting with who I am, being at peace with where I am and not having goals attached to my value or worthiness. Instead of building walls, I now value boundaries and support others to do the same.

At first, placing boundaries felt wrong, as pleasing others was my natural response. I have now come to understand, setting boundaries is an act of love, to myself and others. It allows others to know where they stand and instead of hiding or being what I think others want me to be, I can be seen for who I truly am.

Our environment, with what and whom we surround ourselves with, has a big impact on this. Through finding my tribe, I found the people who can hold me, guide me, cheerlead me and sit with me in my pain without judgement.

To allow others to see me, I needed to first see me. I have taken responsibility for who I am and who I want to be. Leading with vulnerability and openness to change, I have developed healthier relationships. I wasn't rejected or abandoned, I was embraced and loved.

The big secrets that once devoured me are now visible and I am listening every day to my own needs. I still feel the fear but am now able to be in dialogue with it rather than pushing it away. This has led to a more enduring feeling of calm and wholeness. One I hope I can share with everyone I cross paths with by being a guide and not the saviour I once was.

Connection to self is key for connection to others, connection to your dreams and connection to the life you desire and deserve. There is a deep desire for us to feel safe AND connected, and through this work, you can understand what helps you feel this and discover what works for you.

Connection to self is different for each person but the intention is the same. Every client I work with comes to this concept in their own unique way and you will be no different. This is why it is important to listen to your own voice. Each client has seen the impact of this work over our time together, by seeing the big shift they have created in their lives.

One of my clients, Julie, was unsure about how the process would help but, with my support, found techniques that worked for her. She gained a new perspective on situations she thought she had already processed. She found a new space in her life in which she could play.

For Julie, allowing herself to release the emotions and beliefs she carried with her from past abuse, gave her space to create something new. Being empowered to step into this and feel playful in the process, was something she saw in others but never thought possible for herself.

She was able to trust me and, most importantly, the process. She gave herself permission to see the possibilities available to her. She was connected to her embodied knowledge and the power to create the life she desired.

Another client, Rachel, felt isolated and only able to rely on herself. Going through the process, she learnt to reach out to herself and others. This helped deal with her overflow of thoughts and feelings. She could view her life choices from a different perspective and felt more confident opening up to others.

Through the process, Rachel understood that although people in her past may not have been reliable, this may not be the case for those around her now. She began to see the possibilities and, most importantly, the choices she had for fulfilling her need for connection.

Rachel found self-confidence and self-belief to move to a new job where she felt supported and in turn, could ask for support. Her family relationships improved and she found new ways of connecting to herself, affirming that connection can be rewarding and freeing.

By working with me, another client learnt to work with her fears and feel more in control of her life. She felt more motivated and positive and no longer like a victim. What a powerful shift, to no longer feel like a victim but the creator of your own life.

You are not broken; your body is not broken and healing is possible. You can be a survivor AND a thriver. You can have felt pain AND still step into a life of aligned joy. Learn to reconnect, release and reframe your experiences so you can rejoice in your whole self.

I see now how all that has happened was leading me to this point. Each moment, every person was my teacher, and I am grateful for their lessons. I'm not perfect and never will be. I have just learnt to see fear as a friend, rather than my torment.

We all make mistakes, do things out of fear, out of a need to protect ourselves from further danger or pain. So, instead of building walls to protect you from potential threats, I invite you to shape your boundaries. Seek out what feels good, say yes to the life you want and continue being brave.

My sister recently told me her definition of brave – "It's not that you are not afraid, it's that you know it's important and do it anyway." So, it's not an absence of fear but an embracing of fear, an embrace of all you are.

The more time and attention you give to yourself, you will eventually start to hear your voice more clearly. This is the key to moving you to where you want to be. Those places, things and relationships you dream of can be yours.

If any of this resonates with you but you don't know where to start; if you feel you've let yourself down so many times you don't know what part of yourself to trust or listen to; if you want a life where you know your mind and can speak it, know what you need and how to ask for and receive it, let's explore this deeper together. Reach out to me via Hannah McKimm Coaching on social media, or to start your journey now, download my free resource "5 Creative Ways to Reconnect to You".

And remember – the way out is to reach out.

ABOUT THE AUTHOR
HANNAH MCKIMM – MA, ACA MINSTLM, ACSWC

Hannah is a Trauma Therapist & Coach, supporting women who have experienced sexual abuse to release the effects of their trauma by reconnecting to themselves, their dreams and their desires.

Before starting Hannah McKimm Coaching, Hannah worked for a number of years as a Camera Assistant in the TV & Film Industry before transitioning to a career as an Art Psychotherapist. She was keen to support others more directly and was fascinated with what made people tick.

After a successful career helping survivors of trauma, working primarily in the charity and healthcare sectors, Hannah saw the power of combining the learning from her personal experiences and her psychotherapy training and completed an aligned coaching accreditation. Hannah now coaches women to feel safe to step into a life they desire and deserve, by releasing the effects of trauma through embodiment and transitional coaching and therapy techniques.

Hannah enjoys anything involving the sea – such as sea swimming or fires on the beach. She also enjoys hiking and painting.

Hannah is available for Trauma Release Therapy & Coaching, as well as writing projects or speaking engagements requiring a specialist Trauma Therapist & Coach.

You can reach Hannah at:

Email – hannah@hannahmckimm.com
Website – hannahmckimm.com
Free Resource – 5 Creative Ways to Reconnect to You – hannahmckimm.co.uk

facebook.com/hannahmckimmcoaching
twitter.com/hmckimmcoaching
instagram.com/hannahmckimmcoaching
linkedin.com/in/hannah-mckimm111

HANNAH PEKARY
CHANGE YOUR HABITS, CHANGE YOUR LIFE.

I am capable, I am strong, I am worthy, I am allowed.

These words I speak over myself every day and each time I am faced with something outside of my comfort zone.

I am a strong woman, who is now sharing belief with other women to help them feel just as empowered in their lives.

It has been a joy, for over 20 years, to support women in their homes, families and lives. But taking my business to the next level over the last 2 years, has allowed me to walk with clients through their pain and joy.

I have helped dozens of women and their families create healthy habits within their homes, families, careers and businesses, but what I am most proud of in this time, is watching families that were once torn apart through silence find their voices and share them, confidently and eloquently.

Some three years ago, I was a very busy manager within a school, whilst still delivering some teaching.

Fast forward those three years, and I now get to comfortably sit at home and create and work on my business that earns me more money.

I don't rush out the door at 6.30am to beat the rush hour traffic; I now have a leisurely walk with my dog, getting my steps in before my day starts. My day works around school pick-ups, after school activities and gives time freedom for end of summer holiday parties!! Yes, you heard me right! A party to end the summer holidays, why not, hey! (The Spiderman bouncy castle was so big, Spiderman himself looked into the bathroom!) Life is made for making memories!

Since working with my business coach two years ago, my life has been a journey. It hasn't always been easy, as it has asked me to look at parts of my life that I didn't know needed looking at, nor did I know that some of them could change. But today, you read my story in a book that I have dreamt of writing since I first learnt to write!

I have been a business woman for some 15 years. Those 15 years have been fun. Years of supporting families in many capacities, through nannying, nursing, dance, teaching, nutrition, coaching, finding love and joy for themselves, reconnecting with their loved ones and so much more. But some days, I felt like I was wading through treacle and as if I had no value to offer anyone.

I run a successful dance school as well as a tuition business, which has opened my eyes to so much more of the world and what is needed.

I learnt very quickly in my teaching career that there were so many children out there that need to feel empowered to learn and strive for more in their lives. This led to my tutoring business, which encourages children to have a desire for life-long learning.

My dance school has a strong ethos behind it that encourages everyone to dance. We are all dancers. There are no limits.

How empowering to be taught at such a young age that you have no limits in life!

My career in dance has allowed me to travel across the UK and dance on many stages and with many other wonderful dancers. We have welcomed dance companies from Africa, America, Germany and other parts of the globe, to dance with us. As a Welsh company, we took important messages to audiences who might otherwise not hear them. My youth dance company now have the joy of doing the same and creating a legacy in schools, theatres and lives.

My career and businesses have always been creative, and I have made sure they have brought joy to everyone I meet. No child is ever allowed to leave one of my classes without a smile on their face! I felt so much joy when things were good - when my classes were full, when I felt supported by parents or my team. But there was always something underlying in me that knew I could have more.

In my early days of business, I thought this meant that I had to push further up the ladder of my teaching career - to gain more accolades, achieve a masters, take the dance school to such new heights that it would stand out from the rest... All whilst living a busy family life. I put so much pressure on myself to create this life that would look so desirable and make things easier for myself and my family, that I started to not enjoy the moments. I was just going through the motions. This attitude and place that I was living in with my businesses were visible to those around me, leaving me with people telling me perhaps I shouldn't do this business anymore and parents not always experiencing the happy Hannah they used to know. I created a stress for myself, and all I knew to get myself out of this stressed filled place was to create more stress to educate myself and push my way out. Guess what? It didn't work. I burnt out - more than once.

In reflection, if I had been aware of my body's signals of burnout, then I could have taken control.

We don't have to do it all. We are allowed and capable of fulfilling all of our dreams, but we don't have to do it at the detriment of our health.

I suffered with so much self-doubt that I questioned the words I used in conversations with friends. I can still slip into that habit now, but the difference is, I now understand that this is a bad habit and that I am allowed to make mistakes. What I also didn't understand until my coach started to pull back the layers, was how deep rooted my self-doubt was.

I come from a working-class family, and went into my business with a lower than average mentality of my capabilities. I doubted my worth so much that I believed that I should be keeping my 'paid' job while I work my business. In this time, I could see how stuck I was, trying to split myself between keeping a job or two, making sure that I gave them my all so that I kept the job/s, then trying to build businesses on the side in the hours that others would rest, eat and socialise.

I was a business-woman with no life, and stressed too!

I used to believe that in order to create the financial freedom that I longed for, I would have to continue the life I was leading, and wait until my businesses earnt me my monthly wage for me to quit the day job.

Then came the time I had to take the first step in taking decisive action for my life.

I left my teaching job.

I knew it was the right thing to do, but it was still a big decision.

I knew I had to leave behind the state systemic run business, which held no joy for me apart from the families that I was supporting. But I was leaving behind a job that was paying my bills, and giving job satisfaction to those around me that believed this was the path that you had to follow.

Growing up, I always believed that I wasn't 'one of those people' that could have a 4 - figure monthly income, let alone more. I believed that was for those people who drove their soft tops and owned well-known companies. Living that lifestyle was a dream, and as much as I didn't want it to stay there, I didn't know how to strive for more without burning out more. I saw how I supported families as part of my personality, and imparting continuous advice is just something that you do.

I changed my way of thinking to believe that I am allowed to make money from this now, and the life that I had been told is for other people, is one I am creating for myself. I am following my joy-given dreams, passion, heart and desire for more - for me, my loved ones and those I will support through my coaching.

If you recognise your present to be like my past – love on yourself in every moment in every day, even when you feel that you aren't getting very far. Those mental changes are just as big and important as those physical ones which impart the knowledge. We must look after ourselves physically, emotionally, mentally and spiritually.

If I could tell the me before working with my coach anything of value, I would tell her to love on herself anyway. You have done so much that you don't see, that will take you as far as your dreams will.

Moments of self-doubt are perfectly normal as we step into something bigger and more than what we can see ourselves doing. I have learnt to flip this and so can you, with ease and joy, working with your self doubt to understand you better and what you are destined to achieve. Self-doubt can actually help you. I only self-doubt what is valuable. I am valuable and so are you.

I was bullied through my school and work life. It impacted me more than I realised until I was coached.

My bullying started with the simple playground teasing that many would be able to brush off, but everyone knew me as quiet Hannah that wouldn't say boo to a goose, so ran away to cry. My parents loved on me, supported me to build friendship groups, instilled self-belief and hugged my tears away. Somehow, no matter how much they loved on me, the bullying never stopped. They always seemed to find me.

I used to question my school life, as to why I was so attractive to these bullies. I kept myself to myself and had a lovely circle of friends, but guess what? They were just as quiet as me and had never stuck up to bullies either!!

I knew, as a young teenager, that I was an introvert. It had been talked over me long enough, with many people telling me that I was, even though I didn't fully understand the meaning of this, apart from that I was shy.

Fast forward a couple more years of playground bullying, racial bullying, bullying and stigma towards my family, I told myself I wanted to step away from this childish behaviour and took myself to college, where I talked over myself, and found good, loyal friends.

This, I thought, would follow me into university life... only to find that more bullying followed, so much so, that my life was in danger.

This pattern was one that I had resigned myself to. Thinking that you just found bullies everywhere and I needed to build a stronger force field around me.

It wasn't until I did self-mastery and voice mastery, that I learnt that the power was within me to grow, and that didn't mean I needed to grow a bigger forcefield!

Being the quiet one of the family, it was expected by many that I didn't have an answer or opinion, but yet that answer was bursting inside of me, only to have to wait until I got home to be able to share it with my mum, in my safe place. This lack of voice grew to becoming someone who grew a successful dance career because I knew that I wouldn't have to share my voice on a stage in front of many critics. Everyone's a critic, right? There is judgement at every corner. I wanted to stay away from the judgement as much as possible and create a creative outlet that would allow me to hide behind my veil.

I spent a lot of my school life dancing, singing and acting, and loved the opportunities this gave me to be on the stage and have an outlet for my more extrovert side. Whenever I was in a challenging situation that would ask me to use my voice, I would hide behind my veil of shyness and being an introvert. People accepted this of me, loved me for it and spoke for me when my voice was empty. My force field was working.

The force field that I put up for myself, I didn't ever want. I wanted to be like others around me, who seemed so confident and shared their views openly. I wanted to be more extroverted, but how?

I would stand in social circles and still feel that my tongue was sewn to the roof of my mouth, just as it did as a child. I felt so immature, not being able to speak up for myself. How could I create a business that would serve a community and give me my heart's desires if I couldn't speak to them. I tried so many times to create something that would work without me using my voice.

I was hiding. The bullies saw that I was hiding, and they loved that. I hated it, but I couldn't release it as it was so ingrained as part of my identity. This grew to hiding my face from the public and any pictures. My self-esteem was so low that I didn't know how to love on myself. I could see that so many people, who were indirectly in my life, didn't love me either.

Not only did I not have a voice, body dysmorphia took away any love that I could see on me. I doubted my words and my thoughts. I would try and speak up at meetings, classes and social events and people would speak for me because they could see my hesitation. This only caused me to hesitate even more.

I would tell myself that I was ugly, fat, my words were stupid etc. This was my life. Could I change it?

I remember feeling strongly that I wouldn't change myself for anyone else – I had strong morals! But I wanted to change so much so that I could take charge and show more of my desire to be extroverted.

From my late teens, I suffered from burn out. I spent many years believing that I was a hypochondriac, that I must be unfit, that there was something wrong with me because I couldn't keep up with others my age.

I didn't realise for some time that this was because I had an auto immune disease. This would impinge my life, stopping me from being physically and mentally able to focus on my life, work and education.

It took quite some time before my condition was known, and then many more years to really understand how I could support my mind and body.

This came in many forms, but the two that were the most important were rest (managing my time) and supplements. Learning to rest in my teens and 20s was hard! I didn't want to be the one who had to rest after going food shopping or having an afternoon nap after we had had visitors in the morning.

All I could think was that I was old before my time and no one would want to be friends with me when I couldn't manage an evening at the cinema without being so exhausted. I looked like I was going to pass out.

So, I had to step things up and take charge over my body and heal myself from the inside. I remember well my mum taking me to a herbal shop. They took one look at me when I walked through the door and they knew what was wrong with me better than my GP! Consequently, they sold me over £100 worth of supplements!!

From that day, my desire to know more about what supplements we should be taking to support our body, what foods are healthy and not, and how I can live a normal life eating the foods I like but still eating clean foods, was my number one priority.

I was creating my own Healthy Habits, a healthy relationship with myself.

These healthy habits grew to be so ingrained in my day that I still have the same routine now. I have grown to know my porridge oats from my sprouted oats and my cocoa powder from my cacao powder.

The joy and enthusiasm this brought me, to get back in the kitchen and understand food as fuel again, was overwhelming. It held me, until the day I realised that I still had issues with my body dysmorphia. I needed to work on this and the best way for me was to focus on my strength. Changing my mindset brought a reduction in body fat of over 20%. I had never felt healthier, but there was still something holding me back. I just couldn't figure it out.

This is when I started to work with my coach and realised that my health was more than just about food, I needed to focus on my mental wellbeing. Working through the self-mastery course, I finally understood that I was co-dependant, sitting in victim space and hadn't forgiven my past as I thought I had.

My transformation came through knowing that I must work on myself so that I became victor, and forgive others so that I could forgive myself.

This epiphany happened for me when I worked with my coach and learnt the value in all of me, not just what people desire me to be – quiet Hannah that says yes to everything. I have changed from being a people pleaser to focusing on my self-worth.

What I realise now is that I am an ambivert, and I love it! I realised that it is ok to want my own space and to be tired when I am busy holding space with others, to recharge my batteries after social gatherings and to say no to gatherings that I know won't serve me. To hold my worth and value.

My first action was to start speaking my heart's desires and business thoughts and decisions with those that were in my circle of trust. I created a group/tribe around me that would always support me and guide me through the good and bad times. They sang with me in my successes and guess what? They didn't speak for me! Finding women that have the same mindset as you, and will always lift you up to do better, can seem hard, but they are out there.

Thank you, ladies xxx

I then started to create other healthy habits in my business, from setting clear boundaries with clients so that we both knew what to expect from the beginning of the relationship, to setting clear boundaries with myself and my timetable, so that I had time off and I spent that as I wanted to.

One of the biggest things I do for me and my business is to ask for help. This will always be a work in progress for me, as I have a fear that people will think I am stupid for asking a stupid question, (even though we all know there is no such thing as a stupid question) and the bullying and ridicule will step in.

Again, ladies, my coach, and my circle of trust, I am so grateful for you.

From here, I grew to becoming a coach myself, and doing my coaching accreditation with the Leadership of Management. I knew that I had a passion for coaching and the breakthroughs it gave people, but it was important to me that I gain a qualification with world-leading trainers, so that I learnt the best techniques within individualised and group sessions.

My joy for coaching grew more and more whilst delivering pro bono sessions, and this is where I found that my voice for myself and others, and my business grew. My voice grew as I grew a healthy relationship with myself.

Relationships take continued work and energy, but I now don't see this as effort. It is joy to build relationships.

My clients learn to find joy in relationship building, building their self-worth in the process, knowing they have a safe place to do so.

I have grown into my identity as a coach. So, now I have helped myself, I can help others. Helping people build healthy relationships. This naturally grew into moving these relationships over to people's workplaces and businesses.

Clients are now forgiving their past, whether that be bullies, low morale at the office or something else of their individual story. Clients are learning that they don't have to sit in resentment, loneliness, fear etc. anymore. It can all be flipped, through healing, to create the career/business you desire.

My golden nuggets to you, the reader, are: I respect myself enough to love on myself every morning. Loving on myself to eat well and love the curves that have come during Covid. To create boundaries with whoever has blurred ones with me.

Self-love comes first. You can't build healthy habits in any area of your life if you don't love and respect yourself enough to talk beauty to yourself each day.

When I learnt that I was allowed to radiate at a size 12, not just a size 8, I knew my worth didn't come from my dress size; it came from who I talked myself to be and who I created boundaries with to not hold me back anymore.

This took me stepping out of victim space in to a space that allowed me to lead! Wow. I had never been told before that I was a leader, only a follower, and didn't I feel like a lost sheep until I let go of other's words and opinions of me?

Leaving the day job – teaching - was one of my biggest boundaries. I was no longer an employer of someone who felt they could bully me and degrade me. I am Hannah, who is allowed to smile at the person she looks back at on the screen.

Reflecting on my golden nuggets as I grow in myself and watch my business do the same, reminds me of how far I have come.

We are always a work in progress, but I sit here typing knowing that my business is all encompassing of me, and what better way to serve my community than share the world I have created which can support them.

I am now well, and feel energised physically, mentally and spiritually to take my daily practices into my community.

I manage my day with walking, gratitude, prayer, supplements, clean food and treats. As I have found my voice and step out of self-doubt, Hannah Pekary Coaching has grown to now support women in business who are looking to create those healthy relationships and habits, and looking for support and guidance in a loving, hand-holding manner.

Getting out of my own way has allowed me to grow into leadership roles. I now deal with a busier life, but manage it so that I spin my plates equally, whilst giving myself time off every week to love on me.

Unpicking my tongue has released my voice, and wow, is my voice still finding new ways to be used!

I now speak up for myself in situations when my self-worth or boundaries are compromised. I put myself forward for speaking gigs, such as podcasts and interviews. My Instagram page has IGTV's! I speak up for other women who need my love and guidance. I am a vessel for those who can't speak for themselves and need to create their voice.

You can have this too, by just incorporating healthy habits into your relationships and life. Many women are now empowered and have already created boundaries in relationships, and healed some too. Women have learnt to put themselves first and show themselves self-respect. They have learnt to nurture their bodies from the above, and from food, but also to not judge themselves when they have a treat.

My desire was to always be a role model to the children that walked through my doors for dance and education. I spent many years worrying and doubting my words and actions around them and over them. My doubt has stopped, and I trust in myself to bring what they need.

I trust what I bring and have what their parents need in my coaching. Relationship coaching supports voices. Voices are to be heard. I have learnt to share my victor voice.

This is also shown in some of the women that I have helped.

> "I have been having coaching sessions with Hannah for just over two months, and the progress that I have made in so many aspects of my life is mind-blowing. I am well on my way to healing relationships that I never thought I would, I am resolving deep hurt and lifelong learned bad habits that I thought would be with me forever, and I cannot thank Hannah enough."

This individual came to me asking for help with some consistency. This quickly led to the realisation that relationships needed healing and self-love wasn't in abundance. They now have positive relationships with extended family and have reignited a fire within their belly for business that would otherwise have stayed a dream.

> "I first started working with Hannah as I was looking for support with how I parent my two young boys who were going through a challenging phase. Hannah's support, guidance and advice helped me to develop my own parent skills and settle my family down into a better routine. Although I originally worked with Hannah around parenting, this quickly developed into coaching me around all sorts of aspects of my life, such as nutrition, self-care and healthy habits. Hannah's kind, gentle and supportive approach is very empowering and it is reassuring knowing that I have her support. I thoroughly recommend Hannah's coaching."

It is so empowering to show women that in order to grow relationships within the home and family, they need to create a healthy relationship for themselves, and how this transforms family life and business.

> "Life during lockdown might have been very different if we had not found Hannah. We were experiencing a lot of conflict as we tried to settle into a 'new normal' when schools closed down, and Hannah helped us to quickly achieve a happy equilibrium. On a parenting level, I was very grateful to have the support of Hannah and her family coaching. I was lucky enough to be able to continue working throughout the summer, but I often felt overwhelmed. Hannah helped me to calmly deal with stressful situations and conflict and gave me systems and routines to help limit them. At the same time as helping me, Hannah also tutored my daughter, who sat fully engaged for each two-hour virtual session. Hannah is gentle, encouraging and firm when she needs to be, and I highly recommend her."

It can all be so easy to follow advice via social media or the like and feel as if you are in a perpetual cycle of desperation and frustration, but the cycle was broken here, with communication, boundaries and respect.

You too can have healthy relationships in your life, and healthy habits in your day. Your habits don't have to be so strict that you feel you can't live, but structured enough that they become part of who you are.

I can teach you a 10-minute, morning routine, that can have you bouncing into your day so that you feel loved, empowered and ready to share your voice, feeling ready to look after your family and have conversations that you only dreamed of.

Your business can be just the same as your home life.

You can create healthy habits and relationships within that too, so that what you thought were dreams to while away your day on are becoming reality, so changing your future and your family's.

Once you learn to find your voice and help yourself, you will be able to help your family. I empower parents to create healthy, balanced relationships whilst making healthy habits, that impact positively on themselves and their family's wellbeing and health.

Building habits is about relationships. A relationship with you must come first.

You can have it all. You are allowed it all. You are worthy, strong and capable.

Come and join us in my free Facebook book group and follow us on Facebook and Instagram.

www.hannahpekary.com

https://linktr.ee/HannahPekaryCoaching

https://www.instagram.com/hannah_pekary_coaching

www.facebook.com/groups/Alignedrelationshipsinbusinessandlife

https://www.facebook.com/HannahPekaryCoaching

ABOUT THE AUTHOR

Hannah Pekary is a business coach who helps entrepreneurs to create healthy relationships in their businesses and personal lives; creating healthy habits so they are well equipped to work through their limiting beliefs, money mindset and more, so creating their true identity.

Hannah is a graduate coach of the fully accredited Aligned Coaching Academy (ACA MInstLM), and a certified Story Work Coach with Andrea Callanan (ACSWC)

Before starting a coaching business, Hannah worked for 15 years as a dance teacher, and professional dancer, whilst also training to become a teacher and running a successful tutoring business. Before and during this time, Hannah nannied for numerous families, supporting them to create healthy habits. Hannah now helps these entrepreneurial mums to create their own businesses and lifestyles full of freedom and joy.

Hannah lives on the Welsh coastline and loves to take unwinding walks with her dog, breathing in the salty air.

Hannah enjoys baking for any occasion, and loves to spend time with her family.

Hannah is available for Business coaching, both 1:1 coaching, and through her courses.

You can reach Hannah at:

Email – hello@hannahpekary.com
Linktree - https://linktr.ee/HannahPekaryCoaching
Website – www.hannahpekary.com

facebook.com/HannahPekaryCoaching
instagram.com/hannah_pekary_coaching

JACKIE VAN BAREN
COURAGE OVER COMFORT

"Can I just stop you right there, Jax?" he said. "Courage over comfort." Some hardcore Brene Brown fans may recognise this phrase, I hadn't come across it before. This is what my brother Scott said to me when I was moaning about how hard it 'all' felt and how it was like Groundhog day every single day. I knew the life that I wanted and I had the power to change it, but I was stuck and scared. It was the beginning of 2021 and we were in our second lockdown in Wales, with no end in sight.

He said it again..."courage over comfort."

Click! The penny dropped. I realised I have a choice to find the life that I want... there is always a way, and where I was right now was not where I would be for my whole life. My life, my choice, but a fair amount of discomfort and changes were needed to get to the life I had on my vision board.

I called time on our life in a small town in South Wales and travelled with my young family to the other side of the world, with no firm arrangements in place, during a global pandemic. Taking one step at a time.

As I write this chapter, my husband - Pieter, and children, [Dominic (7) and Olivia (5)] and I are on an epic journey from the little Welsh town that Tom Jones hails from, to Queensland, Australia, via New Zealand, in search of the fun-filled, outdoor lifestyle that I grew up in. This is our story as we are living it. We haven't arrived at our destination yet, but we are having an incredible adventure getting to that place.

In the 21st century, you may think that all that this adventure required was passports and money, and we could go wherever we wanted, at a time that worked for us. Thanks to the restrictions that Covid-19 had brought to the world, the journey from South Wales just to Auckland, took us 3 intense weeks and 12 suitcases! Against the odds, we successfully completed 2 visa applications to allow us to enter Australia and New Zealand... when we were allowed to travel that is. We had managed to secure a 'golden ticket' quarantine hotel spot on the NZ government website and we had our Covid tests booked for 2 days before our flight. There was so much uncertainty whether the plane would actually leave, whether our Covid tests would be negative so that we could depart, and whether we would even be allowed into the country.

I shared my anxiety with my friend who had moved back to Australia at the start of the pandemic - that we wouldn't be able to fly to New Zealand as there were so many things that could go wrong. She reassured me that I should "act like your journey will take place as planned and deal with any problems along the way". Well, I held onto that nugget of information for dear life and we packed our bags and headed to the airport.

Now, the New Zealand government had closed the borders to all non-essential travel to ensure their zero-Covid-case strategy stayed strong, and for those lucky enough to board the empty flights to the country, they had to spend 14 days in Managed Isolation or Quarantine (MIQ), in a hotel of the governments choosing. It was completely the luck of the draw which hotel you stayed in... even what kind of room you had. Fortunately for us, we ended up in the Crowne Plaza, in Christchurch, with two interconnecting rooms and a balcony. What a blessing that was! There were people on our floor in the hotel who didn't even have an opening window in their room. Imagine that with two bundles of energy who never sit still!

Let me rewind a bit and give you a little glimpse of what life was for us before we decided to uproot our seemingly happy lives and move to the other side of the world in a pandemic.

Why would you want to sell your house, take your family away from their grandparents and little friends and move to the other side of the world? Truthfully, there have been times since we made that decision when we have questioned our choice and whether it would be easier just to stay where we were... and then in a flash I am transported to the 'place' in our future that we have sketched out on paper and added to our vision board. This 'place' is near the beach and we are living our best life! This is our opportunity to carve out what our days would look like and what our definition of success would be. I firmly believe that what success means is different for every single person in this world. I used to think that success was having loads of money, a lovely large house, flash cars in the driveway, and having beautiful clothes to wear. The more work I do on myself and my mindset, the more I realise that I am actually living my definition of success right now - happy, healthy children, a happy and loving relationship with my husband and an suv business with fantastic clients. However, I still wanted more. And that makes me feel a bit guilty. As a South African who has seen people live with no food, no shoes, no homes, why is what I have, not enough?

Let's pause there for a moment.

For years, my husband and I have been working hard to pay off our debts accumulated when we got married and moved to live in the UK in 2014. I am South African by birth and Pieter is from Perth, Australia. We met in Melbourne in 2011... the year that changed everything for me. Imagine, flying out to Australia 'just for a year', only to return three years later, with a husband and new baby. In fact, the path to marriage was super quick, we met and married within eight months... when you know, you know!

When we arrived in Wales, we had a six-month-old boy, who wasn't a fan of sleeping at night. We stayed with family for a few months and then we managed to find a small house close by. We were your typical, sleep deprived new parents, who were doing our best for our son and surviving the day on minimal sleep. Having just come from Australia where Pieter is originally from, we found it tough when the days ended quickly and it turned dark and cold from 4pm-ish.

Being someone who has been working since the age of 13, I was not used to sitting still and being a good housewife. I like to keep busy (anything other than cleaning that is) and I like to make money. I had a couple of well-paid corporate roles when I lived and worked in London in my twenties, and when my first baby came along, I was keen to get started with some kind of job that I could fit around Dominic.

I started selling Avon products to neighbours. Having no friends in the area, I thought it would be an excellent way to get out and about and meet new people, my neighbours, and make some friends. Turns out, trekking out in the rain to deliver/collect catalogues, not to mention purchasing the products for myself, was not going to make me millions or make friends very quickly! We always wanted our children to fit into our lives and that life was going to be full, fun, and exciting!

I needed something more fulfilling, but we were in a bit of a catch 22. My husband was focused on looking for work too and I was negotiating motherhood, which I found really, really hard. I needed to find work to contribute to our family income. In the UK, grandparents often step in to help their children with childcare while the parents went back to work, but unfortunately for us my mum was working full time. I needed a job to pay for childcare for Dominic, but I needed someone to look after him while I was looking for a job and then working. Looking for a job in a new country is a full-time job in itself, and 10 times slower when you have a little inquisitive boy getting into everything. The only other option was to take a chance and send Dominic to nursery for two days a week. That space allowed me to fulfil the opportunity to work for a family friend as a Virtual Assistant (VA).

I haven't trained to be a virtual assistant but I have worked in sales, marketing, and office management, so I knew I had transferable skills to bring to the party. The best bits about being a VA meant I could use my skills and work from home. All I needed was a laptop and good Wi-Fi and I was away!

When I started my VA business, I was introduced to all the business networks in the local area... I even led a networking group for mums in business in my local area. I said yes to all the jobs that were offered to me even if I didn't like doing them, I was grateful for the work. I used to laugh at the fact that I would help a client organise a conference in India and all the necessary documents to get there one day, and the next day be writing social media posts for a local garage offering MOT's. I didn't have a niche, I didn't have an ideal client mapped out, I just did everything... as long as it was legal, that is! I built my own website, did my own marketing, I had no team.

I was still a sleep deprived mother of a very determined little boy who did not want to miss out on any of the fun downstairs. I was exhausted... and then I fell pregnant with another baby, just when we planned to wait for a few more years so that my business could grow a bit more and life would settle down a bit.

For years, I worked as a lone wolf, building up my client base, being all things to all people for a very low hourly rate. The one thing you get with trading your time for money is that you hit a limit very quickly; that is, you hit a ceiling with the number of clients you can support on your own, and my stress levels were beginning to take their toll.

There had to be a better way to have the family life that we wanted and a successful business that didn't drain me. I think I realised during that first year of living in the UK with my beach and sun loving husband, that we would only be in the UK for a short time, so I needed to work on establishing myself and my business.

If you are reading this and thinking, "well, that's alright for you Jackie, you had (enter the thing you feel you don't have in your life)", please know that if you want to do something badly enough, if it is all you can think about, dream about, talk about... then you have what you need inside you to take that first step towards your goal, your dream life.

If you are working in a job that does not bring you any joy whatsoever, taking small steps towards that dream, that new business, that new life is all you need to focus on...

One small step at a time.

Before we embarked on our adventure to the other side of the world, we spent years talking about when we could move. My husband kept his ears and eyes on the news in his home country, we worked and saved as much as we could so that we when we left the UK, we could afford to buy a home near the beach!

With that dream in mind, and my little mantra of 'courage or comfort', we set to work to make our dream happen.

We had a lot of work to do to be able to leave with as little stuff as possible. We needed to sell our first ever house, our cars, our bikes and a whole heap of children's toys and clothes that we had been accumulating in our loft. The thought of having to sell our house and emptying our loft almost put a stop to the whole move and adventure. Those of you with children who are Frozen 2 super fans may appreciate this little bit of inspiration that we took from Anna, when she sang, "Take a step, step again, it is all that I can to do the next right thing." So that is what we did; we started with painting the bathrooms and every weekend we did a little more. I say we, I mean the tradesmen we paid and my husband, Pieter, who worked hard to paint those walls and little touch ups around the house where the children's little 'creations' appeared on the walls!

Once the bathrooms were finished, and the kitchen walls had a lick of fresh paint, the final bit was the little garden out the front. Pieter worked hard on making that home super inviting. Once we had taken those final steps to fix the house, we contacted a few estate agents to let them know we were ready to sell!

The process that we assumed would take months, took less than a week. Thanks to COVID, people's desire to move after being in lockdown for so long, and a very efficient real estate agent who knew what he was doing, our first family home was on the market and sold for our full asking price in just one week. While we were in a state of shock, we were also so relieved that it was sold as keeping your home 'show house ready', with two little kids in lockdown, was super stressful. We had been monitoring the market around us and houses were taking at least nine months to sell, it only goes to show that if something is meant to be, the doors will open for you and the seemingly impossible will become possible. It all starts with taking that first step forward... one small step at a time... and even more than this, it's about having the courage to take that first step, knowing it will be super uncomfortable at the time but hugely beneficial in the long run.

So, that was the house sorted, now we needed to mentally prepare for the move overseas, and also I wanted to keep my clients happy, and wanted to keep my business going during the move so that it would continue to grow while we were finding our feet in a new country.

I could not do it all alone though, I needed to pull in help. Admitting that I needed help in my business and that I could not control everything was super tough. Before working with Andrea Callanan and doing her Unapologetic Self-Mastery course, I thought that no one could service my clients like I could. Not only that, but I worried that a VA or a bookkeeper who I needed most in my business would judge me for the way I approached my clients and processes.

When I first met Andrea, she talked about fear. The negative way you show up for your family or your clients comes from a place of fear. For me, that fear was in the form of control. I could do everything myself. I could be a wife, a mother, a business owner managing multiple clients, and keep it all to myself. Well, it turns out you can't and you are not meant to do it yourself. I am not saying that you have to take on employees. Hiring freelance team members who were specialists in their field was the single best decision I made for my clients, my business, my mental health and my family! The first person I took on as part of my business was an incredible bookkeeper. She knew the systems my customers used, inside and out (and 10 x better than I did), and it meant that I could focus on the other parts of client work that I loved and could support more customers to start to grow their business.

Let's check in with you, lovely reader. Are you still with me? Is there something in your life or business that you would like to change but are just not sure where to start. I am not saying that you have to relocate your whole family and start again like I did, but you can choose courage over comfort. As Henry Ford once said;

> "If you always do what you always did, you'll always get what you always got".

Are you ready to step aside and rise to the life you want? In this chapter I have been banging on about having courage, taking one step at a time, but there are few other things we did that helped us make the move in the first place. Here are my top five tips to getting out of your own way and helping you on your quest for success as a business owner or in the life that you dream of.

1. Get organised. The more you plan how the next few steps will look, the better you will feel along the way. But don't get too caught up in the details so you don't end up taking any steps forward at all. While I am the driving force behind getting us out the door every day, my husband needs to know every single step that we will take when we leave the house. I think we make a good team. Having a plan set out, however loose it may be, will really help you enjoy the journey to your destination.
2. Take time to build up your team. I realised that I only had a certain amount of time available to support my clients and if I wanted to accomplish my financial goals that I had set for myself, as well as move to the other side of the world, I would need to get a team of professionals who knew what they were doing, and dare I say, had the skills to do it better. There is a famous African Proverb that says "it takes a village to raise a child". I think it takes a village to have a successful business too, and that village comes in all shapes and sizes. My village now has a VA, a Tech VA, a Bookkeeper, a social media manager... and that is just for my business. As a family, we had a cleaner when we lived in Wales and even though she only came once every two weeks, the money we spent (or invested in our home) meant we could spend more time as a family on the weekends, or I could dedicate more time to my business or my clients during the week while the kids were at school. I vowed to myself that the more successful I got, the more days I would ask our cleaner to come around and clean our house... Back to you and your business.
3. Have you ever mapped out what you love doing in your

business? What is your zone of genius? What comes so effortlessly to you that you could almost do it in your sleep? That is the golden place to be in and will help your business to grow. Once you have worked out what you love and are effortlessly good at, start delegating the bits of your life or business that do not bring you joy. If bookkeeping stresses you out, hire a bookkeeper. Think of that precious time you spend on the bits you do love doing in your business or spending time with your family rather than reconciling your Xero account.

4. While you are building up your team, I recommend introducing online access from any device systems that you and your team can work on together so that your business can start to run a little on its own or while you are working with other customers. The best systems to start with include a lead generator, a customer relationship management or email system and a sales system. As a female entrepreneur, you have amazing skills and while it might seem like a rite of passage to work out how to do it all yourself, I remind my clients that we are not meant to know and do EVERYTHING. Having online systems that my team had access to meant that I could take the time off, or drop in and out whenever any urgent work that came through could not wait until I landed in Auckland.

5. Ask for help and learn the art of delegating. As I mentioned above, you have amazing skills, you have invested in training and coaching and being the best you can be for your clients. You do not need to spend your precious time teaching yourself the basics of yet another online system. It makes your head want to explode. You know that building an email list is key to getting the right customers that you can nurture, but it's been on your to-do list for months and it's still not done. Ask for help with it. My team and I work with female coaches and entrepreneurs to get them off the starting blocks and

implement good systems so that they can focus on their zone of genius. It could be as small as implementing an email system; you can start building a valuable email list of ideal clients. Let's get this off your to-do list once and for all, so you can talk directly to your customer in their emails.

My final tip is to HAVE FUN! The more time I spend 'on the road' in another country, with very chilled and laid-back Kiwis, the more I have come to realise that life is actually fun! Life does not need to be hard. It doesn't have to be all about how flashy your car is or how many homes you have, and it is not even about what you need to do to get to your business to the magical 6 or 7 figures. What is more important is the memories we have made along the way and the fun we had eating fish and chips in our campervan in a car park in South New Brighton beach, in Christchurch, before we made it to the holiday park we had booked just the day before we left MIQ.

If you are in the entrepreneurial circles, it can feel like you are missing out when the people start shouting out about how much money they have made and how much they did it with (xyz). I have not made it to 7 figures yet, but I will, one day soon. I know that what I have done by taking my family from one side of the world to the other in a pandemic is brave and bold and proof that if you want to make a change in your life, as hard as it may seem at the time, you can do it.

While we are not quite at our final destination yet, we have arrived in Auckland to my sister's house and, at the time of writing this part of my story, the city was in full lockdown. Armed police were patrolling the perimeter of the city, ensuring only essential journeys were taken (The rest of the country was in level 2 while Auckland was in full lockdown). For us, this was an essential journey! We had already endured two weeks in a hotel, only being allowed out for 45 minutes a day to walk around a cordoned off exercise yard... I say 'exercise yard', what I mean is a car park with barriers around it so that you couldn't escape. We were not allowed to run, but we could walk as fast as you could in circles around the perimeter, keeping our distance and not talking to anyone... dare I say it, it felt a bit like being a prisoner.

However lovely it was at the Crowne Plaza and how cushy it felt to have your meals delivered to you and your washing done for you, and all you could do was watch tv and speak to your friends while you were getting over your jetlag, we still had to stay in our rooms, have regular PCR tests and eat whatever the hotel was serving that day. We were so happy when the 14 days were up and all our covid PCR tests taken during our stay turned out to be negative! That meant we could leave and start our next adventure in a campervan travelling to the North Island. We had planned to jump in a campervan and see all the fun activities that New Zealand had to offer, but all we were able to do was to go straight to Auckland to stay with my sister and her family, and wait for however long it took for Australia to reopen their borders to NZ and allow us in. Our final destination is the Gold Coast, Australia, but that final move may be months and months away! I would be surprised if we were allowed to cross the Tasman this side of Christmas without having to quarantine in Australia for another 14 days.

I am not sure how much my children have taken in of the incredible scenery, and gorgeous wineries we passed in our campervan trip from Christchurch to Auckland over the Cook Strait, but I am sure, in years to come, they will appreciate that the hours of travelling, and the sacrifices we have made together as a family, will make their lives all the more richer from the experiences. I don't think I will ever forget the feeling of the van almost being blown over in the intense wind gusts in a Wellington waterfront carpark while the kids snored away! I was so scared; Pieter's arm was a little bit blue from squeezing him so tightly as we tried to sleep!

If you have enjoyed reading about our adventure and would like to get your systems up and running, please drop me an email or a direct message on Facebook (@jackievanbaren/obm) or Instagram (@jvbconnect). My team and I would be happy to help you establish yourself as a leader and kick start your business with an on-brand lead magnet and the systems behind it. Imagine having an automated system that allows you to build up a relationship with your potential customers, with personalised on brand emails that will turn them from potential customers into paying customers and raving fans.

We have worked with inspiring female entrepreneurs who are the best in their field, as well as new coaches and consultants who are looking for their ideal clients and establishing their offer. They come to us as they are ready to start selling their services, but are so stuck with the necessary systems and technology required to start selling online. There is so much technology around and women come to me overwhelmed with the options and ready to give up. They don't care how it is done, they just want the customer journey to look professional and slick when they need to show up and deliver their service to their customer. Once you have reached the level of success that you have dreamed of, but have reached a limit to what you can do yourself, you are well and truly on your way to establish yourself as an expert and you need ongoing support. We would love to be part of your journey.

Whatever your situation is now, whatever you would like to change... or indeed if you would like to uproot your family and take them to another country, I encourage you to seek courage over comfort and just do it! When you look back at your life when you are 80, you can say, I did it... against all odds.

ABOUT THE AUTHOR

Jackie is an Online Business Manager who helps ambitious female coaches and consultants to build brilliant businesses online by implementing efficient systems and processes behind-the-scenes to enable their business to soar.

Before starting a global online business, Jackie had a successful career in IT Sales and Account Management in the UK and Australia. Working for global software vendors, such as Citrix and Microsoft, encouraged her love of technology and systems, and working in a digital media buying agency such as ZenithOptimedia, introduced her to the exciting world of digital marketing. Jackie, with the help of her fantastic team, now uses their skills and experience to support ambitious women launch successful online businesses or courses, helping them to establish themselves as leaders in their field.

Jackie loves traveling and exploring new places with her husband and two young children, especially when there is good coffee and sushi around!

Jackie has brand new packages to help you either kick start your business, start selling and growing your business or a package that is tailor made for you and your brilliant business.

You can reach Jackie at:

Email: jackie@jvbconnect.com
Website : www.jvbconnect.com

facebook.com/jackievanbarenOBM
instagram.com/jvbconnect

11

JANE MACK

Rise Above the Challenges and Reap the Rewards

I look back over my last 10 years and can see many things that I could have done differently. I wouldn't say that I would necessarily change them, because I wouldn't actually be where I am today without them. I just know that I could have made my life easier back then. As a business coach, I support mums in business to gain a better work life balance through a number of techniques I have come across through running my own business.

As a working mum of two boys, aged 13 and 7, life is a juggling act... and I can juggle because I have that wonderful thing called flexibility to help. Being my own boss allows me to do the mum things I need to do and be there before and after school. No one is clock watching me, nor do I have to take annual leave to go to a sports day. Being my own boss also allows me the options to run my business as I want to and take it in the direction that I am most passionate about.

During the last 10 years, I have had some really proud moments. During that time, my husband and I bought a business on the Isle of Arran, moved there with an 18-month old toddler and knew no one. We grew the business, set up a new life and then sold the business for 6 times the cost we bought it for. Now, I have my own business again, doing something I am passionate about. I help mums in business simplify their businesses, and help them to get that work life balance they have always wanted. On top of that, I have learned a new way of doing business and as a result, I have gained a confidence to put myself out there, through online networking (thanks to a global pandemic) and being on social media, through video and 'going live'. Something I never thought I could do.

It has not always been plain sailing and there have been obstacles and bumps along the way. Ten years ago, my husband and I had no experience of the holiday home management industry that we had just bought into. This lead to a very busy work life and little family time. Work life balance was pretty much at zero. We had lots to learn and as our experience grew, we had plans we wanted to put in place and changes we wanted to make. My head was buzzing all the time.

Doing work over the weekend became the norm, and I would be driving around houses, checking them, with the kids in the back of the car with a portable DVD player and snacks, and my husband worked most weekends. At times it felt like a vicious circle, where I had all these ideas and plans that I wanted to put in place. I would start them, but the daily operational side would kick in and these plans were put to the side, but they were still very active in my mind. Unfortunately, this sometimes meant that while I would be out playing with the kids, my mind was elsewhere and I wasn't actually present for them. Everything became a rush and I never seemed to have time to do anything. One of my team once said that one day, I would actually walk out of the office as opposed to run out of it.

Although all this would continue, the business still kept growing, so it became the normal way of working, because everything I was doing was helping to grow the business. If that wasn't enough, then taking time off for holidays was a complete no goer. There was one year that I took off 14 days actual holiday across the full year. In my mind, I had to be there for everything, incase something went wrong. This way of working is not sustainable and always led to illness over the winter months, stresses and sometimes resentment against the business. I now say to anyone in business that if there's one thing you need to make sure you do, it is to take time off, and when you do, your business will not fall apart. In fact, it will improve it, because you come back refreshed, clear headed, motivated and back loving it again. Having joy and motivation in your business is critical for it to succeed and for you to succeed on a personal level.

One year, my husband and I decided to take a few days away with the kids before schools started back and we got two nights in a lovely hotel, that cost a fortune due to the last minute option, but was the best thing we could have done. After that, each year we started taking more breaks away. I wish we had done it years before.

When I look back now and think of all the things that I used to do and believed, I can see how I made my life quite difficult at times. It was the first business I had owned and I suppose you could say that I didn't know any better and had nothing to compare it to.

I always felt that I had to constantly be at work, and by that, I mean sitting at my desk from 9am-5pm, otherwise, I wasn't working and the business would not be successful. The saying 'work smarter not harder' was not around much then.

I would feel guilty if I went to a networking event or conference, because I had left my team to cover and as I wasn't in the office, therefore, I wasn't working, rather than looking at the opportunities and connections it could bring. I didn't actually go to many because I would be too busy, or that was the excuse I would make, but really, there was a confidence piece there and I didn't want to walk into a room full of strangers and start talking to them.

This was also the case for taking time off, as I thought I had to be there in case something went wrong, as it was my business and my responsibility. I always thought that I was responsible for everything and everyone and it all had to be perfect. The houses had to be perfect, our processes had to be perfect and every guest's stay had to be perfect. Take it from me, trying to make things perfect all the time is not only exhausting, but will also drive you mad.

Back then, I didn't have a business coach and didn't think of investing in one, because I didn't have time (I did really, but just didn't realise this) and thought I should be investing money into the business and not me. Well, I was the business, so this was another stupid thought.

I never really knew much about the phrase imposter syndrome, but little did I know it was there in me. When we decided that the next move for the business was to expand into holiday letting and advertising, this is when the imposter syndrome kicked in. I knew it was the best and most logical move for the business and that our owners also wanted us to do it, but all the what ifs started to appear.

What if an owner asks me a question that I don't know the answer to? What if I can't get any bookings for the houses? I don't have a marketing and advertising degree, and the old favourite line: I'm not the an expert in this. What I didn't realise was that I was living and breathing this stuff daily and I knew a lot more than I realised.

So, to play it safe, I decided that we would aim to have about 15 houses on the website to let. I was being cautious, because I didn't want to go big and aim for 30 or 40 in case it didn't happen, because that may have caused disappointment and the feeling of failure. Well, imposter syndrome soon dropped away as the service took off and by the time we sold the business, we had achieved 55 properties on the website to let.

When you are new in a business, it is common to get carried away with watching what your competitors are doing, but then comparisonitis kicks in and you feel you need to be doing all these things too. I had this and had to stop myself from worrying about what everyone else was doing and focus on my business and how I worked with my owners and the service I provided. That's why they choose us as a service provider, after all. Theodore Roosevelt said "Comparison is the thief of joy" and it's so true as it takes away your joy in your business if all you do is focus on others. I keep reminding myself of this.

There have been some obstacles thrown in my path which caused me to think these things. When the decision was made to expand the business into the advertising and letting, I had to come out of a contract we had with a letting agency, as it would have been a conflict of interest to continue working together. Unfortunately, this lead to some untruthful letters about myself being sent to my owners from the agency. Not exactly what you want, just 18 months into your business. This is where I thought, what if I can't do this because this is a large company and I am small; they have been doing this for years and I have never done it, so I don't have the expertise. I don't have the marketing budget that the big companies have, or the large customer base that's been built up over years and snazzy booking systems, so who am I to think I can give the same service.

I soon realised that all these things didn't matter to my customers, because they choose to work with me because of my values and what I could offer. That was a personal service, a local service, a service with connection and integrity. That's what was important to my ideal clients.

The same applied when comparisonitis kicked in from time to time. My competitors would send my owners letters undercutting me and with big offers. They would try to coax them away and I thought that I should be putting out letters as well with offers to encourage them to stay. This went on for about four years. Thankfully, I didn't need to do this as my owners never jumped ship. They stayed with me because of the way I worked. They did not like this way of doing business and were not sold on the big offers. Those were not important to them. Once again, it was my values that were important to them.

So, I needed to stop worrying about how they were doing their business. I would watch competitors on social media where they would be constantly promoting my area and the businesses in my area, and I thought, I need to be doing this. I stressed about it as I didn't have time to do all this social media. What I realised was, I didn't need to, as my website was all about my area and I had built relationships with these local businesses personally. Once again, this was how I did business and it worked, I did not have to do the same as my competitors. My business had its own unique selling points, which were the fact that it was local and could therefore give that personal service. That's what I started focusing on, rather than my competitors.

Even with this focus on how we worked rather than on our competitors, and watching the business grow steadily, I still didn't feel I could take time off, because the business may fail. There were situations where I had to take time off without choice, but the business kept running.

One of these being, that after a couple of years into the business, my husband and I sadly lost our little baby boy during pregnancy and I had to take time off. Thankfully, I had a small team that was able to keep things running, as not only did I need to be off physically, but there was the emotional trauma to deal with also.

The next year, we were delighted to bring into the world a very healthy baby boy. I then took off 10 months for maternity leave. I still did the monthly payroll and took photos for new properties, but other than that, I was off. But still, after all this, I felt I couldn't take a holiday. This was rubbish; of course I could. It wasn't until several years of winter sicknesses, colds, flu, which at one time, lead to pleurisy, and general exhaustion that we finally started to take time off with the kids and got away.

Each year, we took more time and started having proper family holidays again, and guess what happened? The business did not fall apart, it still continued to grow. We felt so much better for it. We felt more normal and started to enjoy the business more. It is so important that you take the time out for you, your family and your own self-care.

The business would also not fall apart if I attended events, conferences or networking opportunities. I couldn't do this a lot as I felt I was not at work, as I was not in the office. For the previous seven years, I had worked for a large corporation in HR roles, and my job was done at my desk and in the office every day. It was hard to get out of this mindset as that was what I was used to and automatically was driven towards.

Running your own business is not all about sitting at your desk all day. Attending these type of events is part of working 'on' your business, as opposed to always working 'in' your business on the daily operations. It brings with it a wealth of opportunities and learnings. I did learn quickly that there are some jobs that I just can't do, regardless of how much I want to know how to do everything and take responsibility for everything. After having several very long conversations on the phone with Google Ads advisors, I realised that I need to outsource this. Although it was a monthly investment, it was a very wise decision. It was actually saving me money and a lot of time, because the company doing it were the experts in it and it saved me time and money. I realised I did not have to be responsible for everything, and actually, letting someone else carry out these tasks saved me time that was better spent on the business.

Wherever you are in your business journey, whether you are a start up business, or have been operating for some years now, there will be many things that come up that you need to deal with in order to move forward. This can be in the business itself, or personal mindset issues that are holding you back. As a start up, you may be working on getting off in the right direction and trying to move forward without worrying about your competitors. If your business has been operating for a year or two, you may have got to the point that you are so busy with the every day stuff that you can't move forward with more customers, or services that you want to do. Maybe you have lost your motivation for your business and fallen out of love for it. These are things that I have experienced and worked through to move my business forward.

From a business perspective, it's always important to remember why you are in business. What is it that you want to achieve and why? What are your intentions? What do you love about what you do? When you start losing your motivation, go back to these questions to get clear on what you want. List it, mind map it, pin it on a noticeboard to see everyday, but keep it visible in your mind and start being intentional about what you want.

Look at your actual business processes and operations. That's everything from the banking and invoicing side, to the products or services you provide to your customers. What will you do to make these things easier for you and simplify the processes? Check that all your processes are necessary, as streamlining some of them can help remove unnecessary actions. This will help save you time, which is something we all need. We can never get our time back.

There are so many systems out there now that I wish I had implemented to make life easier. I use these now and so can you for a quicker and easier option. You may have some services you provide that you could outsource. Although you would have to cover this cost, it can be beneficial in regards to the time it takes you to do yourself and you can spend that time focusing on more important aspects of your business that will bring you joy and a higher income. The more joy you have in your business, the more motivation you will have to move it forward in the direction you are passionate about.

By growing your business, you can enjoy the fact that you can build a team to support you. Not only does this support function help on the day to day running of your business, but it also helps you take time off without worrying about the business. This is so important, to be able to take time out (we know our businesses are always in our heads regardless) and spend time with family and friends in order to achieve a work life balance.

These actions are not the only solid investment you should make in your business. Investing in yourself, really pushes yourself and your business forward. Quite often, we put ourselves to the back of the queue when it comes to our businesses, but you are the business, so investing in yourself is pivotal to your success. This is anything from a training course, to a business coach, mindset coach or any personal coaching that helps you in any other way.

I invested in a Facebook Ads Course with Emma Van Heusen, to help my business. Part of that course included monthly mindset sessions with Andrea Callanan, where I learned that business success is 20% knowledge and skills and 80% mindset. This was quite a pivotal moment as I had never thought of it like that. These sessions are where I realised the imposter syndrome and comparisonitis elements from previous years, along with many other significant mindset elements.

At times, you may feel imposter syndrome sneaking in. Just remember why your customers are coming to you. It's because you know what they need to know. Look at your past customers or client's feedback, reviews you may have got and referrals. Look at results you have achieved for yourself and for others. This is all evidence that you know what you're talking about and you can help others. This will also help with any limiting beliefs you may have about your abilities or skills. You are the expert of you and no one can doubt that.

If you feel yourself constantly scrolling the internet and social media platforms, seeing what your competitors are doing, then remember that people buy from you because of you. You don't need to be the same as everyone else. That would be boring anyway. You offer something that your competitors don't - that is you! Just because someone offers something that you don't, doesn't mean you have to provide this also, especially if it doesn't fit with your business direction. Stick to your values and let these show in your business, that's what's important and people will work with you or buy from you because of this. You want your clients to be aligned to you, so you are both a good fit to work together.

Also, let people see you, don't hide behind a logo. Visibility is key these days and builds trust. Your audience needs to know what you do or sell, so start to build these relationships. I know that the world of social media can be daunting and also very overwhelming with posts, video, stories and reels, and then the strategy to go with it, and when and what to post. There is so much support out there for that and the best thing is to keep it simple and do what works for you. You don't have to post on every social channel or do everything at once. Take small steps to begin with until you work out what works for you, just be consistent with it. Many people choose to use the support of the social media experts so that your business can keep being visible, even when you take that well earned time off.

Let your audience hear what you have to say and let them get to know you. It can be scary putting yourself out there - I know, I have been there. We all have the same worries; I don't like how I sound, I don't like how I look, what if someone says something negative about me or about what I am saying, what if I get my words all mixed up. If you are talking about something you are passionate about, then your personality and knowledge will shine through. We are all human and people much prefer to see that, rather than a robotic video. Be yourself and don't let anyone put you off. Deep breaths, feet on the floor, sitting comfortably and off you go. You don't need to be perfect, just do it. During my times of getting over my 'going live' fear, I always loved the saying "It's not perfection, its progress" so, go and progress!

Building your online relationships is important, but so are the relationships around you. That could be your suppliers, local businesses or businesses that compliment yours that could be a good working collaboration. Building relationships and connections can be daunting, because as soon as the 'networking' word comes into play, it can fill you with fear. It doesn't have to be. What's important is that you be yourself. Whether events are online or in person, remember that everyone is there for the same reason. Sometimes, you may feel like you are going out of your comfort zone, that's a good thing and builds your confidence. The more you do it, the easier it gets. These relationships are where referrals come from, so they can be an important part in growing your customer base.

Is it time to move yourself and your business forward?

Having learned from all these experiences, it has given me a different approach as to how I run my business and feel about myself in my business. While there have been many events and situations that I have had to deal with, it has put me a stronger position now. If I hadn't been though these experiences I would not have decided to set up my own business to help others. I love to share my knowledge and experiences with others, to help them on their business journey. I get such joy out of seeing people succeed and get excited about their businesses. I resonate with the problems that other mums in business face and help them to overcome these.

For these business owners, I am helping them push their business forward so that they can not only be successful in their own right, but growing their business means creating jobs for others and bringing money into the economy. I find my values very important in how I do business because of experiences I have been through. It has shown me that what I believe in works for me and for my ideal clients.

Having learnt that investing in yourself is just as important as investing in your business, I am glad that I took the leap to invest in a business coach, Andrea Callanan, on her 12 month programme. This was not only for my business, but also for myself. This programme has also really helped me get visible, especially online. I now have a new found confidence when talking on video and even putting myself out 'live' on social media. This has really helped with confidence in networking also, which has brought new opportunities my way.

Recently, a friend told me that I was her inspiration to go for a job that she had some apprehension over. This job is a higher level and would involve part time learning to gain a degree. The fact that I had set up a new business and taken on training courses and coaching along the way, made her feel she could do it also. And she did. And got the job. I am so pleased that I can inspire others to progress in their careers.

Now it's your turn. There is no age limit on when you can start a new career or start up a business, in fact, I have seen that more women in their 40s onwards do this now. In the past, I have heard many women say that they are too old now to start over or to go back to education, but that has changed and there are so many opportunities now that women are grabbing and making a better life for themselves.

I worked with a client who was needing support and guidance in their business. They had become very busy and grown quite fast over the first couple of years. This was resulting in them having a poor work life balance, not being able to focus on the important aspects that they wanted to and they didn't feel they were in a position to take on new clients. The business is owned by two ladies, each of them with a young family, so family time was important. During my time with them, I totally resonated with their situation and the problems they were coming up against. Together, we worked on plans to simplify the business and make it easier to operate. This has allowed them to step away from some tasks to focus on business growth areas.

They wanted to be able to prioritise their client's needs and so we put a strategy in place on how they would achieve this. From a personal level, they have given themselves dedicated time off and are now putting themselves first before the business. This has helped in their personal life and own self-care. Here's what they had to say:

> "Jane spent time with us and managed to get to grips with our business and where we needed help immediately. She had such energy and understanding of what areas of our business required attention. This really spurred us on to have the confidence to implement new procedures. She has managed to help us balance work and home life, which is exactly what we needed and I would recommend an injection of even an ounce of Jane's energy into anyone's company - big or small. Jane clearly has a deep understanding of where our business is and where we would like it to be, can't recommend her highly enough."

Another client was looking for some direction for her business, to take it forward and make it more visible. We looked at options that could work for her that she felt comfortable with and could implement. It was a great session and she followed up with the following feedback:

> "I am really grateful for all Jane's advice and recommendations. I found what was missing in my own strategy and needed implementing. Jane is very approachable and I felt at ease

immediately. I appreciate her honesty, clarity and authenticity, speaking about herself and her experience as well as with regards to my situation. Jane has a genuine like and easy connection to others, which I also really appreciated."

It was a joy to work with these clients as I could see how they were getting their motivation back into the business and were ready to take action and move it forward. This is why I love what I do and you should too.

Are you ready to take action? It's never too late to make changes and start over, just follow where your passions lead you. The advice that I have given you should help you to be able to create a simpler way of doing business that gives you more freedom in your business and your life. Business does not have to be complicated, it's us that complicate it. Find clients that are a good fit for you based on your values and how you work and they will stick with you.

So, if you are stuck in your business, or need support moving your business forward with direction and clarity, then you can follow me on Facebook or Instagram at @janemackcoaching.

When I work with you, my values are at the forefront. Transformation, connection and joy is what you will get as I support you in your business growth. Together, we will work on meeting your priorities and achieving your goals by developing a strategy to get there. It's time to grow your confidence and get your motivation and joy back in your business.

ABOUT THE AUTHOR
JANE MACK

Jane Mack is a business coach who helps mums in business to move their business forward with simplicity and gain a better work life balance.

Before starting a coaching business, Jane spent seven years running a holiday let and property management business with her husband. After growing the business, they sold it to a large company and continued working for the business. Jane then decided she would move into the coaching world and help other mums in business move their business forward like she did, and overcome the challenges that she had to.

Jane enjoys running and is always looking for the next 10K run to get a faster time. She also enjoys camping with her family and has masted the art of family fun in a roof tent.

Jane is available for 1:1 consultations.

You can reach Jane at:

    Email: jane@janemackcoaching.com

    Website: www.janemackcoaching.com

    facebook.com/janemackcoaching
    instagram.com/janemackcoaching

KAREN MARIE NICHOLSON
STEPPING INTO JOY

Tuesday, 7TH of September, 2021.

The place to be happy is here. The time to be happy is now.

It's a beautiful sunny and warm September morning here in my hometown of Fleetwood in Lancashire. I am sitting in my garden with a cup of tea reflecting on my last year and a half, since I retired from being a health professional of over 36 years in March 2020. I am listening to the birds singing and I am feeling grateful.

Grateful for my journey of finding my own joy. Grateful for the opportunity to share that journey with my beautiful mum, Margaret, who has lived with me since my dad died in 1999 of lung cancer.

Grateful for the opportunity to share joy with others and to help others find their own joy on my own terms, as the CEO of my own coaching business, Jars of Joy.

I'm feeling extremely grateful for right where I am now in my life.

Today is a real milestone day because today, I will be delivering my first paid session to residents in a newly built, assisted housing development in my community, called THE LIGHTHOUSE.

The first session of six weeks of their journey to finding their Joy and I couldn't be more excited, humbled and honoured to support them on their journey.

I'm grateful for the weather, the day, and the choice and the chance and the freedom to have a business that lights me up and brings me Joy. A business that not only brings me Joy, but actually brings joy to so many other people. A business that a year ago, I never dreamed was possible for me .

I've pinched myself several times today and in recent weeks at the realisation that I am about to do something that until today, has just been a dream held in my heart; planned in my head and consistently worked for my whole life . I am exactly where I am meant to be; right here, and right now. All my experiences and all that I have done have brought me to this place

Let's go back to DECEMBER 2019.

> "You are always one decision away from a totally different life"
>
> — TINYBUDDA.COM

It's a cold, wet, and windy morning in Fleetwood. I'm parked in my car Outside of my office buildings and I realise, not for the first time, that the situation I am in is not going to change anytime soon. I've come back to work after being off sick since January 2018. Everything's changed, but nothing's changed, so, I need to make the change. I need to make the change that suits me. This is my one life. It's no practice, it's time to take the leap of Faith, listen to my heart and hand in my notice to retire.

I've been thinking about this for quite a while, since returning to work in August of this year. I knew it was an option available to me, to leave my career of 36 years and leave with a small NHS pension and what was left of my self-worth, self belief, dignity and optimism that I was doing what was right for ME; that I was putting myself first, for the first time in a very long time.

So, I dialled the number on my mobile phone of my manager and told her, in my most self-assured, professional manner, that I had decided to retire on the 1st of March 2020, and that although I'd wanted to tell her in person, the opportunity hadn't arisen, and so I I had decided to telephone her to inform her of my decision and that I would follow this up with a email to confirm my intention to retire .

At the other end of the phone, I could hear my manager barely contain her excitement at my decision to leave the organisation and then quickly compose herself to sound professional and supportive and managerial in the next steps forward .

Inwardly, I felt sick. I was shaking as I held the phone. My throat was dry and my stomach was doing cartwheels. I had forgotten to put the brake on in my car and almost crashed into the car that was parked in front of me. I was so nervous at making this big decision, but I knew in my heart that I had to do it .

When I put the phone down, I felt relief. I breathed a heavy sigh. I knew in my heart I had made the right decision. I also knew I'd taken back my power and that there was nothing that person could do about my decision.

But those little voices in my head soon got to work and started telling me to doubt my decision. I could almost hear them having a debate: what have you done? What will you do for money? What will you do for work? And then the other voice would say. "Hey, I've got enough money. I'm going to have fun. I deserve it . I am going to travel and spend time with my beautiful family in China and I am going to do something that brings me Joy. I'm going to do something that brings joy to others. I have no idea what it's going to be, but it's going to be an adventure. I just have to get through the next eight weeks and then freedom is mine."

February 19th, 2020

Retirement Day

I knew a speech would be expected and I had tried to prepare myself for a light-hearted reflection of my 36 years service which would hopefully finish with an inspirational message to everyone who remained behind in the organisation.

And then these words were spoken: I WILL JUST SAY A FEW WORDS, AS I KNOW THAT KAREN WILL HAVE PLENTY TO SAY .

I looked around the room, some looking on in disbelief but no one really challenging what was said. So, I took a deep breath and paused… After what seemed like an age, but was probably only 30 seconds, I responded with a much shorter version of my planned speech, still, of course, expressing gratitude to those who had taken the time to come to my retirement lunch, thanking those who contributed to the beautiful flowers and gifts which I had received, and finishing off with an inspirational message about life being a rollercoaster; you just gotta ride it .

I felt I responded with calm, with dignity, and with my self-respect still intact. I had shown great self-discipline and strength, and that victory was almost mine.

But Inside I was dying -dying to shout out "You b****. You couldn't even let me have my last day. You've ruined my 36 year career…" but I was too professional. She had tried for a good few years to push my buttons and cause me to react, and today was no different .

Her behaviour said so much more about her than it did about me .

February 20th, 2020

Afternoon tea to celebrate my retirement with my friends and family. I made the speech I had intended to make and looked forward to the next chapter in my adventure of life with anticipation.

Plans to visit my family in China were looking less likely, due to a virus that had originated there. Although I was disappointed not to travel, their safety was of paramount importance to me. I was carrying the worry and fear of losing those precious to me, as only a mother does.

March 3rd, 2020

Coronavirus is officially declared a Pandemic.

March 23rd, 2020

Lockdown UK: THE PAUSE

In these initial weeks of the lockdown, the weather was beautiful and we spent so much time out in the garden, me and mum:

Reconnecting with nature, being grateful for the simplicity of life and organising the street clap along every week for our NHS, bringing my community together. I felt useful and that I was helping others;. going live on social media, encouraging people with positive messages and my mum's beautiful singing .

Outwardly, my life looked good: afternoon teas delivered, positive social postings...

Inwardly, it was all starting to take its toll on me. I was worried sick about my son, his wife and my beautiful granddaughters, and I could feel I was slipping down a rabbit hole.

I realised that something needed to change inside of me as I had absolutely no control over the events that were happening around me, but I had no idea where I would find the person who could support me and hold space for me, like I supported others.

All my years as a health professional had enabled me to be just that, to be professional and to always look like life was ok, even when it wasn't. I was the go-to person for everyone else.

And then, just as I was starting to give up hope, and not for the first time in my life, a few amazing things happened. The universe sent me a beautiful earth angel, disguised as a coach Andrea Callanan, on a free 5-day masterclass called "Rise Up and Be Seen in Business".

I had no idea what a coach did or how this would help me, as I didn't actually have a business. I was compelled to stay onboard for the full five days, along with some other beautiful women who are also writing chapters in this book

I woke up from a deep sleep like the princess that had slept for a thousand years. I started to remember the time when I had been a high achieving woman. Not only was I high achieving academically and professionally, I was spinning many plates as a wife, a mother, a friend, a daughter, a carer, a confidant. I had all those resources and experiences in me and I'd completely forgotten about them, because I had switched to survival mode without even realising it.

The last few years, even before the pandemic, had taken their toll. I had been off sick from my job as a health visitor from January 2018 to August 2019. I had experienced several symptoms of bodily weakness, tiredness, days where I could barely get out of bed, memory loss, aching bones, back pain, neck pain... I had undergone many blood tests, been given medications that induced panic attacks, gone to exercise classes that made me feel worse - I had been told if I exercised more, it wouldn't be such an effort. Finally, I was diagnosed with fibromyalgia, and more or less told that this was now my life and I could have some counselling if I needed it, which had a six-month wait, at least.

The day after this diagnosis, I saw a different consultant, an endocrinologist who didn't say I didn't have fibromyalgia, but he said he thought I might also have hyperparathyroidism and that he would investigate further. I was hoping that this would be the case, as I could recover from this diagnosis even though it would probably mean having throat surgery.

Through this process of investigations. I attended many appointments, some alone and some accompanied. There was plenty of time to reflect and be grateful for my life at the six-hour appointment in the cancer unit, sitting with people I knew would not see Christmas.

I saw the surgeon in December 2018, and surgery was scheduled for April 2019. The surgeon told me that he was really experienced in this field and that I could expect a full recovery. As I was a good candidate for surgery and he hasn't lost one yet, we joked if he meant a patient or a parathyroid tumour. He told me both.

So my husband and I visited our family in China, packing in as many happy times as we could as I knew I wouldn't be allowed to travel after the surgery for a while.

The day before the planned surgery, the endocrinologist contacted me and said he thought I might have pituitary cancer, so the surgery couldn't go ahead and I would need further tests

I had three weeks of not knowing, more blood tests, and keeping it to myself, then being relieved that I didn't have the pituitary cancer but still knowing I would need the throat surgery. I went on to have this throat surgery on the 21st May, 2019 and had a tumour removed the size of a grape. It was lodged between my trachea and my oesophagus.

When I finally returned to work, I was grateful for the support of a psychologist who encouraged me to practice the simplest of grounding techniques to manage my state when faced with situations that caused me to be upset. There were many of those in the months that followed. I was grateful for these and grateful for her at the time and so many times since .

The second thing that happened, about the same time, was this: I went into my garage looking for something and I saw two jars. They were from my son's wedding in 2014, and they made me smile for the first time in a few weeks. I thought, if a jar with a beautiful memory could make me smile, what would a jar, beautifully decorated and filled with beautiful memories do to help me to STEP into joy when I needed it the most? It's fair to say, I had never needed to step into joy more. I had never needed to find my own joy more than this.

Like so many others, I had always relied on external influences in my life to top up my joy in my life. I had Joy in abundance from my grandchildren, and family, and extended family and friendships .

I was really missing my grandchildren. I hadn't seen them since October 2019 and there was little hope of seeing them anytime soon .

I knew that finding these jars was significant, in terms of my own health and well-being. I just didn't know how significant they were to become, not only to me and my mum, but to many other people in my community on social media... And the foundation upon which I have built my business .

I began my journey with the support of an amazing coach, Andrea Callanan, who saw in me what I could no longer see in myself. I signed up for voice mastery, with the intention of finding my voice and delivering a TED talk to share my story with others. The thought of a business scared me. Previous experiences in business had not been good for me, as I hadn't really been committed to them. I now realise, as I was already in full-time employment, with a demanding job, I treated the business more like a hobby - a hobby that I loved and that brought joy to my life but financially, I kept the job for the security it gave me.

During voice mastery, I had a discovery call with Andrea's husband, Matt, about his podcasting course, which I thought would help me get my message to others.

By the end of the call, I was definitely doing his podcasting course but more than that, I had a mission. I had a mission to have a million jars of joy around the world. This was bigger than me and now I had something to work with - a purpose and my 'why'.

All I needed to do now was find my self-belief, my self-worth, my voice, my courage, my joy.

So, I did what every person scared of speaking in public does. I started a Facebook group and, with my mum as my support and partner in crime, we went live most days during the lockdowns from my summerhouse - a place filled with happy memories of my family, last time they visited the UK, in 2018. We posted consistently every day on social media. We connected a community from all over the world on various platforms and grew an online community of joy. We also made significant connections and friendships with people who shared our mission and our values. We found champions and cheerleaders from every corner of the globe, many in our own hometown.

We spoke about our joys, our small daily wins and what we were grateful for. My daily routine started with gratitude and stepping into joy. This was by saying three things I was grateful for the moment I opened my eyes, and immediately followed by looking at photographs of my beautiful grandchildren, ZiXuan and ZiLuo. They made me smile, and if I did it for long enough, my brain didn't know the difference and released the chemicals anyway.

The two jars from my garage had now been beautifully decorated by a friend of mine, Sheila, and they contained items that held happy memories for me.

I knew if I needed to step into joy at other points in the day, I could take out an item, hold it in my hand and be transported back to the time, the place, the memory, the joy. A process known in NLP as anchoring.

There were difficult days as I began to go deeper into the reasons for some of my limiting beliefs.

They were made more difficult by the passing of a wonderful woman I was blessed to call my friend, Greta Barker. A beautiful woman who was kind, loving and generous with everything she had. She would share all her vast amounts of knowledge, skills, and expertise about health and therapies with anyone who asked and who needed her. Rarely did money change hands and certainly not for the value of her worth. Greta traded in all my values: integrity ,honesty, kindness, compassion and generosity. She gave of herself. She was one of my greatest cheerleaders as she always saw I was worth more and could achieve anything I put my mind to. I was grateful to be included in the 30 people allowed to celebrate her beautiful life with her family, who she loved with all her heart.

At the wake, my mum and I were speaking about what we had been doing in lockdown. We mentioned we had joined a virtual choir, what joy we had found in such difficult times, and that we were learning a song my mum had not really known before called **"Times Like These"**. Unknown to us, it was actually a song they all sang with Greta and we all sang it together. The words really rang true: "**It's times like these you learn to live again. It's times like these you give and give again.**"

I was learning to live again and losing my good friend made me start to value my worth seeing how loved and respected this woman of integrity was by all whose lives she had touched.

I revisited the hundreds of beautiful comments I had received when I retired from my career as a Health Visitor and I realised what a difference I had already made in so many people's lives, and what a difference jars of joy could make in the world.

Whilst writing this chapter, I have recalled the words of another amazing coach I was blessed to meet in voice mastery - Jermaine Harris, who told me "Karen, you definitely have a business; you just don't know it yet. And when people see this amazing woman with integrity, who does amazing things in her community, who gives of herself and gives to others with kindness and compassion, and when you are ready to take on that business role, there is definitely a business there." Having a coach helping me find clarity of what my business could look like, even though I wasn't ready to move that far forward at that time, was pivotal in keeping on my own path, following my dreams and seeing possibilities.

I decided to retain my nursing registrations and revalidated with the NMC. To do this, I needed some testimonials and a mum I had visited wrote this about me.

> "The support I received from Karen was wonderful and came at the right time, from a fabulous woman who knew how to be professional and empathetic all the way through my support. My anxiety had gotten out of control and some days were really awful and Karen spotted this straight away. Karen knew exactly what to advise and over time, helped me to work on my confidence and become me again. Such a positive lady with an amazing outlook on life. I will be forever grateful."

So, sparkly Margaret and I continued on our mission to spread joy and share joy with as many people as we could via social media, on Facebook, Twitter and Instagram, and we have now built a following and social reach of over 3000.

We were asked to facilitate a workshop at KindFest, USA, about joy and kindness in the workplace.

At Christmas, we had 200 fridge magnets made. It was mum's idea to represent a jar of joy, and we sent them out to our friends and family and to people we hadn't even met, but connected with, to spread more joy at a time when people really needed it.

January 2021

We were invited to be interviewed on BBC Radio Lancashire to talk about spreading joy and our mission to have a million jars of joy around the world.

So, on a cold, dark January morning in 2021, we were interviewed on the breakfast show, in my lounge, in our pyjamas. My mum sang beautifully and our mission to spread joy was welcomed by the listeners and the presenter. We must have made a great impression because we were on the show for almost twenty minutes and asked if we could be filmed the next day for the BBC programme, "Make a difference". We even appeared for 30 seconds on a local TV station that same day. Word was starting to spread about us and our jars of joy.

We were invited back to the radio a month later to share even more joy with the listeners, and our community of joy grew even more. We received messages from people saying how much we had helped with their mental health and wellbeing .

What the listeners didn't know was that on that afternoon, on that cold, January day, I accompanied my mum to have a cancerous growth removed from the side of her face.

She bravely and courageously sang to the surgeon throughout the process, as only my sparkly mum can. My mum even asked the surgeon, when preparing the area she was going to operate on, if she could trim her eyebrows as the pandemic had meant they had become a little overgrown. Of course, this made a difficult situation more bearable for all of us.

The next day, the filming took place. Mum had a huge plaster on the side of her face but again, with great bravery, she got on with it, knowing it would help our mission to spread joy.

We waited for the results and continued getting up and showing up on a daily basis, going live and posting a video with an inspirational message every day on social media.

These daily messages and tweets of joy were greatly received by our community of joy, at a time when everyone was going through the biggest storm many of us had ever witnessed. The biggest pause in most of our lives and certainly in mine. We weren't prepared for this and so many people experienced the pandemic in many different ways.

A month later, we received the news we had been waiting for; that it had been squamous cell carcinoma but they had been successful in its removal. Joy. Gratitude. Relief. A wealth of emotions on our rollercoaster journey of life.

We celebrated with a cup of tea and a piece of cake.

Giving to others has really helped with my own mental health, and although I still have not seen my family who I was missing so very much, finding my purpose and helping others to have a brightness in their day, if only for a minute or two, enabled me to attract more joy in my life.

I made the decision to become an accredited coach with Andrea Callanan, and study as an NLP Practitioner, so that I could help others find their way, find their path, find their mission, find their joy.

The next months involved even more self-reflection, studying, commitment, learning, healing and self-discovery for me. Meanwhile, Jars of Joy's public profile went from strength to strength, and our virtual community of joy continued to grow .

Sparkly Margaret and myself were humbled to be recognised as inspirational women in our heritage museum, as part of an exhibition called This Lass Can, in the company of the first ever women's boxing world champion, Jane Couch, MBE, and an inspirational successful business woman, Doreen Lofthouse, OBE, the founder of Fishermans Friend, as well as some other Fleetwood women doing extraordinary things .

Next, we were invited to share our story of lockdown and share our experience of the pandemic, both positive and negative, and our hopes and intentions for the future for our town, to be part of a soundscape to accompany an art installation in our town, which was a tribute to the lives lost in the pandemic.

What happened next was truly unexpected. Sparkly and I were invited to open the art installation on one of the days. We were the only women invited to do this. People came to see us open this installation who had never even met us, but had followed us on social media and wanted to meet the women who had brought them so much joy during this pandemic. One of these was a Lead Nurse who came down to see the installation. He commented on Twitter later that day, what an amazing Sunday morning he'd had in the sun. The massive highlight was having a fabulous conversation with the amazing women from Jars of Joy. Real human connection was made, and I started to see the possibility of this becoming a business where I could not only serve others and make a difference, but also, there was a real opportunity to receive an income from doing something that absolutely lit me up and brought me joy.

Hearing our story out loud had a massive impact on me, and it was an emotional weekend where I again realised that it was a story that needed to be voiced so that those who needed my help could find me.

It was time to reconnect with a champion who had supported our journey from the start and work on one of the limiting beliefs that had held me back from being a business. This coach, Matt Callanan, helped me to work on having the confidence to pitch to an organisation who had been a supporter of our mission since January 2021, and to ask for the financial remuneration the work deserved in terms of the value and the expertise our Jars of Joy would bring to his organisation, his residents, and employees.

The pitch was successful in every way. My self-belief, my self-worth all restored to that of a woman with choices. All on my own terms and not a bit like working.

This coach had helped me work on so much more, including a limiting belief in terms of technology I had held since I was 11 years old.

In studying to be an NLP practitioner, I had also learnt some techniques for myself to manage this too and I am grateful to my fellow adventurers on that journey for their compassion, kindness, love and support shown to me.

When this book is published, I will be an accredited coach. I have been truly blessed and grateful to be coached and to have coached some amazing women who are also featured in other chapters of this book.

Some have helped me more than they will ever know. I consider it to have been my absolute honour and privilege to have seen and been part, in some small way, of their breakthroughs and transformations. I have moved forward in my life, my business and new adventures and new chapters await me. I couldn't be more proud to have shared this incredible journey with my beautiful mum, Margaret Mary Elizabeth Curphey. If I am half the woman she is, I will be so proud. She really is the wind beneath my wings. A true woman of substance, grit, and determination with the kindest, most generous heart of anyone I have been blessed to know.

So today, I have a business that a year ago I never dreamed was possible for me. But as I learnt, through my own transformational journey of many twists and turns, intertwined with my journey to become an accredited coach with Andrea Callanan, with NLP coaching and MBIT coaching modalities, with Sarah Fletcher, if it's possible in the world, it is possible for me. And if it's possible for me, it's possible for you.

If you are looking to be possible, to find joy in life, in parenting, in your organisation, or joy in a business that lights you up so you never have to work again, I would love to hear from you.

Finishing with the words of a true female icon, the amazing Audrey Hepburn, the word impossible itself contains the words **I'm possible.**

ABOUT THE AUTHOR

Ruth@brooks-carterphotography.com

Karen is a graduate coach of the fully accredited Aligned Coaching Academy ACA MInstLM, and a certified Story Work Coach with Andrea Callanan ACSWC

Karen is a mindset coach having recently been accredited with Andrea Callanan and her Aligned Coaching Academy.

Karen Empowers individuals and groups to find Joy in their life and to discover their authentic, Heart-led,

Compassionate, Courageous and Creative self in life, at work, as parents and in business. Before embarking on this new coaching path as the "liberator of the human spirit to create a wiser world ", Karen was a Health professional for over 36 years. During that time she worked as a RGN an RMN a Public Health Nurse and latterly as a Health Visitor with a special interest in Perinatal and Maternal Mental Health. In this role Karen held space for and empowered thousands of parents to make choices in respect of their own and their children's Health outcomes.

Karen is a wife to Paul a mum to Daniel a mother in law to Sophie and a proud Nanna to two beautiful granddaughters ZiXuan age 7 and Zi Luo age 5. She has a fur baby Jasper a border collie who is 4 who loves meeting people and eating cheese.

Karen is a daughter to Stanley (1931-1999) and Sparkly Margaret the co founder of jars of joy without whom she would not be here today . Thanks Mum and Dad x

Karen is available for speaking events ,corporate events .workshops ,121 and Group Coaching.

With Jars of Joy Karen has spoken at Kindfest USA, appeared on BBC 's Make a difference and was recently nominated for a Pride Of Britain Award.

Please consider this as your invitation to join our conscious community of Joy .

Facebook
https://www.facebook.com/groups/278367259900353/

Website www.jarsofjoy.co

Contact us by Email Karennicholson@me.com

twitter.com/jarsofjoy
instagram.com/jarsofjoywithkarennicholson

13

KATHARINE GILLAM

Most days, I feel pretty fortunate. I'm living my life in a way that makes me happy and gives me purpose. I am raising a family of four children, who are becoming independent people themselves, who have the support of a close-knit and loving family. They are my WHY. The reason I do what I do today and live the life I do.

I don't commute to a busy office or work full-time, like I did in my twenties and thirties, which has given me the time and space to become the best parent and partner that I can be, as well as do what I love and retain my sense of identity. I'm well aware that the hands-on parenting years will come to an end pretty quickly and many of my friends are experiencing the empty nest feeling that comes with that passing of time. I now have a new career that evolves constantly, a positive mindset from my work with an amazing business coach, and time for myself as a person.

I choose to work for myself because, like many parents, I had taken a few years of leave and enjoyed being able to focus on family, but as they grew and needed me less, I wanted to regain my sense of self. I wanted to be able to earn my own income (however small in the beginning), to feel that I was myself again. I'm sure some of you will recognise that moment when you become a full-time parent and realise that you are reliant on your partner.

The turning point came as I worked through self-mastery coaching with the leading voice and business coach, Andrea Callanan, to become confident about who I am as a person and less fearful of taking risks and being visible. I'm no longer ashamed of saying I am successful! I think everyone can do this - I love discussing career changes and start up ideas with friends and colleagues and trying to inspire other people just like me.

In the mid 1990s, after leaving Oxford University where I studied English, I worked in PR for various high-powered, dynamic PR agencies, living crazy days that were mostly lots of fun - sometimes stressful but definitely fulfilling. I never really gave a thought to what would happen later... would I have a family and give up work or would I juggle work and parenthood? Nothing was planned out. I had fun in my job which was very creative and largely within the beauty and fashion industry. I travelled round the world, worked really hard, partied hard – press trips and events were often the highlight of my week. I didn't really have that many responsibilities besides paying bills. I worked abroad for a couple of years, got married young and defined myself by my supposedly trendy high-flying career in PR. I don't regret any of my choices - I would say to my younger self, enjoy that time without wider responsibilities.

One day, after my third child was born in 2008, I went on a weekend away with my husband. We were walking through the Peak District – the year's maternity leave was nearly over. I had three children under 5 at this point. I loved nurturing them and being at home all day. Office life literally felt a million miles away at this point. My lightbulb moment came right then - I would leave the hectic job - take more time off... and then... honestly, I didn't know. When you are in that moment of life with tiny children, there is no time to consider the future and everything is in the present.

My final job at Ketchum (a global PR agency), working on top beauty brands was enjoyable, varied and inspiring, but it was also busy and youthful and there wasn't much space for women who needed to get home for a nursery pick up or a school meeting, or care for a sick baby. I was lucky to be part-time as the company was very progressive, but it didn't really work as I still felt that I no longer belonged in this world. Like a lot of women at a similar stage, it was simply time to step off the career treadmill and spend time at home to embrace my children. I knew after my third child I wouldn't go back to work, but I couldn't really envisage what that meant. My fourth child came along soon after and at that point I remember thinking 'I will probably never work again'.

It started for me when I read an article about Digital Mums - the organisation that made it their mission to get women back into the workplace, particularly those with marketing and communications backgrounds. Digital Mums still exists, although it has evolved as a company to offer digital training for all types of women, not just mums, and it now has a huge range of courses. At that time - early 2015 - they were getting lots of amazing publicity as women who had worked in marketing, journalism or even unrelated industries decided that social media could be their new career - it was flexible, could work around family life and every business needed it, right? I remember reading it on the sofa one Sunday and thinking that could be me… it seemed like a big investment at the time but I signed up the following month. The nine months of the course were a whirlwind of learning online and meeting new people. I also worked with a lovely company who made children's shampoos, which gave me the chance to revisit my previous skill-set. Interestingly, social media turned out not to be for everyone in my peer group, but it started or triggered something for me. Importantly, I was using my brain in a different way. Mums, in general, have great skills as they learn to multi-task and think on their feet, so why not use these same skills in your own business? That complex negotiation with a teenager over screentime or the detailed spreadsheet of what to bring to school and when can only come in handy in later life. Think about all those times you had to do multiple things while looking after a toddler and a baby... that's why returnees (as they are sometimes called) can be the most productive and valued workers of all.

I learned a lot about my own skills and how to apply them by taking a course in Self-Mastery in early 2020. These were skills from both my earlier career in PR and those that I had developed over time in my personal life – especially through parenting – but also within other relationships, including with my partner and my family.

So, Self-Mastery. What does that mean? And why would you take a course in it?

The dictionary definition is 'the ability to take control of one's life without being blown off course by feelings, urges, circumstances'

I would never ever have read a self-help book prior to 2019 - I doubt I had even opened one. I used to be skeptical of those slightly ridiculous titles - The 5 Am Club, Live Well Every Day, or even THE original - Chicken Soup for The Soul.

The learning here is that doing something out of your comfort zone can change your life and debunk previous prejudices (mine were certainly anti self-help or life coaches). In February 2020 (just before Covid and the lockdowns), I signed up to a coaching course that definitely changed my life and enhanced my relationships. It began over a glass of wine at a Christmas dinner in London with other social media colleagues (most of whom I had never met IRL), where several women, who had also changed careers recently, sung the praises of a particular coaching course based around mindset to improve your business and your relationships. They told me that it had encouraged them to unpick their lives in minute detail and understand how their past experiences had affected who they are today. One of them had now concluded that the business she was now involved with was not actually right for her after writing her life story. It sounded like a combination of intense personal therapy and a way of kickstarting your life and business for the better.

Once again, this felt like a spur of the moment decision but instinctively, it felt right. I wanted to somehow get back to that person who had a firm identity through what I did and change how I interacted with family, friends and colleagues. To say: I DO this.

By this point, I had tentatively started this new career in social media and marketing but I felt a bit lost - I hadn't quite found the tipping point. I know now that I had a case of what is called imposter syndrome (doubting your abilities and feeling like a fraud) - something that affects high-achieving people who find it difficult to accept accomplishments. It's much more common than you might think. So, even though I had been in brand building and communications for nearly 20 years, I still felt like this. I was working solidly for small businesses, advising on strategy and social media, managing social media accounts and then moving into Facebook Ads management.

I often didn't ask for or expect the salary I deserved. I hated asking for money and I did a lot of work for free - I was definitely playing small! I hated thinking and talking about money, which I related back to growing up and my family always having financial issues. I wanted my own identity but I didn't have it. I was doing something but it wasn't clear what my WHY was and I had not fulfilled my potential.

As children grow up, a sense of self often returns - slowly at first, then more quickly - and if you are a high achiever, as I had learned I was through my coaching course, then you start thinking:

Could I? Would I? What would happen if?

I was consciously reading or hearing about women who do go back to work, or return to previous careers, become mumpreneurs, or simply reinvent themselves. I became interested in the concept of second or third careers - challenging assumptions about a traditional career path for women.

Now I say to other women I meet in the same situation, if you are working, you can change careers, maybe write the book you always wanted to or, if you aren't working, there are still plenty of options to reinvent yourself. The world has changed during the pandemic too - maybe for the better. Remote working is acceptable, even welcomed, digital upskilling is everywhere, flexibility is there for the taking.

When I had my family and gave up 'corporate' life or the traditional career, I simply didn't suspect there was an alternative way. Then, when I decided to explore a return to the workplace, it was not as simple as going straight back to that person in my twenties and thirties. As a woman who has become a mother, you change so much in that time. Having children and responsibilities definitely gives you a different outlook on life. As you come into what is termed mid-life, it actually becomes even more important to explore what you want from life in a deeper way.

Most people I knew simply stopped working (if they were able to financially, or conversely, because it was too costly to keep working) and immersed themselves in the day-to-day life of parenthood. Often, those people we knew who continued the 'juggle' became stressed, unhappy, unable to cope and this I think means that a lot of women don't consider going back to work.

So, going back to my self-mastery course with Andrea. I started to explore my past, my childhood, my academic career, my family - what made me tick, if you like. It was really rewarding and at times, slightly traumatic. It's something everybody can benefit from at this stage of life. In my groups, we each wrote a story of our past with pivotal moments - these could be things like how your parents treated you, traumatic events from your past, financial insecurity, marriage or relationships. It became of great interest to me how a single event in your past, or a series of small events, added up to how you were as a person ten or twenty years later. The course and the coaching expanded my thinking and made me consider why I did certain things, what made me happy, sparked joy, and what made me unhappy or stressed. From there, I moved to a business accelerator with Andrea where we used the learnings of self-mastery to build our business and explore how to achieve the best result for us. The women I worked with learned more about the kind of career or lifestyle they wanted for themselves. We learned about how what happens in your personal life can drive you in your business and explored what was holding us back from 'rising'.

The course taught me that my loss of identity as a parent was a key motivator for me. In what I thought of as my 'past life', I had studied English at Oxford, I had always held down a fulfilling job – which was usually well paid (except for my first job as a PR assistant which paid £11,000 a year!).

I had my own bank account, separate from my husband who had his own independent wealth from his successful career and family. I could treat myself to new clothes if I wanted to or go away with a friend for the weekend using my own income.

Children filled that identity for years - I became THE mum, the carer, the organiser, the one who the family depended on. The happiest moments of my life to date have been a house filled with the mess and clamour of family life, cuddles, family holidays and all the rest that goes with the early years of parenting.

Self-mastery and business coaching in the Unapologetic Success Accelerator taught me that I lacked the confidence to move on from that and rediscover my own identity. I realised that earning enough money to fill my bank account and be able to have a certain financial independence made me feel positive and fulfilled again.

Running my own Facebook ads and small digital marketing business hasn't been easy and definitely has ups and downs - the world of digital marketing changes every 30 seconds (or at least that's what it feels like!). Results from digital marketing and Facebook ads in particular have become less reliable as the world has gone online and more and more brands use this as their preferred form of selling or lead generation. Recently, Apple has introduced ways for people to opt out of tracking and therefore, ads are less consistent. However, it is still a booming dynamic industry that most businesses need to opt into.

Some clients have been harder to work with than others, as is the same in any client facing industry, but my self-esteem and confidence in my ability has grown over the last two years - I have usually achieved amazing results for clients, I have worked with some super interesting people - often female entrepreneurs themselves - and helped those people build their brands. Andrea and her course taught me that you might make mistakes along the way but these are learnings, not setbacks, and you need to accept this.

Another thing I have learned is to be intentional about what I want from my life, career, family relationships and the next stage of life. I decided I wanted more flexibility so that I can take Fridays off if I want to, or I can work on a Sunday and take a day off during the week. This past summer, I was able to spend most of the school holidays working remotely in the USA - a huge bonus.

I wanted financial freedom and also to make time for self-care fitness, which is one of my other passions (I actually considered going into the fitness industry at one point and I may still get involved in a start-up business, but that's another story!). Luckily, I get to work with my dream client every day - Barry's - one of the most popular workouts in the world.

The next big thing for me has been visibility - remind people that you are there and you can help them in your business. Social media, which I always shied away from, became part of my own marketing. I was able to afford to pay someone to help create this for me, which was a huge learning experience in itself. I have used my network to grow my business and this has been an example to others. Connecting with people from my previous career, or encounters with people in social situations, has helped me build a successful business today.

I know that a lot of women are scared to stand up and say this is what I do, or this is what I can help you with. There are so many inspiring people out there on social media, talking on podcasts and writing blogs, all in a similar position to women like me or you. I have loved seeing contemporaries of mine who have had huge careers in journalism or tech stand up and encourage other women to 'speak up', 'make changes', and 'don't accept your position'.

I made the choice to get out of my own way, but it was a series of decisions that led from one another. It started with taking the Digital Mums course in 2016, which gave me confidence that you can learn new things at any stage in life. The women who I did the course with - my peer group - Jane, Alexa, Aline, Helen (we were called the Kate Mosses!) - have all gone on to do new things, not necessarily in social media or marketing. Some of them built upon previous careers - one has become an art teacher; another one works in a non-profit. I believe that it was taking ownership of our lives by doing something that was, in effect, a return to work, that was the pivot that made all of us start new things.

Like them, I hope that I am a role model to other women who can see that they too can develop their own financial freedoms and become more visible. I am still a parent and always will be, but I am a better mother as I am fulfilled in my own career and I understand more about how to behave in conflict and stressful situations. I am in control of my emotions (remember the definition of self-mastery?).

I have a small business that I hope will grow and flourish - I am intentional about my plans and my future. Every few months, I plan out the next stage of the business and my life. Personally, as my children grow older and look towards leaving home, each stage provides different opportunities for growth.

In the last few months and years, I've encouraged people to build their business and not get stuck on one path, whether that be outsourcing admin, hiring someone to work with or for you or expanding what you offer. I have inspired other women to make sure they are digitally competent via upskilling, and to be role models for their own families and also their friends.

Along my journey, self-care has become really important to me as without it, you cannot be your best self. I have always loved health and fitness. I exercise or take time to move every day that I can and I spend time thinking about looking after myself (this was not the way in my early career for sure). I'm lucky that my niche is predominantly in this very industry - health, wellness and fitness.

I honestly believe that anyone who believes in themselves can do what I have done. You might have a job already. You might be doing something that you don't enjoy and thinking "do I want to do this for the rest of my life?". I am approaching 50 – intentionally, I think I should try and spark joy in my daily life as well as making plans for amazing things in the future, whether that be travel or a new hobby. The past 18 months have made all of us appreciate the things that make us happy, whether it is being able to go in person to a swimming pool, fly across the world, or hug a friend.

I enjoy my business because it combines so many things - creativity, strategy, brand building, and writing. I have found my niche and, on the journey, I have discovered the way in which I work best and what I like doing. I also know that this might change - life evolves and so should you.

An interesting exercise that we covered early on in my coaching journey was to create a vision board - documenting what you saw yourself doing in a year's time. This could be a Pinterest board, a video or an old-fashioned mood board with magazine cut outs (my preference). I would recommend that anyone in any industry does this as it gives you that feeling of excitement of what is possible. It could be a trip to somewhere you have never imagined going, a new car, or simply an experience.

So, go back to your old career or your earlier life and think about what it was that you liked about it. Write down what you would like your life to look like in 5 years and 10 years. Create the vision board!

Many women in their thirties and forties might be thinking ahead to children leaving home. Consider what is important to you - one of the lessons I have learned is that what works for other people (starting a company with multiple employees for example) doesn't work for you. It might be you prefer to work as a team or alone – part-time or full-time - depending on the financial contribution you need to make.

Above all, remember life is for living. Celebrate successes whether small or large - don't wait any longer to make the changes that might transform your life for the better.

ABOUT THE AUTHOR
KATHARINE GILLAM

Katharine Gillam is a Digital Marketing Consultant, with a particular expertise in Facebook ads, who helps ecommerce businesses reach new clients and scale their business using paid social media, chatbots and email marketing.

Before running her own digital marketing business, Katharine worked in PR for 15 years, working on global beauty, lifestyle and fashion brands.

After a successful career in Public Relations, she decided to move into digital marketing, which gave her more flexibility and provided a new career challenge.

Katharine is based in London but loves to travel around the world with her family (when the current global pandemic allows!). She is passionate about fitness and wellness, as well as maintaining a keen interest in all the latest health and beauty trends and products.

Katharine currently has a small team who work with a variety of ecommerce businesses, focusing predominantly on lifestyle and beauty. She also offers private coaching and packages to help clients run their own paid social media.

You can reach Katharine at:

Email: katharine.gillam@gmail.com
Website: www.katharinegillamsocial.co.uk

instagram.com/katharinegillamsocial
linkedin.com/in/katharinegillamsocial

14

KERRY JONES
TRAPPED BY SUCCESS

Have you ever felt that you should just be grateful for your 'lot' in life? But although your life looks successful from the outside, you know that you're not in the right place and you should be doing something else? If only you could work out what that was!

I finally found the courage to walk away from corporate and entrepreneurial 'success' because I wasn't happy. I then navigated a period of huge change until I allowed myself to step into my true calling as a Coach. And I'm here to share my story and encourage you. If you are stuck like I was, there is a way to find and take your next step forward!

Success is such a subjective concept, isn't it? I didn't really know who I wanted to be as I grew up. The middle daughter of working-class parents, I learnt that money was essential to happiness. My parents were incredibly hard-working but money was desperately tight, and often non-existent. Seeing how hard life was without money created a strong self-drive in me to be financially secure. That was about as specific as I got! But I was absolutely determined to make something of my life.

Determination and hard work got me a long way. For 16 years, I worked my way up the corporate ladder. I was earning a 6-figure income by my early 30s. But I was deeply unhappy and unfulfilled at work. I eventually left the corporate world behind when I was 37. After a few wilderness years, I set up and grew my own successful marketing business, but still could not escape the feeling that I wasn't aligned. So much of my identity was caught up in being a 'financial success', but I still hadn't found something that lighted me up. It was only when, with the help of an amazing coach, I started to analyse and unpick the past, that it all started to make sense. I was stopping myself from following my heart to be a Coach because I simply didn't believe I'd be a successful Coach! I didn't want to try in case I failed.

I could not have been more wrong!

If we fast forward to today, my life is so very different to only a few years ago! I work from my lovely home in Brighton. I walk the kids to school every day. I then spend my time coaching amazing women as a Business & Mindset Coach. These women are very similar to how I used to be. They recognise they are desperate to make a professional change. I use my experience and skills to help them discover the clarity and confidence they need to do it!

When I look back on my corporate career, a bit of me is still surprised at how successful it was. My family wasn't academic, so no one expected me to do well. But with the unfailing encouragement of some fantastic teachers in secondary school and college, I headed off to university. Here, a whole new world of opportunities opened up for me. I started to see that I could actually create the kind of life that I wanted. It was a **choice**.

After leaving University, I worked my way up the corporate ladder, holding senior marketing communications roles for some of the biggest brands in the world. In my last corporate role, which I held for nearly seven years, I headed up the Internal Communications department for Barclays Wealth Management. I had a team of highly professional managers and was responsible for the day-to-day communication needs of the CEO and over 100 Managing Directors. Although based in Canary Wharf, London, my role was global, liaising with those in Asia and America and regularly flying over to the New York office.

I was good at my job. I was respected. My opinion and expertise were called upon daily and my head was full of confidential projects, mergers, restructures, and other strategic initiatives. I worked long days, commuted two hours each way from Brighton, spending most of the journey working on my Blackberry to keep on top of the incessant emails, all demanding my urgent attention. I was also busy trying to manage my team, mentor up-and-coming talent, and enjoy being newly married!

From the outside looking in, my professional life was a success. The problem was that my job left me feeling pretty empty inside. I knew that I was excellent at my role but I also knew, without a doubt, that I didn't want to be doing it. It wasn't me. It didn't set my heart on fire. It felt pointless. Yes, I was earning good money, but you know what they say about money not being able to buy happiness.

So, you may ask, how come I didn't leave? There were a few reasons – maybe you can identify some in yourself too:

1. Imposter Syndrome – although I wouldn't have called it that! I, like so many other high-achieving women, listened to the critical inner voice that told me I was a fraud. I did not deserve my success. I would get caught out one day.
2. Fear – I had been at Barclays for over 10 years and I was afraid to leave. What if I could not get another job? What if a new employer didn't think that I was good enough or, even worse, what if I got a new job and then discovered that I couldn't do it?
3. Self-Doubt – I found it incredibly hard to believe in my

ability to start again. Was I worth what I was being paid and would someone else pay the same or more? I told myself that I should be grateful for everything I had (I truly was!): I was so blessed to have some financial freedom. I had 'made it'. Who was I to think that I could repeat success in something different?

4. Lack of Vision – I knew what I didn't want to be doing, but I had absolutely no idea what I did want my life to look like! Although I had strong personal values, so much of my identity had, unsurprisingly, become caught up in my job. I had been so busy that I never **really** worked out what set my heart alight. What was I passionate about? What did I actually want to spend my days doing, if I could do anything? I had absolutely no idea.

And so, for years, I put one foot in front of the other, carried on and did nothing.

When I finally left the corporate world to have kids, I seized this as my opportunity to make the change I so desperately needed. But, like so many mums in a similar situation, my whole identity was challenged. If I was not a corporate woman, then who was I? I didn't want to be defined by my job. I revelled in being a present mum and felt so blessed seeing my kids change and grow. I knew for certain that my commuting days were over, but professionally, I was very confused.

Because I had never really addressed my imposter syndrome, being out of the corporate world for a few years meant that my inner critic got even louder. My confidence had taken a battering and I suddenly found myself playing small and started freelancing on a cheap hourly rate.

All the while, I was constantly driving myself mad trying to work out what I was going to do. Should I use my marketing skills and be a consultant? Maybe I should contract locally? Or maybe I could try and set up my own business? One of my strengths had always been my ability to make solid and quick decisions. But I spent about two years living inside my head, completely paralysed in case I made the wrong one. And these were lonely days. I very much felt that no one really understood the chaos in my mind and was able to help.

In the end, I had to make a decision! I decided that setting up my own marketing business would give me the flexibility and challenge I was looking for. I signed up for free courses, worked out my packages, built my own website, started networking and worked hard to make it a success.

That first year in business was tough - working the evenings when the kids were asleep and juggling only two mornings of nursery childcare with a growing client base. But having made the decision to go for it, I felt that I needed to throw myself into it. And it was working. My business was thriving. But if I was honest, it just wasn't working for me. So, I attended more training courses, gained new digital skills and qualifications to offer more value to my clients. But although my clients were happy, inwardly, these changes made little difference to how **I felt**.

I had invested so much of myself in my career and business. Professionally, I seemed to be able to create success. But that success came with a personal cost – happiness. It was then that the penny dropped and I realised that I had never, ever, invested in ME. And that was something completely different!

Now, this may just be my hang up, but I never used to rate coaches! Coaching seemed to be too fluffy for me. Not enough emphasis on strategy, structure, goals and planning. I'd had some leadership coaching at Barclays, but I slowly realised that I needed to invest in a coach who could help bring order to my confused thoughts. I'd been trying to figure it out for years and it had only gotten me so far. It was time to turn to the experts.

I signed up for a four-month coaching container with a leading business and mindset coach. This was a substantial financial investment and I don't mind admitting that I was nervous! But, week by week, I allowed myself to explore what I wanted, my identity and beliefs, in a way I had never before. I showed up with an open mind, took action, did the exercises and trusted the process. And the fog started to lift.

I started questioning everything. I started to understand and own my story. I began to realise why I thought the way I did – why I had placed such limits on my life and made the decisions I had made. Coaching helped me see that although I was very self-aware, I still lacked two key things - Clarity and Confidence.

It feels so obvious now, looking back, but I had very little **clarity** on what I wanted the next chapter of my life to look like.

What were my desires? What did I most enjoy in life? The answer on this was surprisingly clear – I loved connection and I loved helping people. I've always been someone that people find it easy to confide in and to ask for guidance and support. I really enjoyed listening, coming alongside to give advice, sharing my own experiences to help and encourage others who are in a similar situation. With my background, I'd learnt so much about diplomacy, stakeholder management, difficult people, negotiating, planning, management, HR and so much more. These experiences were invaluable to those I supported and mentored. But I couldn't see how these skills, which came so naturally to me, could translate into being a well-paid job.

I remember so clearly the moment when I finally gave myself permission to step into being a Coach. My marketing business was thriving and I was at a place where I needed to outsource some work in order to manage the growing number of clients. After much research, I signed up for a Business Accelerator programme, a substantial financial investment. Logically, my head told me this was what I should do. The business was doing well – I should invest in scaling it. At the same time, I knew some people who were starting a coaching accreditation. And I was jealous! Jealous that they were creating meaningful careers helping people whilst I **had** to build out my current business.

I felt trapped by my own success.

Lightbulb moment!

It was **my** marketing business, just like it was **my** corporate career! I could make any decision I liked. I was refusing to give myself permission to take a different path and do something I loved because I was afraid that I couldn't make it a success. I decided in that moment that I had wasted too many years and, although I could not see every step of the path ahead, I deserved to follow my dream and be happy. Yes, I was scared and nervous, but I could not ignore it any more. I withdrew from the Business Accelerator programme and signed up for the Coaching Accreditation with the Institute of Leadership & Management. This defining moment was one of absolute clarity. This was what I was called to be. I had finally acknowledged to myself what those around me had known for years – I was a natural coach and mentor and that was my superpower!

Having finally got **clarity** on the next step, I then needed to work on my mindset to find some **confidence** that I could make a success of it! Through coaching, I learnt how my imposter syndrome was feeding me lies which my brain had now convinced me was truth. I took a good hard look at my distorted money mindset. I recognised how my perfectionism (a great quality to have in a corporate comms role!) was keeping me in a straight-jacket. I delved into all of my limiting beliefs and where they come from. I started evidencing and creating my own truth. And my self-confidence once again started to soar.

It was really important to me that I was properly trained and accredited as a coach. There is a stigma attached to coaching, that anyone can do it. Excellence and integrity are two of my personal values and I knew from my own experience of being coached that it takes an excellent and skilled coach to bring about incredible transformations. I was determined that my clients would receive the most skilled and life-changing coaching with me.

So, I spent months being professionally trained and accredited. I was already a trained counsellor and had studied psychology extensively. I completed over 120 hours of coaching, wrote reports and a case study and took part in supervision exercises. It was full-on but I loved learning more about the science of the mind and how to connect on a deeper level. As someone who is really quick at processing, I really enjoyed joining the dots in people's lives and being able to have insight into what was actually going on for them.

Once accredited, I used my previous experience of how to set up a business to launch my coaching practice and I was off! But this time, it was finally different - I loved it! My coaching is a wonderful blend of business and mindset coaching, drawing alongside like-minded women who find themselves trapped in a similar situation to mine, helping them to discover clarity and confidence so they can take the next professional step. I was finally using my skills and experience to make a difference.

As I look back, I'm incredibly grateful for my journey because it shaped who I am. I can now see that I was held back by so many limiting beliefs. What were they and where did they come from?

The biggest one was that I should stop wanting something different and just be grateful for what I had. It was arrogant of me to want something else when things were going so well.

Our backgrounds naturally shape us. There was never any expectation from my family that I would excel. It was assumed that when I finished school, I'd get a job (probably in retail) and earn enough money to get by. Whilst my parents did their very best to provide for me and my sisters, I was under no illusion of the crippling physical and emotional impact that not having money had on our family. Money was a looming shadow that was constantly over all of us. So, when I graduated from university and continued progressing, my limiting belief kicked in that I should do everything I could to keep hold of my income. You can't have money and happiness. Don't rock the boat. Just in case it sinks. Sound familiar?

I believed that although some people discover what makes their heart sing, the vast majority don't and you just need to accept what you have and be grateful for it. All of us have met a few people who absolutely love what they do. They are radiant when they talk about it – excited to start work and make a difference. But I have not met many. Have you? Although I knew that it was possible to enjoy your job, I didn't believe that I was one of the lucky ones.

I had a distorted view of what success was. I tried to guard my heart and keep aligned to my own personal values that self-worth had nothing to do with money. But the corporate world rewards success with money. With each promotion, it became harder to hold onto the belief that I was worthy because of who **I was**, not because of what I had **achieved**.

In essence, my self-talk at this time was that I should be grateful for what I had and I wasn't one of the lucky ones who figured out their life purpose. Even if I did, my low self-belief told me that I probably wouldn't make a go of it on my own anyway.

And yet, with this new found **clarity** and **confidence**, I did!

Does any of this resonate with you? What I have learnt, from my own experience and countless hours coaching women in a similar position, is that what holds us women back most is essentially **lack of clarity & confidence**. And I know with absolute certainty that with the right support, both of these are easily overcome.

As a Business & Mindset Coach, I now use my experiences and professional training to empower women to discover their own clarity and confidence. Having coached countless women, here are some simple, and yet powerful, actions that you can take should you find yourself in a similar position:

1. **Get clear on your vision:** For many of us, this is HUGE! You'd think that as high-achieving women, we would know what we want our lives to look like wouldn't you? But interestingly, this is not the case. Corporate women in particular find it harder to dream because we live 'in the moment', delivering at pace, and any long-term vision for our life gets squashed down. But, having a vision for your life is crucial. When you are clear about what you want and why you want it, you can then start to put in place plans to move in that direction. It sounds simple but honestly, how many of us do that? If you find yourself lacking vision, what can you do? There are plenty of different techniques you can try but, as a starter, I recommend these two very effective exercises:

Give yourself permission to dream: Go someone quiet with a pen and a notebook and start dreaming about what your ideal day would look like. Start writing and see what comes out. Walk through your day in your mind, from when you wake in the morning to when you lie down to sleep at night. Where would you be? Who would you be with? What would you be doing? Are you at work? What kind of work? How do you spend your free time? As you write, notice how you feel.

Create that dream visually: Now take some time to create it visually so you can look at it every day. A Dream Board is a great way. Have fun cutting words and images out of magazines that represent things in your life that you desire, or simply use Pinterest. Once you have finished, can you see any themes? How does it feel? Does it feel a bit unrealistic and at the same time fill you with excitement? Great - you are on the right lines!

You'll find that the vision for your life will change over time. Your board will get updated or you'll start another one. That's totally fine – you just need a starting point. When I first did mine a few years back, I found this exercise really hard to do on my own. Talking it through with a friend really helped.

2. Create a plan with plenty of small steps: Once you have a clear picture of what you are aiming for, take an honest assessment of your reality now. Make some decisions on what needs to change. You need to create a plan. But in order to avoid overwhelm, break it down into small manageable weekly actions. And the same for the next week. And the week after. One of the pieces of feedback I get from clients all the time is that agreeing small manageable tasks each week really moved the needle for them because they could celebrate their progress and not feel overwhelmed. If you don't do this, the danger is that it all seems too big and too unobtainable and you simply don't do anything at all.

3. Listen to your narrative and identify your limiting beliefs: When you look at your dream board, what are you telling yourself? What is your narrative and what are your limiting beliefs (beliefs you hold that limit your progress)? Do you believe you can't do it, that it's too hard? That you won't earn as much? That you don't deserve it? Once you have identified your narrative, you need to explore where it has come from and decide whether to believe it. There are many exercises I use with clients to help with this but essentially, it's about identifying what's false and replacing it with truth.

4. Learn to manage your imposter syndrome: Part of your negative narrative is probably due to imposter syndrome. Over 70% of people have struggled with imposter syndrome at some point and it particularly affects smart women. I've yet to coach someone who doesn't struggle with this! With the help of an experienced coach, explore that inner critical voice and what it is saying to you. Do you feel like a fraud at work and are worried that one day someone will discover and expose you for not being good enough? Maybe you are scared of not succeeding (or indeed, actually being a success). As part of my programme, I teach techniques to combat imposter syndrome so that you have more self-belief and confidence in your own ability.

5. Give yourself permission to change direction: You need to be honest with yourself. Don't let your previous roles, jobs and achievements define you and stop you from heading in a new direction. This is really hard, especially when life looks like it is going well. Only **you** are going to be able to change your life. Only **you** can decide and it is okay to say goodbye to things that don't fulfil you or are not aligned with who you are.

6. Get the support you need: For high achievers, asking for support can feel uncomfortable. We have an internal dialogue that we are meant to be able to do everything on our own! Being honest with myself and recognising that I needed some support was an absolute game-changer for me. And that support is ongoing. I have a business coach, who also helps me with my mindset, and a peer group of amazing, wonderful entrepreneurs. We share each other's journeys, encourage and cheer each other on. Do you need some business and mindset coaching? Or, do you need a support circle of likeminded women who have your back? Maybe both! Find your tribe. Find your cheerleaders. And be accountable. There is incredible power in knowing you don't need to figure it all out on your own.

It's been quite a journey to get here but it's wonderful to finally love what I do. Coaching really does make a difference! The more I coach, the more I realise what an incredible blessing my corporate background is. My clients are ex-corporate women who want to take the next step but need clarity and confidence to do it. Many have been out of the workforce for a while and are struggling with what to do next. Some are thinking about applying for a new job or have already set up their own business but are not fulfilled. Others are contemplating a completely different change in direction. I have experienced all of these. I understand and am the perfect person to help them navigate their own path.

Let me share just three examples of how I've supported women on their journey to a more fulfilled life.

My first example is an incredibly accomplished woman who left her corporate role to have kids and was trying to navigate returning to the workplace. Over a number of sessions, we explored what she wanted the next chapter of her life to look like. We got clear on what kind of role she wanted and unearthed how her internal narrative was preventing her from applying for roles she knew she was more than capable of doing. Over the weeks, as I walked her through various exercises, her mindset shifted and her confidence grew. She applied for, and was instantly offered, a fantastic new job, on her flexible terms! She credits so much of her success to our coaching sessions;

> "Clarity of thought is what happens as a result of coaching sessions with Kerry. She has a knack for asking just the right questions to help you crystallise your thoughts. Her toolkit of exercises is illuminating and provides the focus for change."

Let me give you another example. She was a very successful Director for an international financial services company. To her colleagues' surprise, she resigned with nothing lined up because she just knew that she wanted a change. But what? That's when she started working with me. After only a few coaching sessions she said;

> "Kerry helped me shift my mindset and I now feel so much more confident that I've made the right decision. Kerry steered me toward making a plan, and gave me coping strategies for dealing with the anxiety that comes with a huge life change."

And a third example is the CEO of a social enterprise who put all of her focus into work because it was something she excelled at, but it didn't always leave her fulfilled. Of her coaching experience she said;

> "If you are a woman looking to transition to a new role or phase of life, Kerry is the perfect guide to help that transition and also deal with the many emotions that come along with it."

So yes, coaching does work. It's transformational!

If you are reading this and just **know** that you are stuck, I want to encourage you that clarity and confidence is absolutely available to you. It's not just for other people, it's for you too!

You can create a vision for your life and then, each day, take practical steps towards it.

You can be free from the endless cycle of uncertainty and feel excited about your future.

You can make courageous choices that will result in a happier you.

So let me ask you:

- Is it time to make a professional change and do you want some clarity and confidence so you can actually do it?
- Do you need help to create a plan with manageable steps to work towards?
- Would you like to rediscover your personal and professional confidence again?
- Do you recognise that you would benefit from the support and accountability of a coach who has walked the path, learnt the lessons and is passionate about you succeeding?

Then, my friend, it's time to take action and invest in some coaching!

Nothing will change if you don't decide to take some action. My 1:1 coaching programme, 'Momentum', has helped so many women get unstuck and move forwards. Over only a few sessions you will be able to:

- Make the right decisions with absolute clarity.
- Recognise the blockages that have been holding you back and learn how to shift your mindset to feel more confident.
- Create a practical plan of actionable steps to take (with bags of support and accountability along the way!).

This wonderful blend of business and mindset coaching has been transformational for my clients and will be for you too. Reach out. Invest in yourself. Let yourself be wonderfully supported for this next chapter of your life to finally get the clarity and the confidence that you deserve.

To find out more how we can work together and sign up for a free call, simply visit www.kerryjonescoaching.com

ABOUT THE AUTHOR
KERRY JONES

Kerry Jones is a Business & Mindset Coach who helps ex-corporate women discover clarity and confidence so that they can take the next step.

Before establishing her own coaching practice, Kerry spent 16 years in high-level corporate communications roles for some of the biggest brands in the world. After leaving the corporate life, Kerry launched her own marketing company, supporting small businesses, before becoming accredited as a coach with the Institute of Leadership and Management.

Kerry now uses her skills and experiences to coach women who want to make the next professional decision without spending months procrastinating, feeling afraid or being overwhelmed.

Kerry loves living near the beach in Brighton with her husband and two amazing kids!

Kerry is available for 1:1 coaching through her signature coaching programme, 'Momentum'. She supports ex-corporate women to get clear on what they want, helps create a practical plan so they can achieve it, and then unblocks any mindset issues that are holding them back. The result? Confident women with more fulfilled lives!

You can reach Kerry at:

Email: kerry@kerryjonescoaching.com
Website: www.kerryjonescoaching.com

facebook.com/kerryjonescoaching
instagram.com/kerry.jones.coaching
linkedin.com/in/kerryjonescoach

15

KERYN POTTS

THE ACCIDENTAL ENTREPRENEUR

A Deeper Purpose

I'm Keryn: coach, mother, survivor, part-time introvert, the ultimate pin up girl for Lone Wolves. This is a story of how I realised I was meant for more and then learnt how I could pass on my experiences to help other women that could relate.

By sharing my story, I'm hoping that other high achieving entrepreneurial women can learn to connect more with others and become more congruent with their purpose and "why". I'd love for them to ultimately find their own inner peace by breaking through their fears as I did, by becoming more vulnerable.

Can you remember a particular time in your life, or perhaps there are many, where one minute, you were cruising along on autopilot, just living your life, but then it all changed so drastically when either an unexpected circumstance occurred or something just made you realise your situation wasn't for you any more?

One minute, I was working for royalty, waving to the Queen as she drove past the store of her relative, my window displays within her sights, and on other days, enjoying the possibility of bumping into the various celebrities as they walked in. How quickly life changes though... Suddenly out of work with a new baby in tow after being made redundant, unable to find flexible and well-paid work. How did I get here? I wondered. What to do next? I deserved better, but how to get it was the issue.

Have you ever been to a doctor and they just can't pin point what the issue is? You search for many more years, until one day, you find someone who can name it. Not a doctor in my case but through continually pushing myself I realised I was a Lone Wolf. I veer off the beaten track to isolate for various reasons, which ultimately holds me back. I finally had something to grasp on to for the next stage of my progress. I have now learnt to manage these traits much better through a course of self-mastery, which resulted in allowing myself to be more vulnerable by removing some of my armour.

The self-improvement journey I've been on these past several years is like an awakening, giving myself a shake up as I've been having so many lightbulb moments for why I've been doing what I do. I've steadily been reframing my thoughts and how I process them, and always will.

Are We There Yet?

I've always isolated through fear of judgement and hidden my vulnerabilities so didn't progress as far as I could in my life and career. I was always searching for a more enlightened path, kind of like an awakening when you start to see patterns in yourself, realise what triggers you and how you respond, yet didn't know how to help myself. I just knew there was something missing that I wasn't quite getting. I am educated, quite resourceful, solution focused, intelligent, well travelled, yet couldn't quite grasp how to evolve more consciously. One doesn't just google this stuff as you don't actually know what you are looking for most of the time or why you are not as happy as you could be. I feel content now in knowing that so much more is possible. Leaning into one's feelings rather than avoiding them is so important for growth, both personally and for business.

Overly happy people had always been quite foreign to me as I perceived them as fake in the sense that they must be hiding something, pretending life was a bunch of roses when it couldn't have been. I'm drawn to authentic people and didn't see them as that. I used to keep my feelings to myself, but over time have come to realise the more authentic I am, the more trust is built with clients. Our stories are what connects us together. I now realise those happy people along the way were just making the choice to focus on the positive aspects of their life. Bad things happen to all of us, but with a mindset shift, you can avoid being distracted by them. Deal with any problems, let go, then move on.

If I could speak to my younger self, I would tell her not to listen to the opinion of others as they are not the ones that need to live her life. I'd also tell myself that the people judging her are projecting their own fear, failures and experiences on to her, so disconnect. Don't be persuaded to go the path they want you to go. Stand firm in what you believe is best for you and in my case child as well. Create your life with intent and purpose. One also needs to show up along the way of the journey to enjoy all the moments, rather than waiting to get to the destination, as well as make mistakes much quicker so we can then learn soon after that. Don't wait, just start, as you can learn along the way.

Trust In Oneself

I'd always played much smaller than my real worth due to limiting beliefs, yet always felt I was made for more. Surely someone as feisty as me had a higher purpose, I just didn't know how to go about getting there and/or didn't actually know what I wanted. I've often just known what I didn't want, but not what I wanted. My life has just happened rather than been built with intent.

I've always asked questions, seeking more, and it wasn't until I did Andrea Callanan's self-mastery course that I started to find the answers. I am very harsh on myself for not knowing things, as I have always felt judged. Self-sabotage has been a constant in my life as well as many excuses for not doing things. I thought I needed external affirmations, but it's all within. I hid.

One of the many advantages though of being a life long learner, is that it has helped me get to where I am today as it opens up so many more possibilities, leading to a more expansive mindset. I am always trying to work on my fixed mindset to change my default responses to one of growth, as do the many other like-minded women who have something from their past that gets triggered, our subconscious is trying to keep us safe. I help give some clarity to them.

I am quite a sceptical person by nature, due to being bullied at school, and so I do not trust many with their intent. All of that slowly chipped away at my confidence and self-worth. I am much better now, but still tend to dip my toe in with new people as I assess my level of trust.

My lack of confidence and self-worth has been a major factor holding me back. It's up to me though to progress, I'm not waiting for anyone else to save me. I wanted to be invisible, as people wouldn't then see me, so tried to blend in. I often find myself going against the grain in my thoughts though, and for many years, I still tried to fit in by being more agreeable. I've realised now though, over time, that being different is one of my many strengths. The world needs more diversity in its thinking; too many people just go along with the majority, pick on those that are different, then those picked on become too scared to use their voice.

I faced many brick walls in front of me, trying to set up a co-working/ crèche, such as with insurers not even understanding the concept of what we were trying to do. Looking back, it has been a common theme throughout my life, thinking differently. Keep going and pushing through, despite not many people wanting to understand. Even if you stop at some stage along the way, you will have made an easier path for the next person. Inspiring others with your efforts is key.

Self-mastery doesn't just happen overnight, as I well know, and so, it is important to manage expectations with clients from the outset. It's important to distinguish what a coach is, and that is to encourage women to realise their potential, kind of like planting a seed of positivity and letting it grow - with some pruning along the way. Growth takes time.

My coaching programmes aim to give women the space and the tools to gradually understand their behaviour and gain various lightbulb moments along the way. Continued coaching is also on offer with me for those kick-up-the-bum and pruning occasions. I encourage all to have a coach, for accountability and to inspire them, as part of their self-care as this helps nourish the soul.

I'm proud that I haven't just sat idle throughout my life as one thing led to the next, even if I didn't realise it at the time. I can now look back and appreciate what I have experienced. Flipping any misery into a learning has been a part of the reframe process. I still sometimes fall back into my old ways as I'm only human, but nowadays, am much quicker at pulling myself back and trying to understand why I may have such feelings and/or what has triggered me, then, I can move on much quicker, thanking my subconscious for trying to keep me safe.

The Key To Freedom

I am at a point in my life where I can appreciate much of what I have experienced, as it helps me keep moving on. However, wasn't in that place for many years as didn't have the mindset tools to appreciate and see my strengths. My self-talk has been harsh and now, I am trying to be more forgiving for any mistakes I have made and to own my destiny.

As a result of being bullied at school and having an overly critical/uninterested-in-a-girl type father, plus many other life experiences thrown into the mix, some of my drivers in life now are integrity, kindness and trust, to name a few. I'll also dive in to any moment when the scales need balancing between the sexes. Having a girl makes me even more aware.

When I look back at all I've experienced, I see now that at the time, I didn't feel there was an alternative, yet there was one all along. I just needed to give myself permission to feel a certain way and to realise it wasn't my fault for many things - it was other people projecting their own issues and insecurities on to me. For years, I self-sabotaged. I didn't feel good enough as that was what other people had told me. What would be the point then in finishing anything, as it wouldn't be good enough? I often disconnected from others due to a lack of self-worth, and self-deprecated before anyone else said anything. However, my sense of humour and casual nature has now turned out to be one of my strengths as sometimes, I feel that life is taken a little too seriously and therefore we should lighten up somewhat. There are serious moments in life, of course, such as an earthquake, but need to find the positives too.

My experience of being in a major earthquake when living in Kobe also brought with it much resilience, and a solution focused mindset developed from much of what occurred. This likely stems from having a single mother as a parent, doing what was needed and getting on with it. She showed me that women are just as capable of doing everything, and to just get on with it, and this is what I did after the earthquake. I work with clients to help push aside their limiting beliefs, to gain faith in their abilities.

In Kobe, I had to leave my home as it was likely to topple. I lived in an evacuation centre for a week, shared our rations of food with others, found our way out of the city as all usual pathways to the airport were either damaged or ruined, but due to living with an American friend, we were found by their embassy and then led to where the airport ferry was. We literally sailed off into the sunset. I am just so grateful for these people that trudged through the rubble to find their citizens. It was a very surreal experience to arrive at Osaka airport, as they had not been affected and life went on. We arrived disheveled, as we hadn't been able to wash for a week. We most likely smelt and emotions were high. A poignant moment firmly embedded in my memories from that day was that you just get on with life, and then do what you have to do to survive and/or thrive.

I had claustrophobia for quite a while after the earthquake, and had cognitive therapy to help somewhat, but the memories will still catch me by surprise on the odd occasion, if the exit and path is not clear. I can appreciate now how far I've come with it and that is a part of self-mastery. I realise too that I've always had a positive mindset, but just had to dig deep to find it again. It's a work in progress and much in life will bury it, but I'll dust it all off again and keep going. At first, I thought it was all rather silly saying gratitudes, but through practise and daily routine, it becomes easier.

At one stage, shortly after the earthquake, I lived in London for six months and would keep getting off buses and trains on my way to work, but kept getting back on as needed to be somewhere. The solution I found at the time was to give myself more time to get where I needed. My life had changed and so it was best to adapt. There was no point hiding as I would have ended up staying in my bedroom, afraid, for the long term. Travelling by plane has definitely been the hardest when suffering from claustrophobia, as you can't get off, but I love travelling and so pushed through the temporary ill feelings and panic attacks. I think I carried a plastic bag with me for many years just in case I threw up. This was the feeling I had straight after the earthquake gasping for air whilst sat in the middle of the road wondering what had just happened due to being woken up so suddenly. This bewilderment in life was to become a pattern.

I believe that by continually looking ahead at the time, it helped me get to where I am today, where these memories now only sometimes bothers me as I have much better coping strategies in place to help. I have gained many strengths during my life experiences but due to lack of confidence in my abilities, I suppressed who I was.

Although I was shown independence and resilience from an early age by a single mother, it was the financial abuse I witnessed growing up that affected me. My father withheld money from my mother and so I always had a distant relationship with money, more avoided it as was the cause of so many problems.

It's just so fascinating when you start to realise why you don't charge your worth, as it often goes far deeper than many women first believe. I have unravelled many layers in my self discovery journey.

Part of my coaching process is to ask my clients: Why don't you charge your worth?

Come Out Come Out Wherever You Are!

If much of what I've been mentioning resonates with other women, I offer coaching programmes to help.. I find it much easier to pinpoint what they are experiencing as have been there myself for much of it, in some form or another. I would start by asking "What happened to you?" Next, I ask "What is your vision/ purpose?", then, after all that, I reverse engineer from all they have said. I find that from years of self-sabotage and making excuses not to do things, it has ended up being a great strength to help troubleshoot and look at the finer details I am told by my clients. I get right in there and have a poke around. I'm the queen of excuses and so know where to focus with others.

I've been investing heavily in myself, even more so in the past few years, and so, changes for the better are happening. I'd recommend that others do the same as when you open yourself to change, then that's one step forward already.

Be open to what offerings there are and be proactive to get involved in your growth community instead of isolating from shame, lack of self-worth and fear, to name a few. The more you look around, the more you will see that you are not alone in your thoughts and experiences. You just need to start, just do anything rather than nothing. Where do your kind of people hang out? Go there and/ or create the space yourself.

I've often felt different to others, not just as a 6-foot tall female with red hair. I also diverted from the path most take as I have endlessly travelled in between my studies rather than settle down. My life has been more wanderlust than anything else, looking for fresh starts, always searching for more, doing it on my own, yet coming back to the pack every so often. It can be a lonely existence, and so I make sure I don't wander off too far. However, I try to balance this with my strong freedom driver as don't like to be hemmed in.

I think that the skills I need to be content have been within me all along, not buried deep down between the hills of Mongolia, nor the top of Mt Fuji. I now just appreciate the journey along the way as the focus, rather than the destination I've been craving. I help women do the same.

Business isn't just about making money, as most of the high achieving women I work with have similar voids. They could have done any of the following: earned the big bucks, climbed the ladder in their career, have a nice house, great partner, good bunch of friends, travel, be social, have kids… and yet, they still aren't 100% happy. There is more that they desire; they just don't know what it is. So, I help coach them to understand themselves and gain clarity. Giving themselves permission to deserve much more is so important. It is usually their purpose in life that hasn't been fulfilled, and so we work on that to achieve peace within themselves. Having a 'servitude to others' mindset plays a huge role in bringing about change.

There is a huge freedom driver for many women, wanting to be financially independent, yet not earning enough to do or be that because they get in their own way. They do actually have that sense of servitude, yet don't know how to go about utilising it. This is where coaching comes in. Women want to thrive, not just survive, yet need help to get over the hurdles for loss of purpose/ identity, confusion, procrastination, fear, self-worth, imposter syndrome and other obstacles. Having a child for me really did put so much into perspective.

Showing up is so important, in attitude and in person, and that's how I help women progress to a more joyful and fulfilled life. Peace being the ultimate goal.

Anyone can change, but they have to want to do this. I'd been stuck for so long, wanting to do better and progress in my business and just be happier, but couldn't figure out how to go about it. I realised along the way, that many more women feel the same. I've never been a big sharer in that regard as I was always told to be quiet when younger by my father, however, it draws more people to you when they can connect and relate. You just isolate yourself further by keeping your story all in.

I had been to multiple business workshops to progress in my career, and, as helpful as they were, they never quite got me to the aha moments I needed until I started on my self-mastery journey with Andrea, kind of like an awakening where all the pieces of my life started fitting together like a jigsaw. It wasn't too woo woo either, as I would have backed off, but just enough to pique my interest to then want to delve further in. I don't think many people google self mastery, more a process of osmosis where when you search for more, it eventually finds you at the right time. For me, I had started to study social media with Digital Mums and FB ads with Emma Van Heusen and then, one day, there she was, the shining bright star of Andrea Callanan. A person so engaged in life that I wanted to find out more. I knew that she was the kind of person that would understand me by what she was saying. This is why it's so important to share your story with people, so they can see the authentic you. This is why I am here in this chapter. We all crave connection, right? Someone who gets us, surrounded by like-minded people, away from Debbie Downers telling us we can't do something.

I've learnt, over time, it's not just about doing a business course to progress, it's about mindset and positivity. "What makes you happy?" "What is your passion/ niche?" And, "How will you help people?" are questions that are explored in my coaching sessions.

Any programme one signs up for should include both and that is why I offer these two, so I can help women get more visible, find their voice, gain confidence, become more vulnerable, break through any fear, step up their self-worth and work on self-care. Women are then able to get more visible in their marketing and social media. I offer specific help with this too.

What has been holding you back?

What makes you isolate?

My Beautiful Failings

I feel that I now have a sense of purpose and am able to help other women who resonate with my story. I have invested heavily in myself for the better and my offerings come with many a coach on my shoulders, passing their wisdom along: Andrea Callanan, Niyc Pidgeon and Brendon Bruchard to name a few. I feel like I have made progress in my growth, which then helps in my business. Mindset and business are completely intertwined.

I hope that my entrepreneurial spirit can help inspire others, such as when I opened a co-working/creche in London with my wonderful friend, who opened the doors to her lovely home with the aim of creating space for various women as they tried to find a way to transition between leaving their jobs and having children. We didn't let the matter of location/funding stop us with our idea as wanted to have a trial first before we invested our time and money further.

I was surrounded by so many inspiring women who wanted something more. Making it into a viable business model though was the challenge, and so we closed it after six months. I may not have been able to find an instant solution to change the world or remedy our patriarchal society, yet I was able to help make a difference. I am slowly realising that all I do is not a failure, more a learning. We inspired many others to do the same in their homes. It just takes one person to make a difference... or, in our case, two. My business ideas were furthered along with the encouragement from my mentor at the time, and so I will always carry this support along. Hang around successful people as they will try and prop you up rather than bring you down. I have continued with this mindset in my coaching. Community is so important, rather than always isolating as the lone wolf.

I have also come to realise through my coaching, that it doesn't necessarily matter what someone's job is or once was in order to help them, as that is secondary to the mindset journey they are on. It is the thought process and experiences that many women have that connects us. I want to help women transition from one stage in their life to the next, with the skills they possessed all along, but have been holding themselves back due to trying to avoid what they need to do next to level up. My approach is direct and targets limiting beliefs head on. Self-worth and courage is there for the taking.

I laugh now when I think what I'd always imagined my spiritual awakening would be, full of joy and content throughout, but that is more towards the later stages. One needs to push through feeling uncomfortable because until those feelings are accepted and released, it will keep popping up throughout one's life as we are triggered.

Helping someone become more self-aware of themselves is one of the greatest gifts you can give someone. Thanks to Andrea, I can now pass that on. Going over one's story and life pivots is just the beginning. One needs to start with the vision then work backwards from there. Finding time to reflect and tune into yourself is part of the process, so try and schedule in more ME time. I'm working on it, as I've not quite mastered it... yet. I'll forgive myself though, if it doesn't happen straight away. I do know for sure that if I don't take care of myself, I am of little use to anyone else.

Gather Round Lone Wolves – Finding Your Tribe

I have helped various high achieving women realise their potential with my direct approach, stripping away the layers to get to the core of why they are stuck. This brings more peace and contentment in their life and business.

Limiting beliefs often stem from childhood trauma, such as from a parent/ relative/ teacher, bullied at school and/or one's boss and colleagues at work. Many women leave their employment after having children or just not happy where they are and so then move away from the security of employment and go it alone, with a hope and prayer that their idea works, or actually no clue at all. There is a lot of success for some women along the way as they change direction, but then they get stuck and unsure why. Many highly skilled and high achieving women get stuck due to some or all of the following: fear of judgement, shame, no purpose and/or why, lack of money/ abundant mindset, don't yet know their ideal clients or niche, branding, self-worth is low... and with all these, they start to isolate themselves. They then don't have the structure or support to get themselves out. Through coaching, I help give such support and a community.

One of my aims is to get women out of the child state and into creator mode by gaining an understanding of how negative thinking slows down brain co-ordination, therefore making it difficult to be creative and find more solutions. Cortisol floods the synapses for the flight or fight response when in the child state of negative thoughts, and so women will just keep getting the same response as they always have and have no head room available to create. My focus is to help them change state and to give them the facts on how to do so.

Changing state and becoming more self-aware helps bring peace and a more contented life. Once you understand that you are no longer searching for what once didn't make sense, you are then able to progress with more specific intent and purpose.

I also help clients overcome their money mindset issues to realise why they don't charge enough for their services and skills, why they procrastinate and to help them overcome their fears. This then leads to further progress in their business as more ideas flow when they stop working on the processes instead of the bigger picture. We break the seal together and then it all just flows from there. My clients become more independent in figuring out much on their own with the new structures and strategies in place, after a few aha moments from our sessions.

One of my clients had been two years without a lead magnet and a clear sense of direction and my sessions really helped her with that:-

> *"If you are looking for a coach that has the ability to understand exactly the support you need on any given day; a calm, approachable manner and results-orientated focus, give Keryn a call! In six sessions, Keryn has elevated my approach to my own business. (I thought I could casually transfer my skills from 20+ years in corporate to going solo but the experience was overwhelming at times and tough to focus.) Keryn expertly cut through all the noise and reframed my mindset. By the end of each session we identified manageable steps to move my business forward. It was exactly the business support I needed to make the change from corporate life to going solo."*

Open For Happiness

If any woman resonates with my story, I'm able to support her on her journey by my particular focus and style of coaching. I have the insight and experience to know where clients need to focus and will help coach them to discover more about themselves. I mirror coach and so very aware what they are dealing with in their lives. There will be many an aha moment for them too, slowly but surely, as they put the pieces together about themselves. Self-awareness opens so many more doors.

So much can be achieved by opening one's mind to further possibility with a growth mindset, which involves focusing on the positive, as well as walking through discomfort to reach my client*s ultimate vision. She is ready to explore any reoccurring patterns in her life and will stop playing small so she can sit in her higher power.

Focusing more on the positive has been the turning point I needed, although still a work in progress, I stopped making as many excuses. I limit my time with the Debbie Downers as the energy they zap serves no purpose. My boundaries are always improving with other people and what I allow to be acceptable. I created a community where like-minded Lone Wolves can gather. They are not alone.

I've been continually pushed by my higher self to create a space to help women take their business to the next level and break through their fears. I have been making way to allow myself to be more in creator mode through positivity and abundance. This is what I am proudest of, besides having my daughter of course.

ABOUT THE AUTHOR
KERYN POTTS

Keryn Potts is the No BS Mindset Coach. A fully accredited coach who empowers and supports high-achieving female business owners with her straight talking and casual approach, she helps to break down those blocks, walls and armour that hold us back in our lives and businesses.

By helping women become more authentic and confident they can progress forward into what they really want to create. Keryn's interest is peaked by women that isolate themselves through FEAR which reflects her own journey to success - including the 'beautiful failings' that we learn so much from!

Before starting her own business, Keryn had a vast amount of experience in creative and retail senior management, graphic design, teaching and customer experience. She's a lifelong learner and now helps other women find their why and purpose and get out of the wilderness that she has long trudged.

Keryn enjoys time with her daughter and family in Sydney, soaking up the everlasting rays of the sunshine while looking for her next adventure. She's emigrated multiple times between London, Japan and Australia, so she truly understands how important freedom drivers are!

Keryn also provides social media strategy to support women to get consistently visible.

Keryn is available for 1:1 coaching and strategy sessions, as well as group sessions, guest speaking and workshops.

You can contact Keryn via:

Email: kerynpotts@gmail.com
Website: www.kerynpottscoaching.com
Instagram: https://www.instagram.com/kerynpotts/
Facebook: www.facebook.com/groups/heylonewolf

16

LUCY CIARAMELLA

UPGRADE YOUR LIFE TO FULL COLOUR

Upgrading my life to one in full colour is the best way to describe the journey that I've been on. I've never particularly disliked my life but I've always been conscious of it being what I make it. It has taken a lot of healing, mindset work and facing my fears to get to where I am today, but I can safely say that it has been 100% worth it. I have now designed a life that is truly aligned with my greatest value - freedom. Freedom of who I want to be, who I surround myself with, where I spend my time and in what I do.

As an Energy Worker and Healer, energy plays a massive part in my life and I now know that all the decisions I make align with the energy of who I want to be and what I want to attract. Choosing to upgrade my life has allowed me to call in the desires that used to be merely a dream for me. I now live by the sea, have turned my passion into my career and purpose and have become an entrepreneur that gives me the perfect work/life balance to fit around my young family. My day is spent doing what I love and working with the most incredible and inspiring people. My mission is, and has been since I started this journey, 'to live the best life and inspire others to do the same' and I now live by this every single day.

I would describe myself as independent, intuitive and very emotionally aware. I like to see these as the superpowers that have been with me for as long as I can remember. Growing up, I knew when something felt aligned and even when it went against expectations, I chose to follow my heart. I've always been described as a bit of a free-spirit and independence and freedom has always come up high on my list of priorities.

From a young age, I looked up to my Dad, who had his own business and the freedom that came with it. I wanted the same but, unlike my father who knew from the age of around 12 what he wanted to do, I couldn't work this part out. Along with this major issue, I also had a severe lack of confidence and self-belief that I would be capable of starting my own business. I felt there was a massive pressure as I was leaving school, to choose exactly what I wanted to do and be, study for it, get a job and then many years later, if I were truly successful, self-employment might be a possibility. There seemed to be a stigma attached to being an entrepreneur and I didn't quite understand why.

Art and design was my strength at school and after spending time pondering on the decision to study Interior Architecture or Psychology (human behaviour has always been a passion), I chose the former. I was hoping that this would give me a skill that I could continue for the rest of my working life. The course and all the people on it were amazing, but I knew in my heart that this wasn't going to be my life-long career and purpose. I knew that something else was out there and I made it my mission to go and find it.

During this quest, I did what a lot of 20 somethings do and travelled the world. This was a phenomenal experience and I will forever feel thankful that I made the decision to do it.

On return, I spent the next seven years flitting between various roles in sales, customer services, design, mortgage advice and even continued to travel as Cabin Crew. As soon as I lost interest, I found myself moving onto the next role. Finding out what I wanted to do was a process of elimination. My instinct knew that there was something more aligned out there for me and all of these roles were leading me to where I wanted to be. What became apparent was that the office setup didn't inspire me; travel was best done with those that you love and being passionate about what you do on a daily basis was essential. I knew for certain that none of the jobs that I had had fulfilled me enough to give me the desire to work my way up the career ladder.

I broke free of this cycle when I became aware of the pattern. After doing some inner work, it became apparent that I was the one standing in my way. It was ME holding myself back as going from job to job was the easy option. I felt safe as I didn't have to step up and do or become something that I, deep down, didn't think I was capable of. Starting my own empire around something that I was passionate about, to make it my purpose, brought up FEAR within me. Fear of failure, fear of rejection and fear of judgement. I didn't want to leave my comfort zone and experience these emotions and instead chose to stay in the safety of what I knew. Looking back, the cycle of hopping between jobs was a form of procrastination that I now know is a major sign of fear.

I was unaware that help was out there in the form of a coach or mentor if I needed it. Someone who could have supported me, helped me set goals and empower me to take action. A person who could have pointed out that it was down to me to make the change and that I had everything within me to do so.

At the start of the recession in 2008, I finally started my journey of breaking free from this cycle. Redundancy gave me the push that I needed and I embarked on a course that would change my life. I enrolled on a Holistic Therapy course, specialising in bodywork and energy healing. This course ticked the boxes and allowed me to use my creativity, intuition and natural healing powers to help others.

The healing journey doesn't happen overnight and can often bring up shadows from our past. Like a lizard sheds it's skin, when we have moved on from one layer, something else may crop up. At the start of the journey, I remember becoming a lot more self-aware and thoughts I had suppressed, started coming to the surface. I soon realised that behind the bubbly, strong-willed and determined facade, I was a girl with very limiting beliefs who had a massive fear of being her true authentic self. I was looking for permission to rise and was waiting for that perfect time to step into who I wanted to be. I was keeping myself small and conforming to the beliefs that I had about myself and thought others did too.

The limiting beliefs that I had about myself mainly came from stories that I made up in my head. Unlike my Father, who excelled at everything he did and always had done, I had to work hard to achieve good grades. I tried to follow his way but knew deep down that I could never reach his standard of academia. I was very hard on myself and even though he never criticised my progress, I felt whatever I did wasn't good enough and that I could always do better. I constantly told myself and believed that I would fail. This brought about a lot of stress and anxiety and over time, slowly chipped away at my confidence.

Right at the start of the impressionable teenage years, a few years after my parents divorced, we moved home and with this came a change of school. To try and blend into my new environment, I started to play small through fear of judgement and rejection, which meant that my grades took a nosedive. It was also at this time that I fell victim to a spell of bullying and would spend my days with a heightened awareness of what was going on around me. Even though I wanted to, I failed to voice my emotions at home as

I didn't want to be a burden, so I just sucked them up and got on with things in the hope that it would improve.

Before doing the inner-work, the feelings I had of low self-worth also manifested in my relationships. To seek the love I needed, I looked to others to provide it for me. I needed a partner to prove that I was worthy of love and affection and in doing this, I made relationship choices that did not align with my values. I chose partners who failed to respect and support me emotionally which in turn, reinforced my limiting beliefs.

I married in 2011 and knew deep down that my husband and I weren't truly aligned. We came from different cultures, with different values, and the cracks soon started to show. This, in itself, was a challenge, but along with it came a person that wasn't capable of being emotionally available. I wanted the relationship to work as it would confirm my worth, but instead the cultural difference created a lot of arguments and a toxicity within the home. Loneliness kicked in and I started to feel like I wanted out, but the thought of being by myself brought up a sense of fear. Even though I was only in my early 30's, I couldn't see a way out and felt like it was too late. Guilt also kicked in as I felt a sense of duty to keep the little family setting that we created, together. In hindsight, I wish I had known that I already had everything within me to make the change that I needed and was capable of giving myself the love and affection that I craved.

The behaviour and belief that I wasn't enough continued until the pivotal moment in my life when I hit rock bottom and had to either sink or swim. This moment came a couple of years after my youngest son was born. At this time in my life, as mothers do, I had immersed myself into motherhood, putting the needs of my children first. Support was scarce as I didn't have family in the area and my ex-husband spent the majority of his time at work. I found the sole responsibility very challenging and felt burnt-out. The toxicity with the relationship had become worse and our marriage was rapidly breaking down. The relationship was very controlling, which meant that I had completely lost sight of the person that I used to be. It was then, at this critical point in time, that my fight response kicked in and I found the strength to change. No longer did I want to live this way. I realised that life is short and for the sake of myself and the boys, I wanted to choose happiness and would do what I could to get it. I knew deep down that if I was happy, it would make them happy too.

This change all started with my mindset. I started researching motivational speakers, listened to self-development podcasts and sought out positive quotes and affirmations. I started making this a daily habit and found that it very quickly lifted my spirits and increased my energy.

By following these simple steps, my thoughts soon started to become more positive and the limiting beliefs that I had about my capability and worth started to improve. The clarity that I was severely lacking started to resurface and I could again start to visualise and believe what was possible for me to achieve.

In September 2017, as soon as my youngest started nursery school, I set to work and reintroduced some of my passions back into my day as I knew this would be a fundamental step in helping me find internal happiness and rediscover my identity. Before marriage and children, fitness had been a massive part of my life. I joined a gym and started going to classes with high energy music, like-minded people and sweat inducing exercise, and the person I once was, started to return. I couldn't get enough and knew deep down that the shift I had with my mindset was expanding to other areas of my life. I was doing something I loved that was making me feel great on the inside and strong and confident on the outside.

With my confidence levels at the highest they had been in a long time, and the feeling of burn-out dispersing, I was able to set goals on where I wanted to go in the next stages of my life. I returned to work as a Holistic Therapist in a local spa and got tremendous joy from helping others create positive wellbeing. I was no longer willing to settle for anything in life that failed to bring me happiness. The time had come to end my marriage and the loneliness and hurt that I faced on a daily basis. If I was ever going to live by my mission of 'living my best life' then I would need to break free.

This wasn't an easy ride and things got far worse at home before they got better, but the inner-strength that I had mastered through raising my frequency, following my passions and gaining confidence, got me through.

Like a domino effect, our life continued to improve. After the divorce, my long awaited desire to start my own business came to fruition. Inner-Action Wellbeing was born to cater for clients that were looking to treat the mind and body holistically. It catered to a market who wanted spa quality treatments in the comfort of their own home. This soon expanded to providing treatments at retreat venues and corporate settings. It worked for my family's needs, as it created a great balance that allowed me to be there for my boys. The guilt of not being able to attend sports day, prize giving and school performances that I had once experienced, was now in the past.

If you want to expand and grow, you have to continue to learn. Adding further modalities to my offerings and qualifying as a Yoga Teacher, EFT Practitioner and most recently, as an Accredited Coach, has meant that I can now take my services online to serve a wider community. The pandemic, as awful as it was, taught us many things and one was the power and convenience of modern technology and the need for flexibility. Pivoting my business seemed the logical thing to do, both for myself and my clients.

One of the best moves I've made was to invest in a coach to empower me to uplevel my life and business. Justifying the cost took a while, but investing in a resource to enhance your future is one of the best things that you can do, and for anyone who is on the fence, I urge you not to think twice about it. It is guaranteed to change your life.

Becoming an online coach has brought with it another set of learnings and personal challenges. The shadows of low self-belief and confidence have again cropped up with the need to get visible to market my business. I've had to get comfortable with the discomfort of being online and getting myself out there. The limiting beliefs and fear of judgement, rejection and failure have all raised their ugly heads and I've had to seriously tap into managing them. Unlike in the past, before I started working on my mindset, I now know that I have all the tools within me to work on myself to push fear aside, believe in myself and take the actionable steps that will get me to where I want to be.

I remember when I was younger, thinking that I wanted to be a coach and the voice inside my head telling me that I needed more experience and certainly wasn't capable or good enough. I am so proud to say that she's here! Lucy Ciaramella is now that coach who she aspired to be and is living her purpose of empowering others to achieve their dreams.

So, if you can resonate with wanting to add a little more colour to your life, you are probably asking, where do I start? The starting point is with you. Give yourself some space to gain clarity on who you are and what you want to attract into your life, where you want to be and who you want to become.

In a coaching session with me, we focus on all aspects of your life, from your environment to your career and relationships, and discuss your feelings around them. We identify areas that aren't in alignment with the life you want to achieve, and together, we create clarity and actionable steps to move you closer to your future vision.

Take some time to think about the areas of your life. Is there an area that you feel takes up a lot of your energy and depletes you?

Are there people around you that don't bring out the best in you? Are you no longer enjoying your job or business and long to find something that lights you up?

When you start working on yourself, the best place to start is by feeling good about who you are. Many women take a back seat and feel selfish for practicing self-care. I can confirm to you that self-care is not selfish; it is essential and is needed for us to be the best version of ourselves. It is needed to lift our spirits and raise our frequency. With a higher frequency comes a higher level of manifestation. According to the laws of attraction, you get what you put out, so coming from a high-vibe place of abundance and positivity will attract more of the same into your life.

It doesn't have to come in the form of bubble baths and massages, even though these can be very rewarding. It can come in the smallest and easiest of ways e.g., practicing gratitude and using positive self-talk. Along with joy and happiness, gratitude is one of the highest frequency emotions. Making a list of all that you are grateful for can be a great way to start the day. Initially, you may find it a little hard to do, but with persistence you will find that over time, the things that you are grateful for will flow from your mind onto the page.

Time is one of the most valuable gifts you can give yourself. Time to just be - to be present with your thoughts and feelings; to tap into your creative energy and to pause and fill up your cup. Being in control of your time and blocking out sacred space to breathe and be at peace will not only benefit your mind and body and how you show up in the world, it will have an impact on those around you. You can do whatever you feel called to do in this time, whether it be meditation, to calm the mind; movement, to create energy; or reading, to unwind and relax. This time is yours and with the right planning, can be a game-changer in creating a more harmonious life.

Clarity is often a stumbling block for many of my clients. They struggle to know how they would like their life to look. Life is busy and it can be so easy to get swept up in the daily routine to even consider how it can be any different. Visualisation can be a great tool for helping to create a destination and therefore, a roadmap of how to get there. It can be done in a number of ways: in the form of meditation, drawing, or by creating a vision board out of pictures and quotes to represent your goals and dreams. By visiting one of these methods every day, you are setting the intention of attracting that which you desire and are starting the process of manifestation. You are telling your subconscious mind exactly what you would like and subsequently, every conscious decision that you make will support your request.

The art of journaling daily can help you to explore your thoughts and feelings. It can allow you to discover who you truly are and what makes you tick. You may come across shadows and areas that you need to heal, but this is all a valuable lesson. We cannot truly move on with our lives if we have negative beliefs and emotions from our past holding us back. We are certainly not going to be aware of these until we start exploring them. Journaling doesn't have to be a struggle. Getting the thoughts out of your head and onto paper can feel very cleansing and can create space for more positive thoughts to enter. Healing can also occur as the words are transferred onto paper and the energy that is associated with them is released.

To design a life that you love, you will have to start living your present life consciously. Being aware of where you are, the energy that surrounds you, and the habits that you have created, will allow you to reassess where change can be made. Delving deeper into how you feel about these and being honest with yourself about what you do in the present will help to serve the future you. Are the habits, feelings, people and places you have in your life helpful for you to create the life of your dreams? Or are they holding you back? By living consciously, you can be aware of the steps that you can take to create change and start implementing it. You can start living intentionally by showing up and making decisions that support the future version of yourself. How does she show up in the world? Where does she frequent? And who does she surround herself with?

Working on and improving your mindset every day is invaluable. Just like working on your body will get you fit, working on your mindset daily will expand your mind with new learnings and positive suggestions. Working on your self belief, confidence and worth will have a direct impact on the decisions that you make and how you show up. This can be done at any point of the day, but for me, this is the first thing that I do whilst drinking my morning coffee. There are many ways that you can do this and it all comes down to personal preference. There are millions of podcasts, audiobooks, Youtube videos and books out there that you can choose to help you. Not only will they inspire you, making these part of your daily routine can change your life. The easiest way to create a habit that will improve your life is to learn from those that you admire, who have taken the path ahead of you and who you can relate to. By taking their advice and implementing it into your own life, you to have the ability to get to where they are. With the right tools and a mindset full of self-belief and confidence in your ability, you can achieve anything that you set out to.

Fear is a primitive emotional reaction created in the brain that sends a message to our body to activate a response to keep us safe. Known as the fight, flight, fawn and freeze response, this automatic physiological reaction occurs to protect us from potential danger or threat. This was positive back in the day, when our ancestors fought to survive, but nowadays, this fear can play a part in inhibiting our growth and development. It can keep us stuck in a cycle that will prevent change. The only way to conquer this is to face it head on. Get comfortable with being uncomfortable and work through the emotions. Make a habit of doing the things that frighten you often to help break through the feeling. It can be the most liberating thing that you've ever done and can create the biggest change.

Lastly, I'd recommend moving your body. Move it, feel it and enjoy it. Put some of your favourite music on and let the energy flow. Lose yourself in the sensations and embrace the body that you have been given. Feel how the energy lifts you up, makes you feel alive and in the moment. Notice how creative and light you feel and how it can be an instant boost to your mood. By moving the energy around your body you are playing a part in freeing any energy blocks that you might be holding onto through negative beliefs and emotions. It is great to allow these to be released so you can move forward.

When the time is right and your desire is strong, you will know when you are ready to make a change and as long as you work on it daily, there will be no stopping you. If this is you, I'd like you to start working on the belief that you CAN, as I have been there and know that if I can, you most certainly can too.

It has taken a lot of work and dedication, but I now wake up seizing the day. The quality of my life has improved greatly with an understanding that I deserve it, as do my boys. We are worthy of living the best life that we possibly can. I now have the freedom of time to enjoy an exceptional work/life balance, to be there for the boys and follow my passion and now, my life purpose. I'm now more comfortable with the feeling of judgement and rejection as I have realised that the only way to conquer it, is to face it. I have faith in who I am and what I do and make it part of my habit to live a conscious life.

Hitting rock bottom was the best thing that happened to me. It gave me the drive to make a change. I am now the most comfortable that I have ever been in my own skin and the most physically fit. Waking up, I now know that my day is going to be full of passion and purpose and I'll be surrounded by people who lift me up and only want the best for me. I know that with this mindset, I will only attract what I put out and now live by the affirmation that only abundance, joy and success surrounds me.

I have made the conscious decision to get out of my own way and realise that I matter, I'm worthy, and I'm very capable. I know that my life purpose is to help others believe that they can also achieve anything that they want. I work with my clients to help empower them to believe that with clarity, vision and self-belief, they can focus and take actionable steps to create the life that they desire. Being my authentic self means that there is no longer any hiding. I can show up as who I really am, with my unique gifts to the world, like I am meant to. I now realise that by hiding, I was doing a disservice to my community as they weren't aware that I even existed to help them. As parents, we are role models for our children and along with inspiring other women, I want my boys to believe that they too can be and do anything that they desire and to know that this life is for living.

I would like to share with you some life-changing results that have come about from some ongoing coaching sessions I've recently had with a client.

When Joanna first came to me, she was lacking in direction and clarity in where she wanted her life to be. As a single mother, she was living pay cheque to pay cheque, stuck in an unfulfilling job that was just making ends meet. She was putting the needs of her children before her own and just couldn't see how she could make a change. She felt like she was on a hamster wheel with no way of getting off. The relationships that she had been in didn't seem to go anywhere and she had a deep sense that something within her was holding her back. She had forgotten what her passions were as she had been living in survival mode, and so, wanted to find her life's purpose.

When we first started working together, we focused on her relationships, what she used to do in her spare time that lit her up and on what she wanted her ideal day to look like. To seek clarity, we did some guided visualisation to identify what she wanted to attract into her life and to allow a space for her to get excited about her dreams. Throughout the sessions, we discovered that her own limiting beliefs were blocking her from moving forward. She hadn't been allowing herself to gain clarity on what she truly wanted as she didn't believe that she was worthy of achieving it. This had come from a childhood trauma that made her feel like she didn't matter. It knocked her confidence and had subsequently made an impact on her current reality. We worked through some of the negative emotions that were holding her back by doing an Emotional Freedom Technique session to shift her beliefs. Together, we set actionable steps on what she could do to move forward and create change.

I am so proud of what Joanna has achieved from our time working together. She has enrolled on a course to become a hypnotherapist, as she has always had the desire to help others. This decision will allow her to work flexible hours and create more time with her young family. It will also elevate her finances to allow her to travel and do more of the things they love together.

As for her relationships, she has shifted her mindset after realising that she was attracting the wrong type of partners, who were merely a reflection of how she felt about herself. She now realises how talented, strong, capable, worthy and loveable she is and tells herself this daily. By doing this, she has attracted someone that can also see those qualities in her. Someone who is aligned and brings out the best in her, as she now believes that she is worth it. She is no longer playing small and floating from one day to the next. She has vision, drive and is excited for all that is to come. Making the decision to invest in a coach has certainly paid off for her and by working on her mindset, she has had a massive shift in how she feels about herself, what she wants and who she wants to be with.

The road to change always starts with you. You are in the driving seat heading towards your destination and your intuition knows the right direction to take. Having the right mindset is a great foundation, having a vision will allow you to gain clarity and consciously planned action will allow you to take the steps to get there. Negative beliefs or emotions need not hold you back and by either shifting them or facing them head on, you can create more space in your mind for more positive thoughts to enter, and move forward to focus on your goals and dreams.

You are capable of being and doing whatever you dream of as long as you are clear on how you are going to get there. Being mindful of your energy and that which surrounds you will support your growth and encourage more of what you want. Your mind is always listening and therefore, you become what you believe, and others will treat you according to how you treat yourself.

Creating a conscious life will allow you to find your passions and life's purpose. You will be able to design a life that works around you and your loved ones and one that is fully aligned with your values and mission.

To seek clarity on what you would like your life to look like, identify the things that light you up, heal the past and find a way to achieve your dreams, then joining one of my 1-1 coaching packages is a great place to start. Each block offers a number of coaching sessions and, depending on your needs, can include an embodiment practice of either Energy Healing, Emotional Freedom Technique or Yin Yoga, to help release any stuck emotions or beliefs that you might be holding onto.

If you are ready to upgrade your life to one in full colour, step aside from fear and rise to be the person that you're meant to be, visit lucyciaramella.com or reach out to me at lucy@lucyciaramella.com

ABOUT THE AUTHOR
LUCY CIARAMELLA

Lucy Ciaramella is a Life Transformation Coach who helps women that feel stuck in their life or career gain clarity, confidence and momentum to become the best version of themselves and manifest a life they truly desire.

Lucy is also a trained Holistic Therapist, Yoga Teacher and Reiki Master who has worked in the Wellness industry for 13 years. She combines her coaching practice with the holistic energy healing practices of Reiki, Yin Yoga and EFT, to help her clients heal from events of the past and embody the change that they want to make.

Lucy spent years searching for her ideal career before she turned her passions of personal development, holistic wellbeing and fitness, into her purpose. Throughout this time, she gained invaluable experience in various roles that have all helped her get to where she is today.

During the early years of motherhood, Lucy found herself hitting rock bottom. Her marriage was falling apart, she was exhausted and she had lost her identity. All of her energy had gone into ensuring that her young family's needs were met and she was left with none for herself. Something had to change. A shift in mindset, prioritising self-care, re-introducing fitness and making positive nutrition a way of life, all helped to turn Lucy's life around.

Since this time, Lucy's mission and purpose has been to help as many other females who are in a similar position to where she was, uplevel their mindset and turn their life around to create more fulfillment, abundance and joy.

Lucy, originally from Scotland, now lives in Sussex with her family. Being a true Piscean, Lucy is drawn to the sea and her favourite place to be is at the beach. She is a lover of fitness, food, long walks in nature, travel, music, reading and dance.

If you are ready to make a change and uplevel your life to one in full colour, Lucy is available either online or in person, for 1-1 or group coaching sessions.

You can reach Lucy at:

Email: lucy@lucyciaramella.com
Website: lucyciaramella.com

facebook.com/lucyciaramellacoaching
instagram.com/lucyciaramella

17

MEL WAKELY

BE A PHOENIX AND RISE

Today, I'm on a mission to be a cheerleader for business-owning mums - the high-achieving, badass, entrepreneurial women who deserve to be the best they can and be unapologetic about it. So many of these amazing women are in fear of getting visible online. The thought of showing their faces and being vulnerable gives them the jitters.

Instead, they choose to hide behind the safety of their beautiful styled-out branded photography instead of showing the real them.

The pandemic has created a shift in how people want to consume social media and be entertained. Video content has always been important, but now, I believe it has to be an important tactic for any female entrepreneur who wants to grow a personal brand online. The growth of TikTok is testament to this and Instagram quickly followed suit with Reels in August 2020.

In January 2020, I was a "hiding" woman. I was petrified of going live on social media or even doing a pre-recorded video. I was happy in my comfort zone, earning just enough to pay the bills and have a nice life. But deep down, I was bored as a social media manager for events companies. It didn't light me up. It was a freelance 'job' and not particularly aligned with my values.

Sadly, the events industry was hit hard by the pandemic, and I lost all my clients.

Was this serendipity? Did the universe have plans for me?

I've always loved to have fun and not take life too seriously, but at the same time, I always wanted to be successful. Finding a way to align these two values never happened in my 20s and 30s.

I had a career in PR and marketing, and although I loved some aspects of it, other parts, left me cold. Earning money and going to work was always just a necessity to afford my lifestyle, rather than a passion.

In October 2020, I began Andrea Callanan's Unapologetic Self-Mastery container. I was a different woman then from the one I am now. When I started the course, I was armoured to the hilt. No f**ker was going to 'see' me. I spent the first six weeks of the three-month course hiding in the Facebook group, in utter fear. I was being triggered by other people who were so comfortable 'going live' all the time and sharing their story. So many times, I told myself it was the wrong decision: What the hell have I signed up to? I want my money back! But thankfully, I stuck it out because in the end, it was life changing.

At the beginning, I was not ready to share anything except the version of me that I'd edited and that kept me safe. Only my besties got the real me. My coach had her work cut out!

This is my Phoenix story. Lean in and learn why I made the decision to "Be a Phoenix and Rise" and how I transformed myself from a woman armoured to the hilt, standing 100% in my masculine, to the soulful, smiling woman I am today.

Discover how this Generation X party girl, mother, and wife found her soulmate coach who, over 12 months, helped me to get vulnerable, get visible and get happy by finding my purpose as a Mindset and Visibility Strategist.

What does "Being Seen" or "Getting Visible" mean to women who are not natural extroverts or who can't bear the thought of what others may think of them if they do show their true selves? It means something scary. Something best avoided. Something to hide from.

Let's rewind to 2020, when I was hiding. The thought of putting myself out there on a livestream, pre-recorded video or even my face in photos gave me the heebie jeebies. I was in fear. Fear of what other people would think of me – she's fat, she doesn't know what she's talking about, she's making a fool of herself. Does this resonate with you?

I had many limiting beliefs that I had no real awareness of and even now, often find it hard to articulate my feelings. Having done the subconscious work, I understand they were formed during my childhood. My dad was career R.A.F. This meant that from toddlerhood until I was 10 years old, we moved around every 2 years or so. The transient, nomadic life meant that any friendships I formed were short-lived. I grew a thick skin and learned to be wary of developing deep friendships. Aged 10, I went to boarding school. This made me strong and independent, but also fearful of being rejected. The fear of being rejected has played out in my adult years with patterns of co-dependency in relationships and even with clients. Even now, I only have a few very close friends, although I am getting better at being more vulnerable and opening up to new people I meet.

I've been self-employed, running a freelance business since 2010, when my first son was born. For the first 5 years (2010- 2015) it suited me, with kids under 5, to have easy part-time freelance work. But from 2015 onwards, when my eldest started big school, my stubborn personality and fixed mindset kept me stuck in my business. I like to call this time my 'fannying around' period! I knew, deep down, that I was meant for more, but I was too comfortable and, if I'm honest, too lazy to do anything about it.

The social media marketing consultancy work I did for my clients paid me just enough. It was easy but dull. I needed inspiration. I needed someone to ignite the entrepreneurial fire inside me. Two pivotal moments happened in 2020 that started my transformation.

First, I decided to invest a lot of money in a Facebook Advertising course which I hoped would add a new revenue stream and an in-demand skill to my business. On this course, I met a mindset and voice coach, Andrea Callanan. The second thing that happened was a global pandemic.

Being a female entrepreneur is hard. But being a female entrepreneur and a mum is harder. It's hard emotionally, mentally, and physically.

Emotionally, we have mum guilt. Mentally, we have *all* the mental load and the multitasking. Physically, we have periods, hormone imbalance, peri and menopause plus the actual childbirth and breastfeeding.

In 2021, I celebrated my 49th birthday. In previous years, I would have been a bit in the doldrums about the speed at which I was advancing towards 50. But this year, I decided no more of that rubbish. Instead, I set two intentions. The first was to hold a big 50th birthday party with a live band and all the trimmings! Second, I told myself I would like to make a million before I'm 60. I heard the other day only 2% of female entrepreneurs make 7 figures and 90% make less than 6 figures a year. Why isn't it okay for women to create wealth? This should be something that's acceptable, but even in 2021, a gender wealth inequality still exists.

Since I set this intention, I haven't been afraid to share my vision with friends and family members. Some say, "good for you" and others laugh, like they don't believe me. Maybe this is because I've never considered myself to be a "high achiever" – not in the traditional sense anyway. I never got the top grades, I didn't make prefect or head girl, didn't excel at sports or make the school team. Not me. I was the cool girl. The rebel. The rule breaker. I was more interested in having fun, wearing the latest fashion, listening to the top tunes, and blagging my way to success. I always did 'just enough' to get on in my life. And for much of my life, this was enough. Until it wasn't.

Let's go back to January 2020 again and a wake-up call I had in Heals (the posh furniture shop). I was playing that imaginary game – you know the one... where you pretend you have an abundance of cash to spend. I'm trying out a gorgeous, eye-wateringly expensive sofa, dreaming of my dream abundant life, when my inner critic pipes up.

"What the F are you doing Melanie?" (My inner critic is so potty mouthed).

"You're made for more than just daydreaming".

"Nah," I say, "I'm perfectly fine. I'm so comfy".

"But aren't you just a bit bored, Melanie?"

"No, I'm fine," I say. But you know what? Deep down, I was bored to tears.

By October 2021, I only had one of my event industry clients left. I'd been working with them for almost four years. They were a lovely, retained client, who paid me well. I felt aligned to them and their business, and we got on brilliantly.

The client often praised me (significance driver for me), which I loved. I was just fine. I had enough time to be a good wife and a great mum. It was all tickety-boo. BUT WAS IT?

Is 'just fine' enough? Does it mean you're happy? Does it mean you're fulfilled? Does it mean you're striving for more or does it mean you're coasting? Do you know what I mean? Have you felt like this too?

I wanted more, but I didn't know how to make the change. I was stuck in my comfort zone.

I remember waking up on New Year's Day, 2020, and feeling full of excitement for the year ahead. I'd made a pact with myself that 2020 was the year for my business to grow. I'd invested in a Facebook Ads course, with the fabulous Emma Van Heusen. I was ready to level up and grow my business.

My inner critic was right. I am meant for more. ALL WOMEN ARE.

In 2020, I was a freelance social media manager, working three days a week with clients in the events industry. I was earning 'just enough', and the work was easy but a bit boring. It wasn't stretching me, and it certainly wasn't filling me with joy. I got my kicks from family life and partying at weekends.

I was at a crossroad in my life, unsure of the path ahead.

It's hard to find the courage to take a leap into the unknown.

Since leaving Goldsmith's university of London in 1993, I've worked only in sales and marketing.

First, I sold press advertising to record companies for mags like iD, Select, and The Big Issue.

Next, I did guerrilla marketing and PR stunts at Cunning Stunts. The agency that projected a naked Gail Porter onto the Houses of Parliament for FHM Magazine.

So, when I lost my lovely, retained client in March 2021, I felt backed into a corner. I didn't know how to do anything except social media and marketing. With the help of my coach and the amazing women I've met through my group coaching networks, I realised what I needed to do was to get as visible as possible online and the way to do that was through using video.

Marketing has changed an awful lot since I started working in the early '90s. When I started selling advertising on magazines, I didn't even use email - shocker, I know! Working in music and style magazines during the Britpop years was a lot of fun. We wined and dined advertising agencies, with these ridiculously expensive lunches in swanky London restaurants, never returning to the office for any work later. I had backstage access to all the best gigs, including Oasis at The Astoria and Knebworth. I worked with an amazing man called Andrew Creighton at The Big Issue and later at iD magazine. He went on to create the Vice Media empire...

But while on the surface it all sounds very fun and glam, I don't ever remember feeling particularly fulfilled or having a purpose that was meaningful. It was just a means to an end. Money to pay for partying and rent. Before doing the inner subconscious work, I used to spend hours beating myself up about these lost years with no purpose. Now, I celebrate the life experiences, and anyway, isn't that what your twenties should be about?

I'm grateful for all the life experiences and stories it's afforded me, but let's be honest, you can't dine out on pinching Liam Gallagher's bum at an after-show party forever. I was never going to be some skinny groupie, hanging around, waiting to pull and find a rich husband. Ha-ha!

In 2007, I was working as head of events at a PR firm in London. My main client was a London destination. I was responsible for a £1 million budget for their 6 weeks of Christmas events extravaganza.

It was the toughest client and event I've ever managed. Nothing I did was ever good enough for the client or my boss (both women). I worked tirelessly through the night, in freezing temperatures, managing the installation of handmade decorations designed by film set designers that looked amazing, and the next day the client would stride around saying "nah, don't like them". The final blow came when I got a phone call from an important local stakeholder. There had been a mix up with the schedule and we had agreed that our performances wouldn't clash with his services... the night in question, we had The Gay Men's choir performing and the stakeholder was livid. I lost my temper with him and, as a result, got fired.

I was on the verge of burnout. My self-worth and self-esteem were destroyed from the bullying. I vowed to never to work in an agency again. I'm proud to say that I've never worked in corporate again, apart from some freelance work, completely on my own terms.

My learning from this experience is that not all women are supportive, but there's always a reframe. Mine was to use this as an opportunity to travel. My husband and I made a big decision to take a year out to travel around the world. It was 2008, and as the financial recession hit, it was a brilliant time to escape. It was amazing. So many happy memories.

This is just my (fairly low brow, but fun) career path; every mum has a path.

We all make decisions along the way – from important-at-the-time GCSE choices to following a boy to university, to getting married or not, and ultimately deciding how to make everything you've worked for in your 20s and 30s, work with your family in your 40s.

I'm friends with bankers, business mums, photographers, TV producers, stay-in-corporate mums, stay-at-home mums, Insta-mums, Instablaggers, mum side-hustlers, designer mums, the don't-give-a-shit mums, the school-swot mums, and everything in-between mums!

The unifying thing for all of us is the struggle to retain our pre-mum identity, and to find work we love that fits family life with little compromise.

We're lucky to live in a digital, internet led world. This world has opened the doors for mum entrepreneurs to sell their thing online, whether it's print-on-demand t-shirts, artisanal food, or hypnobirthing classes... just a few of my client's choices for flexible working that works with kids.

There were some pivotal moments during my 20s and 30s which shaped my path and which I probably wouldn't even have had awareness of if I hadn't done the inner subconscious work. I'd like to share three of these with you:

The first is that not all women are kind and supportive.

The second is, to succeed as a woman in business you must be single-minded about your intentions and goals while at the same time, coming from a place of integrity.

The third is there's more to life than having a career. Much, much more.

It's okay to have fun. It's okay to enjoy being the centre of attention. And the hardest one for me is, it's okay to be vulnerable.

But the biggest one is accepting and being okay with how much I love to have fun and realising that you can have a successful business and have fun at the same time.

I love that despite ALL the challenges women face, we are massively on the rise as entrepreneurs. Like myself, women are waking up to a realisation they can have success without compromising family life and without apologising.

The thing I love the most about my work now is seeing women getting a dopamine hit from going live and making social media videos that really connect with their audience.

For me, the Gen X party girl, the buzz is not dissimilar from being at a rave or gig with 1000s of people – remember that?!

I see them get that buzzy feeling after they've had an Instagram Reel get over 1000 views, or a live stream with lots of comments from their followers. It's this that motivates me to carry on in my quest to help as many women like me, to do the mindset work and unlock this feeling for themselves.

I love seeing my client's faces, when they have that 'a-ha moment'(so what I think if you're over 40, knackered, feeling a bit saggy, drained from trying to remember all the STUFF), they realise they've found a way to get back that feeling and that lost identity of partying in your twenties. If you want it, the online space is wide open for the taking, you just need to have the desire and the expertise to rise and standout from the crowd.

You need to embrace the fear and be courageous. *Courageous* means having, showing, or doing *with courage*—the quality of being ready and willing to face negative situations involving danger or pain.

I know this is easier said than done. Our internal "Little Miss Fear" a.k.a., our subconscious mind or inner critic is there for a reason - to keep us safe. But the subconscious mind can be reprogrammed through courage and mindset. I have told myself I'm good enough so many times now, that my subconscious mind has started to believe it's true. This self-belief gave me the courage to do my first live on Instagram – which was far from perfect, but I celebrated that I had done it and progress is always better than waiting for perfection.

In 2021, when I relaunched my business, I didn't realise how many women there are who, like me, are Generation X, successfully running their own businesses but scared to embrace social media marketing. All of them in fear of making a fool of themselves, of being laughed at by the peers and of failing to grow an online personal brand.

For a long time, I've believed there's something extra special about women of the '90s rave generation.

We're young at heart and spirited. We're wise from all our living life to the full. We know we won't ever look like we did in our twenties but we're definitely not ready to be classed as 'past it'. We're on the rise later in life – probably because we had children in our late 30s, early 40s.

Some of us are embracing social media and leveraging its power to grow our personal brands online. But some of you haven't yet embraced social media. Some of you don't understand how to use it. Some of you think it's only for Millennials. Is this you?

Do you have a vision of a future that gives you freedom? Not only financial freedom, but also time. Time to enjoy your family life, and run your own business, a business that makes you feel 100% fulfilled but not overworked.

Believe me, it is all there for the taking. All you need is self-belief and expert knowledge in something that solves a problem or fulfils a desire for someone.

I'm nearly 50 and only just embarking on my entrepreneurial experience. I don't think it's too late for me. In fact, I think it's the perfect time for me to rise and share my expert marketing knowledge with the world. The Global Pandemic has changed the way we work and use the internet like nothing before. The growth of online learning and services is in huge demand – recent stats show **e-learning is expected to grow by over 250% between 2017 to 2026** (*Source: Business Wire*).

We are all experts in something. What is your superpower? Are you ready to share it with the world? Are you bored of your 9-5? Are you fed up serving your clients one on one and working your butt off? Do you want more than being a mum with a part-time business?

Do you have a story to share that could help others? Do you want to reignite your 'before kids' identity? Do you want to make money and have fun again? Do you want to get a dopamine hit from working on your successful and growing business? Do you want to give yourself permission to have fun and make money? Do you want to rise and be seen?

Did you say a BIG FAT YES to any of these questions? Don't wait a minute longer. Give yourself permission to find the thing that lights you up. I invite you to just do it and enjoy the experience of getting visible and sharing your amazing expertise and knowledge with the world. What have you got to lose?

I hope this resonates with you. Have you always felt you're made for more? But for some reason, you're still sitting in your comfort zone, feeling 'just fine', even though deep down, you've got this itch for more? More freedom. More financial security. More time.

If you're in your mid to late 40s and thinking it's too late for you, please think again! There's so much you can do in your later years. I'm proud to share with you my story of discovery and learning since working with my coach. I hope that my insights and thoughts will help you to overcome your fears around being seen so you too can step aside and rise.

Why do women like you and I get stuck in our comfort zones? For me, I lacked confidence and self-belief after having children. I think a lot of women lose some of their pre-being-a-mum identity, along with their self-esteem, confidence, and courage after having kids. One of the most pervasive and harmful notions we perpetuate in our society is the idea that, once a woman has a child, she ceases to be a woman and is, from that moment on, only considered a mum. That doesn't happen to men who become dads. Dads are still allowed to be men with their own separate personalities and lives

Isn't it interesting, if you're determined to make a success of something, the universe sometimes has other plans for you? Have you experienced this? You make an important decision for your business. One that you strongly believe will help your business to grow. But it isn't to be.

Three things happened in 2020 that sent me on a different path:

The first was the numbers. You need to be good with numbers to be able to leverage the best results for your clients with Facebook ads. I have a problem with numbers and therefore, a problem with Facebook Ads Manager. I hated the maths but loved the creative and strategy side.

The second was being in the Covid Cohort. Go figure!

The third thing that changed my path was meeting my mindset and business coach.

Here's a thing... At the time of the first lockdown, I was totally directionless, like a duck treading water. Juggling a business in lockdown with home-schooling to manage was a tough gig. I salute all the business owning mums that did this. I see us as the unsung heroes of the pandemic.

My coach helped me to find my purpose. I grew awareness that having fun is an important part of my identity and rather than feeling ashamed of it, I should celebrate it. If I wanted to build an aligned business that brings me joy, I needed to find a way to cleverly blend my need to have fun within my business model.

Over the next 6 months, I broke through layer upon layer of some of the thickest armour you can imagine! I had been protecting myself for years, but my coach's Unapologetic Self-Mastery course was a life changing experience for me. I became part of a group of women who all had issues with their self-worth. We all had something in our stories that caused us to be stuck in our progression. These are things like self-judgement, procrastination, self-sabotage, perfectionism, and ego, that so many high-achieving women, like me, need to work through.

I've learnt that mindset is a daily practice, and this inner work is very much still in progress, but now, instead of beating myself up about it, not feeling good enough and feeling like a failure, I've learned to see things differently:

There's no such thing as failure, only learnings to improve for next time.

It's better to progress than wait until you decide it's perfect.

We are all good enough.

Being vulnerable is a gift and it's important to share your vulnerability with the world to grow your personal brand.

When I lost my lovely client in March 2021, my first reaction was panic. But after a few days, it dawned on me that perhaps this was serendipity. After all, I was ready to embark on a new and exciting chapter in my life.

I re-launched Mel Wakely Marketing and launched a new business for start-up mums in business, called 'Social Media Ravers'. See there how I've added in the fun element?!

I followed my heart and decided to focus on the thing that I love more than anything else. My passion is to empower mum entrepreneurs to embrace social media and improve their online visibility through one on one and group coaching. Working with me will help them destroy the mind monsters around showing their faces online and instead, they will start to love the buzz of going live and have fun creating short-form videos, which are one of the easiest and quickest ways to grow your audience online.

Do you feel like you're made for more? Are you stuck in your comfort zone? Are you ready to level up and get into the growth zone? Does this sound like you?

- You have a successful one on one service-based offering and are doing *just fine,* but you yearn for more freedom and income in your business.
- The thought of going live on Instagram give you the jitters.

- You think Reels and TikToks are only for Millennials.
- You don't want to show anything of your 'non-professional' life, so stories are all about your business and nothing behind the scenes.
- During the pandemic, you got to grips with Zoom and worked successfully with your 1-1 clients. This has opened your eyes to a new and more flexible way of working online and possibly, 'one to many' group coaching.
- You're on social media (Instagram, Facebook, and LinkedIn) but you don't enjoy it. It doesn't feel natural to you, so you outsource the day-to-day management via a virtual assistant or social media manager.
- Because you're not showing up as yourself, your audience only sees the polished brand photography and pre-agreed captions that your team posts – they don't get to know the real you
- You know, deep down, you should be doing lives and social media video, sharing your lovely authentic story in your own voice, but you've always got an excuse like I'm too busy; too old; people will laugh and judge me; it's not for me, it's for millennials; it's stupid, all that dancing and pointing and lip syncing; I don't know how; I don't understand the tech; I just don't want to.

In the last 12 months, I've transformed my online visibility by strategically focusing on video content in Instagram Reels, Lives and Stories, using video and I've seen steady growth every month with these year-on-year stats:

- 450% increase in followers.
- 3898% increase in reach (this is the number of unique accounts that have seen my posts), 2124% increase in profile visits.
- 1971% increase in website clicks.

If you're a female entrepreneur that's scared of showing your face on social media and doesn't understand the tech to make great Reels and stories, let me help you!

- I support women like you with one-on-one coaching focused on leveraging your story and your beautiful self, so that you start to show up on social media using your own authentic voice. This will enable you to get more visible, grow your personal brand and increase your impact, influence, and income.
- You'll get super confident with training on how to create Reels, Stories and Lives that feature YOU (and no dancing or pointing is required if that's not your thing).
- We'll work on your personal brand strategy so that people get to know and love the real person behind the polished 'branded' photos.
- We'll destroy the mind monster around fear of judgement, fear of not being good enough, perfectionism and self-worth.
- You'll start believing that you're amazing, good enough and learn that being vulnerable is the best way to grow.
- If you do the work, you'll start enjoying it. Getting visible and being seen gives you that dopamine hit that all of us old '90s party girls crave from our clubbing days.
- Soon, you'll have more IMPACT, INFLUENCE, and INCOME, by harnessing the power of social media to grow your online business.

Even though my new business is in its infancy, I bring to the party over 25 years of marketing and life experience to share with my clients. I absolutely love helping women be the best versions of themselves online. So far, I've been lucky to work with many mum entrepreneurs, all of whom have experienced a transformation of their online visibility.

My first client was a Personal Trainer who wanted to level up her online presence to grow her business. She said:

"You're a superstar! I feel so supported, especially as I am 100% technophobic! Thanks for sharing your social media strategies and tips. My Instagram and Facebook pages are growing quickly, as are my Zoom personal training sessions. Your recommendations have made a massive difference to my business during Lockdown"

Next, two amazing women with over 40 years of experience between them as personal impact coaches, but 100% 1-2-1 model offline. They said:

"Pre-Pandemic, our business model was all face to face and any new business came through recommendations. Then everything changed. We started working online and realised the flexibility and potential we could offer clients...

We knew nothing about how to leverage social media to launch online.

Mel showed us a new way to build a business.

She created a launch strategy that's practical and manageable.

Mel knows the online world inside out.

She's been a massive inspiration with loads of creative ideas.

Our confidence on Instagram has grown from zero to hero - and we can even do Reels now!

Mel's persuaded us out of our comfort zone into our growth zone - and we can't wait for the adventure ahead!"

Now, I'm a different woman. Everyone in my life has noticed and commented on my transformation. Now I smile a lot - that's a biggie. AND, even better, I'm not divorced, which I probably would be if I hadn't learned about the drama triangle and how to step out of it. I invested £6,000 in my personal development in 2020, and even though I lost all my events clients in the pandemic,

I have zero regrets. In fact, I invested even more this year to join a business accelerator and as a result, my business is going from strength to strength.

Now, I'm kicking myself that I didn't invest in myself sooner. It simply is the best gift you can give yourself, so if you're thinking of investing in your own development, just bloody do it!

Truth bomb! There's no magic wand. Growing your personal brand online is all to do with mindset, strategy, and technical know-how.

If you work with me, I can show you how I went from hiding and in victim mode, with low self-worth and no clients, to how I am today. I embraced the fear. I ignored my inner critic and decided I didn't care any more about what other people think. I stopped comparing myself to others, reminding myself daily that we are all at different stages so it's impossible to compare. I taught myself how to master video to grow my personal brand on Instagram.

Let me hold your hand and share everything with you so that you too can have fun on Instagram, while at the same time increase your visibility, audience, and clients.

Be honest with yourself. Are you hiding and in fear of showing your face like I was? Do you know, deep down, this is the one thing that's holding you back? I invite you to get in touch if you feel inspired, to see if together, we can get you unstuck with an Instagram growth strategy using the power of video in Reels, Lives and Stories (no dancing or pointing necessary if that's not your thing!)

If my clients can get over their fears of showing their faces online, being vulnerable, finding and sharing their authentic brand voice, then so can you!

I invite you to step out of your own way and instead, like me and the women I work with, BE A PHOENIX AND RISE.

ABOUT THE AUTHOR
MEL WAKELY

Mel Wakely is a Marketing, Mindset & Visibility Strategist *with a difference.*

She helps female entrepreneurs unlock their fears around being visible and show them how to leverage the power of social media to grow their personal brands online.

Mel brings to the party, over 25 years of sales and marketing experience gained whilst working for marketing and PR agencies on accounts including MINI, Tango, FHM, PlayStation and Smirnoff.

She has experience in sales, PR, experiential marketing, and event production.

In 2010, she set up a marketing consultancy working exclusively with events companies offering business development and marketing consultancy. In 2016, she trained with Digital Mums and fell in love with social media. Mel brings so much amazing value and insight to her female clients. Supporting them to get over their fears around judgement and self-worth so they can start being seen authentically online through the power of social media video.

Mel has transformed herself by doing the inner subconscious work. She has found her life's purpose and is on a mission to share her value through mirror-coaching other women on the mindset and visibility strategies that have transformed her business and life.

Like Mel, the women she helps have limiting beliefs around self-judgment and self-esteem. They are likely to be perfectionists or procrastinators, who routinely hide and self-sabotage because they don't believe they're good enough.

Mel still loves to be the life and soul of the party. Her kitchen discos are legendary, but a little bit less wild than in the '90s. She absolutely loves living and being part of an amazing community in Walthamstow, East London, with her husband and two boys. She loves English beaches in winter, all kinds of music, from rave to Britpop, festivals and music gigs, Spanish red wine, and Marmite on toast.

Mel is available for one-on-one coaching sessions, via Zoom or in-person. She has several packages to suit all budgets. She is also the founder of Social Media Ravers – a supportive community for women who raved in the '90s and now run their own businesses and need help with their social media.

You can reach Mel by emailing mel@melwakely.com or connecting with her on LinkedIn or Instagram.

Did you party in the '90s and now run a business?
Want to improve your socials? Join my free Facebook Community
SOCIAL MEDIA RAVERS

instagram.com/melwakely
linkedin.com/in/melwakelymarketing

RACHEL HARVEY
A JOURNEY TO SELF-BELIEF

The woman I am today is an entrepreneur who has developed multiple brands in the education, E-commerce and social media marketing sectors. I consider myself a lifelong learner who loves to learn new skills and integrate these into my businesses and personal development. Along the way to becoming the woman I am today, I learned a truly integral lesson: that my feelings of self-worth must come from within. I must not rely on anyone else or the results from my business for that validation. It's this story that I'd like to share with you. I hope in reading it, I can show you that you too can overcome any current obstacles or stories you've told yourself about not being 'enough', so you too can "Step Aside and Rise" to become the woman that you want to be and have the business that you desire.

I'm proud that, as a single mother and woman of mixed race, I raised myself up and put myself through university. I achieved a 1st class honours degree in primary teaching with science, and also a distinction in a masters in education - the latter whilst working full-time as a teacher, in an atmosphere of bullying and intimidation.

However, I knew I was meant for more. I went on to build those successful six-figure businesses and I also purchased my first home, creating the life that I'd dreamt of for myself and my son.

I used the traumas and adversity I have faced throughout my life to develop the resilience to continue, even when I felt I couldn't go on. It drove me firstly to create an education business that has helped and impacted the lives of students whom my business served, and still drives me now, with the businesses I help to grow and scale through my Facebook and Chatbot marketing agency.

I have invested in myself, with both business and mindset coaches, to help bring me to the place I am today. I always think of myself as a work in progress. There are always more people to learn from and I have an insatiable appetite for learning. I have a love of reading and the list of books I've read would probably fill a book!

I want to give credit to the coaches I've worked with. As well as the many books I've read and communities I've joined. These have given me the tools and accountability that enabled me to reach the current place of happiness I now reside in. It's not always easy and can be a roller coaster of emotions, but I want you to know that you too can Step Aside and Rise to your own place of love, happiness and fulfilment, whatever that looks like for you.

My life didn't always look like this however. At the age of around 15, I developed a burning desire to work in the Fashion industry as a model. I plastered my bedroom walls with covers of magazines, desperate to look like these beautiful ladies - especially the mixed race women I identified with (these were very few and far between). I loved make-up, skincare, fashion and anything to do with this industry. Having been told I was "ugly" as a younger teenager, this, I felt, was beyond my achievements at the time. But as being mixed race became more acceptable, and I grew older, people suddenly started asking me if I was a model! This gave me the impetus to take the steps to join an agency and my life as a model began.

From the outside, it probably appeared that I was living an exciting life. I was going on fashion shoots, shooting music videos and commercials, travelling, and even working on major movie productions. The highlight of these was probably being an air hostess in the Bruce Willis movie, The Fifth Element.

I got to hang out with various celebrities and had a busy social life - clubbing, drinking (too much!) and always on the go. Although at times, this was, of course, fun, on the inside, I wasn't happy.

The lack of self-worth and self-belief that I had developed as a child and learned to believe was true, impacted my thoughts and behaviours daily. The external validation I sought from others, through my work and my personal relationships, only compounded the beliefs. From being told I was "too dark skinned", "too light skinned" or too "exotic" on model castings, to being cheated on in my toxic, co-dependent relationships with men. All this just fed what I thought of as my truth. It confirmed all the horrible comments that I had heard about myself growing up and fed my feelings of no self-worth and of not being 'enough'.

I still remember the day I learnt that I needed to love myself, believe in myself and that I was enough. It was a cold, crisp Monday morning in December, and I was in the throes of a deep depression, wondering what the point of my life was. I felt stuck, with no way out. As I sat at my computer, I remember working myself up to the discovery call I had with a coach I was considering working with. It was on that short call that my eyes were opened and a shift occurred...

In the space of 20 minutes, Andrea, who became my coach, was able to show me my life was full of abundance and I had plenty to be grateful for. This was the day that I began to rise up and get out of my own way. I realised that I had been looking for validation in the wrong places and from the wrong people. The only person whose validation I needed was my own.

Of course, this was, and continues to be, a journey, but I want you to know that, if I can get out of my own way to create the life of my dreams, so can YOU.

It took many years, and going through different traumas, to reach the stage where I finally understood this. I hope by sharing my story with you, it will help you leapfrog ahead to the learnings that I would love to have understood earlier and get you to the place you want to be sooner.

I spent many, many years on the hamster wheel of 'not enough'. You name it, I lacked it! Belief in myself; my worth; my intelligence and my appearance. I had imposter syndrome, thinking everyone else was better than me, that my work was not good enough. I let people treat me badly and speak unkindly to me, but probably the person who ended up being the most unkind to me, was me!

The stories that I told myself that were true, were all based on other people's opinions of me, or how I didn't fit in with their view of acceptable. Of course, now I know that the issue was theirs, not mine. But as a child, I didn't have that kind of understanding. So I grew up assimilating the negatives and weaving these into my story of who I was.

These beliefs followed me wherever I went. They were there through school, college, modelling, university, teaching and into my first business success (My, that's a long list!). I often thought I would be happier when I had achieved X and Y, or had this much money. Then I would feel better about myself. Of course, that never happened!

I found myself playing small and settling for less. I had money mindset issues; my skills couldn't possibly earn the money I wished I had. I not only put limits on my earning potential, but also on finding a partner who would love me for me (if I was slimmer, prettier, more successful, then someone would love me).

I drew people to me that I let fan the flames of these stories I had told myself, until they were huge fires that were out of control.

Where did these beliefs stem from? When I was a child, I often drew racist comments about the colour of my skin. The neighbourhood I lived in was predominantly white and although there were a few other families of colour, none were mixed race and looked like me.

I remember watching an episode of Oprah one day as an adult where she interviewed Mariah Carey. As a woman who is of mixed race, she said as a child, she had felt invisible. Neither fitting in with white children or children of colour. She even wrote a poem about it. I really identified with this as an adult and it answered some of the feelings I felt back then.

As well as this, I didn't have a happy home life. I was often told I was "naughty" and "bad". If someone tells you something often enough, you believe it. I now know that this was a poor choice of wording. Had I been told it was my behaviour and not me, I might well have told myself a better story, but as it is, the one I told myself was that I was not good enough to be loved.

Moving into my teenage years, I started being rejected by boys because of my skin colour. This built on the feelings of not fitting in, not being good enough to be loved, and a lack of self-worth. When I did start to have relationships with boys, then men, they didn't go well!

Fast forward to the relationship that created my pride and joy, my son, Aaron. I had come to the end of my modelling career and was attending acting lessons (I had such terrible stage fright, that I used to shake and never managed to go to an audition!). We met, fell in love, got engaged within a couple of months and I moved in. He didn't want me to work and at that time, my lack of self-worth and imposter syndrome was happy to go along with it.

Once I fell pregnant, everything changed. He very obviously started cheating on me with an ex-girlfriend. This caused me so much stress, that I went into early labour and my son arrived nine weeks early.

To cut a long story short, I was left with no home, huge debts (I let him use my bank account and credit card, as he had 'offshore' accounts) and a baby still in hospital. We were eventually housed in a hostel and I filed for bankruptcy. It took me years to rebuild my credit, which no doubt contributed to the money mindset issues that I had already developed.

Once my son and I had moved into our council flat, I started to think about how I could provide the life I wanted him to have. I wanted to set an example for him and show him that he could achieve anything he wanted from life. This is when I first felt that I was meant for more and found my 'why' and purpose.

I took myself off to university for the first of my degrees. My son was around 3.5 years old at this time. It was hard work but I met wonderful people and other 'mature' students like me, who were aiming to improve their lives and those of their families.

I think I always felt imposter syndrome during my teacher training. I now realise that this is because I am a high achiever and want to be the best I possibly can, to serve and help others achieve their potential and fulfil their dreams. So, once I nervously started at my first teaching job in an independent Catholic boys school, I was already carrying my stories of lack and imposter syndrome.

Instead of a nurturing environment, with an outlook of teaching and improving the newly qualified teacher that I was, I instead encountered senior staff who bullied and intimidated me. If it wasn't for all the lovely teachers who supported me through this tough time, I don't know that I would have lasted the three years I spent there in order to finish my masters in education.

With the end of my degree in sight, I knew I had to leave the toxic environment I had found myself in and couldn't imagine working in another school. The experience had left me with a longing to be free of this sort of establishment. But I had spent the best part of five years learning and developing skills in education and I didn't want this all to go to waste.

I had loved the feeling of being self-employed as a model, so I started scouring Google trying to find a way to use my education skills in a self-employed way. This is where I found my first business opportunity.

An education franchise. Perfect! The opportunity to build my own business, use my education skills and be my own boss. Or so I thought...

What do I mean by this? What I came to learn, after working with my self-mastery coach and reading many self-improvement books, is this: That until you have the self-love, self-worth, and self-belief in yourself, all the stories that you have come to believe over the years will go with you to each new job or business you build. Truth bomb! What?!

So, there I was with this successful business, not feeling happy or fulfilled. Still not feeling worthy and that I needed to be more. It felt like I needed a change, a new business to make me happy. I began to study again. More and more courses, this time developing skills in the marketing world. First email marketing, then Ecommerce. I built a new business selling products on Amazon. My new partner became involved and helped me grow and scale the business (whilst still running my education franchise).

It was at this time that I came across the law of attraction and joined my first mastermind. I began to learn about why I felt the way I did and how to do something about it. This helped for a while, but I didn't keep up the practices and I soon slid back into my pain and unhappiness.

I continued on, trying new ways to find happiness through work and learning new skills, whilst at the same time, feeling guilty that I wasn't spending enough time with my son. It was a perfect storm. Guilt, lack of self-worth, money mindset issues, living for the future yet stuck in the past.

This is when I came across a course in my Facebook feed advertising a course on social media marketing. "Ooh this looks perfect" I thought! I would be able to start a new business solely based around working from home, sell my franchise and get to spend more time with my son.

I went and bought the course. All good. But I soon realised that this was not quite it. Enter a renowned Facebook advertising coach. This was it! Finally, a way to earn more money, work from home and be able to sell my franchise. I put my franchise up for sale and began to build my new Facebook advertising agency.

It just so happened that as part of this course, mindset masterclasses were included. I was introduced to the amazing Andrea Callanan. She restarted my journey of self-discovery and her Self-Mastery course gave me the tools and belief that I was limitless. She took me from a place of fear and darkness to a place of belief in what's possible.

During this course, I began to untangle my story and the beliefs that I had told myself were true. I still, to this day, continue to use the tools she gave me. I have learned that when I'm about to level-up, I hit a new glass ceiling that I need to break through. Having the knowledge and strategies from her course and the subsequent books I have read, help me smash through those ceilings and continue onwards and upwards.

What can you do to Step Aside and Rise? If you resonate with my story and are letting your own lack of self-worth, self-belief and feeling 'less than' get in your way, my advice to you is to think about investing in yourself and work with a coach who can help you.

You may feel 'in lack' over money and think you can't possibly afford it. I used to feel that way too. Once I thought about it in terms of investing in myself, and that the return on that investment would increase my earnings, it became a no-brainer.

There are many different types of coaches out there and you'll need to read and research carefully to find whose story speaks to you. Finding a coach who has been through what you're going through will allow you to learn more quickly than going it alone. They will be the bridges that guide you across the mountainous landscape of building a business, helping you heal past traumas, learn from your story and release the mighty woman that you are.

There are also amazing mindset coaches out there who are astute business coaches too. They will propel you and support you through developing the right mindset to break down your personal barriers and help address any issues of 'lack'. They will also show you how to plan and execute the growth of your business.

Make sure you check testimonials and ask for recommendations. Check out their social profiles and websites. Try their masterclasses or challenges and see if you're a good fit. You could even join their free community and stalk (in a nice way!) them for a while. But do make sure you take advantage of a free discovery call so you get a taste of what they are like in person. After all, working with the right coach can be a real game-changer. It was for me.

Why am I telling you all about mindset coaches when I'm not a coach?

Coaches are not just for service-based business owners. If you're building a product-based business and sell online, or even in a physical store, you'll know that each level of growth needs the foundation of a positive mindset to push you through the pain barrier. Having a cheerleader and a community of like-minded people behind you is invaluable in the ups and downs of life as an entrepreneur.

What's mindset got to do with Ecommerce and Facebook advertising?

I know from my experience of having an Ecommerce business myself, and also working with clients in this space, it can take an unshakable belief to take those next steps, especially when you are working to a five or ten-year plan of growth. Not for the faint hearted!

You need to have all your money mindset issues dealt with so you're not worrying about paying staff, suppliers and yourself! You need to be able to trust in yourself and practice positive thinking.

One of my favourite quotes is from Napoleon Hill. He wrote the book 'Think and Grow Rich' in 1937. He said, "Whatever the mind of man can conceive and believe, it can achieve." A forerunner of the self-development movement and many of the self-help and law of attraction teachers that we know of today.

You might be at the stage when you know you're ready to level up from where your business is currently at, however, your mindset is telling you that selling your product en masse would be 'selling out', and you'll lose your small business ethics.

Try reframing the thought that you might be 'selling out'. Your independent brand has grown from a small loyal following to the point where the next step in your growth is paid advertising. If this makes you feel uncomfortable, I invite you to think of the changes that you're making as growth instead. Think of your ability to have a greater impact in how you serve and help your customers.

Of course, you may be ready and feel comfortable to take the next step in advertising your business. You'll be fully prepared in the knowledge that it can take a few tries before you get it right. Remember the saying "the faster you fail, the faster you succeed". It is by trying, and in the case of advertising, testing, that you learn and grow and increase profitability.

With this knowledge and experience, you will implement new processes and systems across your business, giving you greater efficiency and return on investments. This is true for all business owners, not just Ecommerce.

If you've developed your growth mindset and smashed through your limiting beliefs, but don't know if you're in the right place to invest in advertising to grow your business, these are the elements that I always ensure my clients have in place before my agency runs any paid advertising (these points also apply to service-based businesses too):

- Engaged social media channels to show the platform algorithms that you produce good content that people are interested in (also a great way to test content for paid advertising);
- Email marketing setup with automated sequences and consistent campaigns;
- A fully optimised website with a smooth, frictionless customer journey from landing on your site to making a purchase (or booking a call);
- Maximised average order with cross-sell and upsell (for Ecommerce);
- A proven offer that people purchase;
- The systems in place to fulfil the increased orders! (for Ecommerce).

If not, we offer our clients advice on what to do to get to that place, and assist with this, if wanted.

Just as it's crucial to find a coach whose values and beliefs align with yours, the same should be applied to any advertising/marketing agency you work with. If your business is not ready to amplify your direct sales with paid advertising yet, the agency should let you know and advise you how to get ready. If they promise you the earth, beware! There are no guarantees with advertising but you will be able to get predicted results based on certain statistics.

Working with an agency should feel like they're a trusted, extended member of your team. It should be an enjoyable experience for you both, with great communication. Book a free call and see how you feel when speaking with them. Check out their proposition and client reviews. Do they solve your problem or meet your desire?

So, when you have reached a growth mindset, having gotten out of your way and are ready to rise up to your next level, find an aligned agency, like mine, to help you fulfil your vision.

What does that vision look like?

For my clients, that looks like having a complete funnel in place that is tested and optimised at every stage for maximum profitability. You are confident that specialists are engaging your audience on social media, your email list is growing and making sales. Your website has the smoothest of customer journeys and is designed to maximise order value, as well as rank well on Google. Your advertising is targeted to the right people, at the right time, in the right place. As an Ecommerce business owner, you want the time to be able to work in your zone of genius, knowing that your sales funnel is taken care of for you, whether that place is being the CEO of your company, or feeling the joy of designing new products. You get to spend your days doing what you love because you know other aspects of your business are taken care of.

What did my change in mindset and need for external validation mean for me?

I went from being a model with mindset issues to a six-figure business owner in both service-based and Ecommerce businesses. I finally found my voice and passion.

It hasn't been easy to become visible and overcome the many stories I have told myself to be true, but I have worked through my traumas and beliefs to build an unstoppable mindset. I have finally got out of my own way to rise up and become the confident leader in my business that I always wanted to be.

I have developed a CEO mindset and I know and believe that I am 'enough'. With this 'can do' mindset, I know I am worthy and I help people to achieve what success looks like to them in their Ecommerce business. I support their vision, their impact, and this ripples out with every order they fulfil, bringing joy to people's lives with their products that delight, and, in some cases, creating wonderful family memories to treasure.

I love to be a part of these women's journeys and it brings me such pleasure to see their growth.

I know that I too will continue to grow and expand; to build brands and allow myself to be all that I desire. The shoes with the red soles that were on my vision board are now on my feet. I intend to keep achieving each item from my vision board and visualisations. I know I have more businesses of my own to build and grow and many more women to serve.

One of the best parts of being where I am today is the knowledge that I have had an impact on my son. There is no better feeling than being told that you are your child's inspiration. After all, Aaron has been my 'why' and has given me the strength and purpose to continue, even in my darkest of times.

I have demonstrated to him that building resilience, positivity and believing in yourself is key to living a life you love. That loving yourself and feeling good is at the core of your ability to attract what you desire.

I love that, at the tender age of 19, he already has multiple business ideas and we will be starting a joint venture together in the near future. He definitely has an entrepreneurial spirit!

The ability to set my own schedule, and the freedoms I now have, are all thanks to taking that first step and investing in myself. I hope you'll do the same for yourself.

What's next? My continued mission is to help women grow and scale the business of their dreams; for them to become visible and to assist them in making the impact they desire, whether that desire has an impact on their family life through increased income or more time with their kids, or on their own self-care, because they've been able to give themselves the gift of time through increasing their team members... Or even a global impact, from spreading the word on the products they sell and their brand values.

I love to see the progression of businesses as they start to scale. The excitement women feel as the brand they've worked so hard to build gathers momentum and attracts more loyal followers who spread the word.

Women like one client, who achieved a 490% return on her advertising budget and was then able to take her proof of concept for further funding. She went from no sales to getting an average of £8 back for every £1 spent - that's an 8x return on her budget.

How did she do this? By getting out of her own way and being able to apply the advice she was given to optimise her website, adverts and social media platforms. Taking that leap of faith because she had faith in herself and her business, and had found an aligned partner to work with. Trusting that my agency would treat her advertising budget as if it were our own, because she had taken the time to find out if we were a good fit. We used strategy and carefully thought through audiences and messaging, and we were thrilled to provide results beyond her expectations.

It's all about trusting and believing in yourself and your business. Another client that my agency worked with achieved a whopping return on investment of 945%. She had belief in herself and the services that her business provided. She knew that the treatments she gave women, and the results they achieved, needed to be shouted about from the rooftops! So, we went to work, designing her advertising campaign to show the results her treatment could achieve. By precisely targeting the right audience in her location with a message that resonated and a video to show how the treatment worked, we brought in her dream clients. This helped to fill the appointments that were available to maximise her return on investment.

If you've got a product or service that you know transforms and benefits people or fulfils their desires, you owe it to them to let them know! So put yourself and your business out there and serve those people who are waiting to hear from you. Believe in yourself and rise up!

I hope my story has shown you that you too can achieve whatever you desire. I know that you too can overcome any past traumas, feelings of lack and not being enough. You can live in the present without worrying about what the future holds. You can build a business that impacts many (if you want) or creates the family life you've dreamt of. You just need to take that first step on the journey to self-love, self-validation and belief in yourself.

You can travel and have the experiences you've always wanted. You can feel safe and secure around finances with a strong money mindset. Be the CEO of your business and lead from a place of kindness and strength. Be the boss you wish you'd had and a mentor to others. Nurture your children, your partner, your employees (if you have them). I have no doubts that you can do this and more.

Be the inspiration for your children and everyone around you.

If you'd like to find out if your business is ready for paid social advertising, download my guide at:

https://thebigimpression.com#fiveelements

ABOUT THE AUTHOR
RACHEL HARVEY

Entrepreneur and former fashion model, with a profound love of learning, Rachel Harvey has bootstrapped her successful Ad agency and training business to dizzying heights! Over the past decade, she has developed multiple brands in the education, e-commerce and social media marketing sectors.

Rachel has two degrees with distinctions in teaching and education, and has successfully transitioned her classroom teaching skills to helping others learn how to strategically manage their social media platforms. Having trained with some of the top global Facebook experts in the arena, today she runs The Big Impression, a specialist Facebook Ads agency which manages paid advertising for e-commerce businesses, achieving staggering ROIs of 945%!

Driven by the pursuit of excellence and single-minded about success, she is passionate about helping her clients birth their dreams and leveraging their businesses to a new level.

Away from the world of business and her beloved statistics, Rachel loves spending time with her son Aaron, who is a chip off the entrepreneurial block! At only 19 years of age, he's got multiple business ideas in the pipeline, including a joint venture with his mum! Rachel is also a self-confessed cat lady and a lover of shoes with red soles! Fun fact: Rachel appeared in the film The Fifth Element, which starred Bruce Willis, as one of the air hostesses. If you're of a certain age you may remember them!

You can reach Rachel at:

Email: rachel@thebigimpression.com
Website: https://thebigimpression.com/

facebook.com/BigImpressionHQ
instagram.com/big.impressionhq
linkedin.com/in/racheljharvey

19

ROSE BROWN

A MENTOR, MINDSET AND A CHESHIRE CAT

Here's me - a born high achiever, a people-pleaser in rehab. Imposter syndrome still creeps in from time to time - I'm only human, after all. But after 12 years of feeling in the wilderness, feeling disconnected from the 'old' me, from having little in the way of direction or purpose, I'm maybe more 'me' now than I ever was...

So, what changed? Well, I rediscovered things about myself that I'd long forgotten during the process of growing up and becoming that 'other' me - Mum. Yes, children change your world forever and yes, you'd never send them back (especially since they never come with a bloody returns label), but as you discover new things about yourself - like how much sleep you can survive on before delirium actually sets in and that you really do have endless amounts of patience - you also lose a bit of yourself too. And that, for me, was FREEDOM.

Nowadays, I have the freedom that I'd always craved and I am so grateful both for where I've been, and for where life still has to take me. It took a long time to get here, considering I essentially live in a country where the majority of us experience freedom daily. But, to me, freedom is CHOICE. And I now have an abundance of choice in my life: for my family, where I choose to work, when I choose to work, who I choose to help, who I align with, how I spend my time, how I charge my value.

Choice.

When I hit my first ever £5k month in my business, I felt grateful. When I take my children to school, take time off for sports day (and my god, my littlest is sooo competitive) or when my kids are ill, I feel grateful. When I sit down to speak to a client or my business bestie, I feel grateful. Because that freedom gives me choice.

Rewind two decades and I was a 20-year-old without much of a long-term plan. My father had just passed away from cancer, I was having to sell my beloved pony because we had to move away from my family home - the farm where I had grown up - and, to top it all off, I was in the middle of an undergraduate degree at Liverpool University. Despite having always been a high achiever and, in all honesty, someone who relied on their natural talents and memory to get them through, I was lost. Everyone around me had always expected me to go far, I'd never struggled at school, but I started to lack the self-confidence to really push myself.

> *Alice: "Would you tell me, please, which way I ought to go from here?"*
>
> *The Cat: "That depends a good deal on where you want to get to."*
>
> *Alice: "I don't much care where-"*
>
> *The Cat: "Then it doesn't matter which way you go."*
>
> — ALICE IN WONDERLAND, LEWIS CARROLL

I love quotes, and I've come back to this quote many times in my life. It always felt so apt - I didn't care much for the journey, but the destination remained fuzzy for a long time. I knew I was meant for more but didn't really know what 'more' looked like or how I'd get there.

If I could go back in time to my 20-year-old self, I'd tell myself not to worry about not knowing what to do and trust in the universe, that even when things aren't clear, everything happens for a reason. But, instead, I stayed in my comfort zone and played small.

And for the next 13 years, I qualified and worked as a Veterinary Nurse. Without wanting to sound arrogant, I was good at my job and I became Head Nurse during that time. My high achiever was back with a vengeance, despite asking my boss at the time if she thought I was good enough to do the role that she had promoted me to. But along with it, my people-pleasing 'skills' really took off. I'd give so much of myself at work, often to my own detriment. It could be hard to switch off - something I've really had to work on along the way - and I hated to disappoint anyone (I still do, to be honest) so, after having child no. 1, I found myself gradually working more and more hours to help my bosses and also the money situation at home.

The crux of it is, I stayed in my job for way too long. I'd lost my passion for it a long time before, but my fixed mindset told me that working 10 minutes away from home with a young family was worth compromising both my value and happiness for. I was in my comfort zone at work and couldn't bring myself to hand my notice in for fear of upsetting and inconveniencing anyone.

In reality, I should have put more faith in myself and my abilities, but the irony is, I could have chosen to leave my job at any time, I just didn't feel that I had the financial freedom to do so.

I'd like to think of myself as the eternal optimist, always trying to see the best in people or situations. I often wonder where I picked up this fixed mindset that always seems to result in a paralysing fear of change that keeps me stuck, people-pleasing rather than following my desires. Ironically, I'm also someone who very much likes change... just not uncomfortable change it would seem.

I'd love to say that it was a consequence of something in my childhood - and maybe it was. But I can't remember what. Maybe someone once told me to stop showing off and that made me feel like I didn't have a voice, I don't know. But as a consequence of this behaviour, I was controlled and bullied at primary school, which certainly cemented my need to people-please, keep quiet and do as I'm told.

Fast forward to another point in my career. After having child number 1, I set up my own ecommerce business, as I wasn't so keen to return to my current job. I did this and learned a lot of new skills which are really invaluable in what I do now, but playing small reared its ugly head here too. I was too scared to grow my business beyond me for fear of it just getting too difficult and complicated. I couldn't see it at the time, but my fixed mindset really meant I'd never grow my business enough to really make the most of the opportunity I had in front of me.

So, I returned to work until I was so despondent with my job, I decided to have child number 2. I thought 12 months would give me plenty of time to find something else to do, and I was right. One night scrolling the internet I came across an online course for mums, called Digital Mums, where they train you to become a social media manager. The investment wasn't small for me at that time, especially as I was just about to finish to go on maternity leave, but I felt excited for the first time in a long time.

I enrolled and started the training when my daughter was six weeks old. Yes, it was tough, but the love of learning something new was enough to keep me going. I'd find myself sat in front of my iMac, breastfeeding a baby in one arm, whilst typing up assignments with my free hand. Tired. Out of my comfort zone. But with a group of women who were going through the same as me (minus the baby).

I talked to a friend some years later, who said she was proud of me for taking such a big risk that had paid off. But every risk I saw as a managed risk. It was never 'just throw caution to the wind'. I had nine months of paid maternity, so I had six months to train and some time left over to find a paying client. I told myself if I did that, then I wouldn't return to my previous job.

Lo and behold, my training client kept me on! Bingo! On to phase 2 of my working life.

I embraced flexible work completely, to the point where I couldn't believe I'd worked 30 hours per week at the vets and also run an ecommerce business at the same time. But I was still playing small. After all, I'd only just learned all of these new skills, without a background in marketing like so many of the others had. Imposter syndrome would often creep up on me, especially around money and seeing my worth.

Sound familiar?

I was earning more than I had done at the vets (despite having a qualification, management role and 13 years' experience!!!!) but my salary was capped by time. I had a ceiling. And I still believed I was worth more. I wanted to specialise in something. Social media was great but there are a lot of platforms to keep on top of. I wanted to get really good at one thing so I could feel like an authority on that and, therefore, have more earning potential.

Enter a mentor...

Emma was an ex-Digital Mum who had niched into Facebook ads. I paid for a 1:1 with her and immediately knew this was what I wanted - to feel like an expert in one thing and to be able to charge more for my knowledge and skills. When I found out she was releasing a course on how to train to do what she did, I didn't think twice... but it was full.

I honestly think it was divine intervention now, as I was really down about it for a few days, then she opened up a couple more spots on her beta course and I was in! This was really the turning point for me and my business, which up until now, had ticked along fine but was nowhere near providing the financial freedom and ease I desired.

Going through that course reignited something in me - a love of learning, of really understanding and mastering a subject. It also delved into mindset - and why having the right mindset is, ultimately, what stops you from playing small. There was a whole new world opening up to me. A global world full of clients that needed my skills. An optimism that I could earn what I chose to earn, to find the clients I wanted to work with. And all I needed was to see that someone had done it before me.

Every experience in life brings value in some way. Sometimes it's not the value you expected, but a life lesson that you can take with you and use in the future. I felt I was suddenly on the right path. It still didn't matter to me how I got there, but I had a goal (to earn £5k in a single month) and this path felt like it could definitely get me there.

This was also the start of my self-development journey. I never had any awareness of coaching prior to this course, but the mindset side of things really motivated me. I find psychology and understanding people's behaviours fascinating. Applying those principles to myself and my own mindset, and simply believing that I could achieve what I set out to do, had a big impact on me. Having a coach keeps you motivated, accountable and on your own path, which is what you need when you're running your own business. It makes a big difference to your rate of progress when you can learn from the mistakes of others and fast-track your own successes.

There is always something new to unpack about yourself. As you continue down the self-development route, you learn so much about yourself and the way you work. Your strengths and weaknesses. Your why. Which parts of your work light you up and which parts are better left to someone with more expertise and passion than yourself. A shaman I met at a self-development day once described life as a spiral, and those things that get to you - imposter syndrome, trauma, losing your voice, playing small - get uncovered as we travel down it. That we will think we've dealt with something, only for it to come up again further down the spiral, ready to teach us something else and new about ourselves.

Fast forward to today, and I now run a successful business with a small and knowledgeable team. I choose which clients I want to work with, which is generally in the ecomm space, and I love it. It really helps that I had the experience of running my own (albeit very small) business in this space, which is why I believe that nothing is ever a wasted experience, the reasons just show up sometimes down the line.

And my turnover this year should hit the six-figure mark, which sounds unbelievable to me considering six years ago I was working for someone else for just £10 an hour (my 1:1 hourly rate is now 26x that!). But here's the thing, this doesn't happen overnight. You have to work for it, just like anything that is worth having in this life.

And when I say work for it, I don't mean simply that you have to be chained to your desk for 12 hours a day to make your business work for you. I've had to constantly remind myself that business can be easy when you experience ease in it. Getting to the stage where everything is in flow; that you have chosen to work with people who have the same values as yourself and that you understand your own value and stand in your worth; when you're aligned to the prices you charge and the services you offer.

The old me knew that I was destined for more than what I had at the time. What the old me didn't know was how to get there. Once I stepped onto an aligned path, it didn't matter how I got there anymore. It felt natural, inevitable. Like Thanos... (I am also a pretty big comic book nerd). As I said at the start of this chapter, yes I still suffer with imposter syndrome from time to time. I think that's natural when you are someone who always wants to show up as their best self. I still have money mindset issues, but I've done a lot of work so I'm much better with this side of my business now. I still have to resist the urge to always people-please (because don't we all love feeling valued and, dare I say it, indispensable to others) and to protect my boundaries (which is also a work in progress, but half the battle is just starting, isn't it?), because if I don't, my clients don't get the best of me. But here is the biggest difference now between the me at 20, 30, even 37... I am aware of my limiting behaviours now and can recognise when one pops up. In short, I now have a choice in how I deal with those behaviours, rather than simply reacting to them.

And 9 out of 10 times now, I choose to flip them to my advantage. Boom!

So now (if you've got this far, and if you have, I truly am grateful to you), I'd invite you to take a look at where you are up to on your journey. Have you lost yourself in a sea of children and long to rediscover that person you used to be? Are you at the very beginning, and knowing you're meant for more but without a direction or any idea how to get there? Are you limiting your success because of the fear of stepping out of your comfort zone as I did? Are you trying to people-please or be there for everyone, without really considering what you ultimately desire or want to achieve? Are you failing to understand your own worth and what uniqueness you bring to the table and so, keeping yourself small?

Then I would invite you to consider how you want to feel. Right now. At this moment. If you had the Infinity Gauntlet (nerd alert again) and could click your fingers, what would you desire? What is your why? Who or what do you want to do all this for?

My why was freedom. Freedom to choose. Freedom to spend time how I wish - whether it's with my children or work, whether it's taking an afternoon off when I feel the need to, to make sure my children take priority when they need to. Financial freedom - because I believe that when we have financial freedom, we are free to make better choices. I want to be able to choose sustainability over convenience. Reusable over disposable.

And then think about your core values. What is important to you? What are your non-negotiables? After much thought, I realised that I can only work with clients who are honest and act with integrity, as those are massively important to me too. Communication is also another one of my core values, along with knowledge, and these are all things I bring to my client relationships. These core values are the basis for any client relationship we have at Juno Six, and so we only work with those clients who value them as well.

Which brings me back to my why, as this is exactly what I aim to give to clients too. Freedom is my driver, and through my work, I offer my clients both freedom of time so they can work on the parts of their business that light them up (hint, it's not usually the Facebook ads) and freedom of money (in increased revenue).

Once you have a connection to your goal or purpose, it becomes much easier to feel it, believe it and achieve it. When you think of your day to day, are you making the most of your time? Are you trying to learn a skill that you could just as easily outsource to someone with more knowledge about it than yourself? Are you stuck in inertia because the fear is preventing you from moving forward?

Are you truly understanding the value you offer to others? Are you standing in your self-worth?

A continued love of learning and wanting to offer clients more value means that I can now advise on so much more than just Facebook and Instagram ads. Forging true partnerships with clients means being a sounding board, making recommendations on how to improve not only their marketing and paid ads, but also their website, conversion rates and overall business strategies at times. So, the only way to do this is to invest in myself - which I do. I believe if you learn from the best then you're choosing to invest in yourself in the best way possible. That kind of investment doesn't come cheap, which is why, now, I do step into my worth, as my clients are getting something they can't get elsewhere, and that's me and my experience.

There are thousands of business owners who are playing small (I know, because I was one). But it's time to stop playing small. I achieved so much more than I thought I would, but I'm so damn proud of the younger me who went through some traumatic times. And it all started to come together for me when I decided it was time to get out of my own way and create bigger goals for myself.

So, you need to ask yourself, what can you do now to change your narrative? How do you want to feel? And what do you need to do to make that feeling your reality?

Being surrounded by the right people - your people - really makes all the difference in this life. They give you freedom. The freedom to be yourself, the freedom to follow your dreams. When you're surrounded by people who make you feel 'less than', who don't nourish you or let you thrive, it's hard to focus on the path ahead.

I've learned this in both home and work life. My family and friends are the people I'd surround myself with again and again because they share my core values and they are the people I can be myself around. They get me. They tell me how proud they are of me, and I have a voice around them because they love me without condition.

But your circle includes your work too, and I firmly believe it's essential to surround yourself with the right people here as well. For too long, I surrounded myself with the wrong people at work. The ones that drain you. Having people to turn to, even when you work virtually, is the key to staying sane and on top of your game. If it's true that you are the average of the five people you spend the most time with, then a few of those are likely to be work associates, so it's essential to consider who you want to share your energy with here too. You need aspirational people in your work life, preferably someone who has already achieved what you want. This could be a coach, mentor, or it could be the groups and memberships you surround yourself with. Choose your work partners wisely. If you surround yourself with people who play small, then guess what? Exactly! I'm very careful to only surround myself with people who share my values, or who support me on my journey in the right way.

One of my biggest drivers now is simply this: am I showing my children that they can achieve their dreams whilst staying true to themselves? That they can have both choice and freedom? That they don't have to play small in life?

Learning has always been a passion for me, and I equally love to share knowledge to help people get further, which is why I love what I do - using my knowledge to help ecommerce business owners be more profitable with social media ads, helping them across different areas of their business, offering support and to be that sounding board, and helping them grow to their next level. In short, I offer them what I crave myself - the freedom of choice to make more money and have more time.

However, when you are a service business, you will naturally have different ways that people can work with you and this, for me is consulting. I love this side of my work because it taps into my love of sharing knowledge, educating and helping others to achieve more in their businesses too. And, for me, this includes mentoring both business owners and other paid social marketers. After all, if I can do it, why can't you?

My team and I have now worked with lots of ecommerce business owners, in both a consulting and full management capacity, to increase their revenue through the work we do. We helped a small business surpass their VAT threshold for the first time, increased the monthly revenue for a travel experience brand by 200% and increase sales for a homeware brand by 134% in the first month alone, to name just a few wins. Our passion for ecommerce brands that have a physical product or experience means we make sure to add value at every point in our partnerships, and so we choose who we work with carefully.

However, I love when we're a part of the journey for a business. When we can make a difference, not just to the bottom line, but to the business as a whole, including to the business owner, who typically has a lot on their plate and is looking for support.

So, if you know you've been playing small. If you know you're worth more than your current situation. If you have the desire to reach a future for yourself and your family that revolves around freedom. Focus on that goal. That end vision. Don't worry about the journey, after all, any road will get you there ultimately... Get clear on what you want your outcome to be. Find your Why and take small and consistent steps every day.

I am proof that it is possible to get out of your own way to achieve things you never imagined. We each have our own Why, and I believe it's what you do with yours that makes the difference. Always stay true to yourself, it feels much more authentic than trying to be something you're not. Make time for yourself every day, because if you don't, who will? And if you feel lost, re-find yourself, bet on yourself and make every day count. Whether that's to set out alone, grow your business, outsource and free up your time - connect it to your Why and never look back. The universe has your back.

ABOUT THE AUTHOR
ROSE BROWN

Rose Brown is a boutique agency owner who thrives on helping and developing other business owners, be it through proven digital strategy creation or coaching them to get the most out of the campaigns they're already running. There is nothing she enjoys more than getting positive results for her clients, and has a drive for helping ecommerce businesses, especially those on Shopify where she feels she can make the biggest impact.

With 10 years experience of running her own side-hustle ecommerce business, and the last six years focusing on social media marketing and niching down as a paid media buyer, she has positioned herself and her agency as a great resource for business owners to leverage.

She is also hugely passionate about supporting other media buyers and helping them to get 'unstuck' with their own campaigns, which she does by 1:1 coaching and also as a mentor and ecomm specialist in a high-profile Facebook Ads membership group.

Her values are key to the work relationships she makes, and her agency, Juno Six, attracts exciting, thoughtful, mindful and value-based brands that have integrity and honesty at their core.

As a big lover of nature and space (the stuff up in the sky), she has a passion for sustainability and making better choices for our planet. Her other interests include gaming and heading to Comic-Con wherever and whenever possible - an interest she happily shares with her family.

Website: www.juno-six.com
Email: hello@juno-six.com
Instagram: @instarosieb

instagram.com/juno.six

linkedin.com/in/brownrosemary

SAMANTHA PATEL
CHANGE YOUR MINDSET, CHANGE YOUR LIFE

If I could use one word to describe my life right now, it would be fulfilled.

I have a business that gives me joy, family and friends who make me smile and support me and a beautiful, funny daughter who lights me up every day. Life is pretty damn good.

I have the freedom to work when and how I want and the ability to choose who I want to work with and for me. That's living the dream. I don't spend hours commuting, I don't work with people who don't respect me and I don't sit at my desk in an office, gazing out of the window wondering "What if...".

I get to CHOOSE. And choice is the ultimate freedom, right?

Every day, I get to coach incredible women who are ready to transform their mindset after experiencing divorce or a relationship breakdown, and that's pretty awesome! I am very, very lucky.

BUT...

It wasn't always this way. Only a few years ago, I went through a pretty dark time. My self-confidence was rock bottom, I was angry, hurt, and had a head full of limiting beliefs that told me I'd never be a success. I was a single mum, working part-time and spending all my time and salary on commuting and childcare. I never thought I'd make anything much of myself.

And then I came across a brilliant coach who helped me find the tools to allow me to smash those limiting beliefs through mindset work. I started my own business, got visible online and created an awesome life for myself and my daughter.

Impossible became "I'm Possible", and I truly believe that every single woman reading this book can have the life they choose. All you need to do is change your mindset.

I like to refer to the years before I discovered mindset work as BM (before mindset).

Growing up, I had so many limiting beliefs and my money mindset was awful. I was painfully shy, had no self-confidence and thought that my life wouldn't amount to much. Don't get me wrong, I had ambitions, but they weren't very, well, ambitious. I wanted to go to university and get a 'good' job, but I never thought I would earn more than about £40k a year, and I'd certainly never rise to the top of my chosen profession. I wasn't clever or confident enough.

I lived on a council estate in North London. My dad was unemployed for a lot of my childhood, so money was always tight. We qualified for school uniform vouchers and free school meals and I remember how mortifying it was to have to queue in a separate line for lunch and to pay for clothes with vouchers. I felt like a second-class citizen and this was a theme that followed me throughout my teenage years and beyond. That feeling that I was never quite good enough. Not clever enough, not confident enough and not wealthy enough. And wealth didn't mean flying first class or going skiing. It meant being able to afford to go on a school day trip or go out with my friends to McDonalds! I remember my cousin asking me to join them on holiday in Spain and I said no because I didn't have any summer clothes and couldn't afford to buy any.

I had a firm belief that I would never really amount to anything. People like me didn't. We were this army of invisible people who had average, invisible lives. No one ever told me that I could amount to more, that I could be good enough, that I could be confident or that I could have ambition and drive. And that I didn't need to come from a wealthy family to do this.

I only really discovered my dream career in 2021, at the grand old age of 49, when I started my coaching accreditation. I thought the coaching would be a bolt on to my social media consultancy business. As soon as I started coaching other women like me, I realised how much I loved it. It was so exciting to be able to pass on my mindset knowledge to them. I also realised that the women who I wanted to coach were those with a similar story to mine. I'd experienced what they were going through - traumatic divorce - and I knew that I could help support them to create the life they deserved.

If I could speak to my younger self, I'd tell her this: Don't ever let anyone put you in a box because of where you lived, how you spoke or where you went to school. I spent far too long thinking that a working-class girl living on a council estate could never be successful. I had to play small and stay small.

Where I lived, having money meant you were a drug dealer or you'd won the lottery! No one made money from owning a business or by working their way up the corporate ladder. You either earned it illegally or you won it. You were a criminal or just plain lucky. My dad, now in his 80s, still plays the lottery every week and still believes that his numbers will come up!

"Money goes to people with money" was something my dad always said. So, I grew up with this belief that I could never be wealthy or successful.

I also believed that confident people were "show offs". This was something that was instilled in me by my mum. Confidence was seen as a negative. It was much better to stay small and be invisible.

My mum, who was born deaf, was painfully shy, which meant that I too was painfully shy. I would never speak in class, talk to boys or do anything that would remotely embarrass my mum (which was basically everything). I never had a teenage boyfriend - firstly, because it never crossed my mind that a boy might like to spend time with me and secondly, because I knew my mum wouldn't know how to react and I'd be embarrassed by her embarrassment!

My list of limiting beliefs were as long as my arm:

I wasn't confident enough;

I wasn't pretty enough;

I wasn't wealthy enough;

I wasn't clever enough;

I wasn't sporty enough;

I wasn't thin enough...

...I wasn't enough.

My daughter's bookshelf is heaving with books about self-confidence and mindset and I often think what might have happened if I had read a book about believing in yourself back then. I had no self-belief and I think that was because I had no one believing *in* me. Of course, my parents loved me dearly, but they didn't have any ambition. And I want to make this really clear, it wasn't because they didn't care. They did, passionately. And they were fiercely proud of me. But this was the 1970s/80s. Things were so, so different. Women were still not really valued in the workplace and they were fighting for equal rights (no change there, then!) and my parents had both come from similar working class backgrounds - it was part of their conditioning.

Back then, I always settled for less than I deserved. I went to university but lived at home. Why? Because honestly, no one ever told me that I could leave home and have the best time living as a student.

I always wanted to be a journalist but never fulfilled that dream because my university tutor told me "I was too shy" to be a good journalist! Seriously! How did being an introvert affect my ability to write?! So, I settled for a career in Public Relations. It was an OK career choice. I ended up staying in PR for 20 years, so it wasn't all bad, but it wasn't what I *really* wanted.

Imposter syndrome has plagued me my whole life. I never felt comfortable around people who spoke more eloquently than I did or people who were more intelligent than me. I also felt inferior to people who went to 'proper' universities. The story I told myself was that I wasn't very clever, wasn't very articulate and grew up on a council estate. Yep, that council estate held me back a lot. It defined me for a very, very long time.

I just blended into the background. I hated talking in public, ran away if anyone paid me any attention, felt inferior to anyone I deemed "better than me" and never believed I could be anything but average.

Basically, I was invisible.

And I stayed invisible for a very long time.

I started to become a bit more visible in my 30s. I met my future husband, was working in a job that I really enjoyed and was a teeny bit more confident. But there was always this niggle that things would go wrong. That I would end up back on that council estate, living that average life.

Foreboding joy is the term coaches use for this and I was an expert in it. I'd worry constantly about losing everything, or that my boss would find out I was an imposter and useless at my job. By this time, three of the PR campaigns I had worked on had been nominated for awards so I did actually know what I was doing!

I'd often wonder when my husband would find someone better than me; when he'd realise that I was a fraud. Even after we had a gorgeous daughter in 2009.

And then 2014 happened.

2014 was a pivotal year for me. It was definitely the year that the universe decided to throw all her shit at me and, when I reflect back on that time, I honestly don't know how I got through it.

My doom scenario became reality. In September of that year, my husband told me he didn't love me anymore and that he was leaving me. I was completely and utterly blindsided. My life turned upside down in one evening. Our daughter was in Year One at school. When he told me he was leaving I passed out. I was devastated.

I was slap, bang in the middle of my own drama triangle. I thought I was the victim; that this was the life I deserved; that it served me right for getting ideas above my station. Of course he was going to leave me - that was always going to happen!

Then a few months later, I was made redundant. So, I'd lost my husband and my job in the space of a few months. My employer had a brilliant work from home policy, which meant that I only needed to go into the office once a week. This was way before working from home became the norm. So, now I had the added worry of finding a job with a similar work from home policy. My daughter was only six at the time and working from home meant I could pick her up from wrap around care easily. I couldn't go back to commuting into London everyday. It just wasn't feasible from a financial perspective or from a time perspective. After school provision closed at 6pm and there was no way I could make it back in time from London.

Whilst all this was going on, I was dealing with some other major family issues - the kind that wouldn't look out of place on East-Enders. The issues were so bad that I never talked about what happened outside of my family and a very small group of trusted friends.

It was the most stressful time of my life and I was dealing with it all on my own. I felt like I had the weight of the world on my shoulders. Then, I was diagnosed with a condition called Immune thrombocytopenic purpura (ITP) - my blood wasn't clotting and if I had been involved in an accident or cut myself, I would have probably bled to death. This condition was likely caused by an infection or stress. I think I know which of the two was at play here.

Fun, right?

It was a pretty shitty time and I was bloody angry at the world. I had just started my own business - a social media consultancy - around this time, so I'd be sat on a hospital bed once a week for treatment with an IV in one arm and a laptop in the other trying to juggle work with illness.

I was in lack. I felt like I was the victim. I had no self-confidence. And I didn't know what the hell I would do.

I consider myself to be very fortunate, as my ex-husband and I came to a settlement which meant that my daughter and I could stay in our family home until she was at least 18. But I worried every single day about what we would do when this agreement ended. The thought of losing my house at any point in the future scared the hell out of me and I spent a long time flitting between abject fear and worry. My anxiety got so bad that my GP prescribed me antidepressants. It was a horrid, horrid time. I wasn't sleeping and I was living on Rice Krispies because they were the only thing I could eat without throwing up.

And then I made a decision which would quite literally change my life. I decided to invest in myself and work with a mindset coach. I'd come across Andrea Callanan on another course I was doing and I loved how she worked. I wanted to create a positive future for myself and my daughter. Mindset coaching allowed me to leave my pity party for one and create a new way of thinking.

I became grateful. I started a morning routine. I focused on how abundant I was and I started to see a massive change in myself. The ball of anger in my stomach disappeared. I started to forgive all the people in my life who had caused me so much stress and most of all, I started to respect myself and see what an awesome life I had AND see the awesome life I could create. I had a house, brilliant friends, there was food on the table, my daughter went to a great school... I was missing all this brilliant stuff in my life because I was focusing on the negative.

Changing my mindset changed my life. But it didn't happen overnight, and it took a lot of inner work to get there.

If you feel invisible because you have no self-confidence or because the universe has thrown some shit at you over the years, know this: **IT WILL GET BETTER.**

But you have to put in the work.

I was like you once. I thought I'd never amount to much, I'd be trapped in a job that I didn't like, I'd be angry at my ex-husband until the day I died and that the universe would always deal me a crappy card. Because why wouldn't it? What had I done to deserve a life of abundance? I wasn't a Grade A student, went to a two bit university and didn't really know what I wanted to do with my life.

But that's all changed. I'm not angry anymore - it's a waste of energy. What's done is done. I have a new story to tell. And it's this one.

I always envied people who said that they had had an aha moment or had found their calling. Imagine how it would feel?

And then it happened to me.

My aha moment came when I realised that my past story didn't have to be my future story. I was in charge of my life and I could create my own future. I could rewrite my past story. Not to erase the shitty stuff but to embrace it for helping to make me the person I am today. Now when I think back to the dark times, I can see how they shaped me. I'm strong, resilient, ambitious and above all, an awesome role model for my daughter. I'm proud of who I am and what I have accomplished in my life so far. And you can be proud of yourself too.

I encourage you to rewrite your story. Be the victor not the victim! Write down all the shitty things that have happened to you over the years, the limiting beliefs that you have carried and the thoughts that have held you back and decide whether you want them to be part of your future. Become intentional, set goals and start imagining your new life. Create a vision board and fill it with images and words that will be part of your future. If you can see it in your head, you can hold it in your hands.

All those moments that have left you reeling have made you who you are today. Want to start your own business? You totally can! Want to retrain and have a new career? Yep, you can do that too. I did both! Use that inner strength and resilience that you've accumulated to propel you forwards. Release all those negative feelings and all that self doubt. You are the author of your story and you can create your happy ending.

Coaching women who have gone through a divorce or breakup and supporting them on their journey is a privilege. It brings me joy every single day. When I was 21, I worked for a car magazine. I was surrounded by petrol heads who loved cars and I often used to think about how lucky they were. They got to do the thing they loved - drive and talk about cars - all the time. And now that's me. Work never feels like work. I could talk about mindset all day, every day!

But how did I change my mindset and become visible?

I started believing in myself.

The more I learnt about mindset, the more I realised that my own mindset needed changing. And so I put in the work. It was hard and sometimes it felt easier to just "sit in the shit", as my coach Andrea would say. Sometimes, being the victim felt good. I could feel sorry for myself and wallow in self-pity, but who was that serving? Not me, that's for sure.

I started to see that I was worthy, that I was a brilliant mum, that I was intelligent and kind, that I was a hardworking and creative woman. And once I started to believe this, I became more confident, more ambitious and more visible. I didn't have to lurk in the shadows; I had lots to offer the world - and especially, to offer women like me.

My advice to you is simple: Believe in yourself too - you CAN do it. If you want to change your mindset, read as many books as you can. Listen to podcasts and work with a coach if you can afford one. If you can't, then follow coaches on social media. Join Facebook Groups like mine 'Reclaim your life after divorce' - they are often free and you'll get so much out of them. You'll learn lots and be surrounded by women like you.

Have a growth mindset. Focus on Can not Can't. Take action every day - you won't create change in your life if you do nothing. Be accountable. Become self-aware and learn to spot what makes you feel crappy. Once you understand your triggers, you can put things in place to help you deal with those triggers and how they make you feel.

One of the single most important things you can do for yourself is be grateful for what you have. Every day my daughter and I talk about what we are grateful for. If it rains, we're grateful that we have water, if the heating breaks down, we're grateful for the blankets we have, if we don't feel well, we're grateful for medication. We are lucky. We have a house, she gets to go to school, there is food on the table... Even when you don't feel very grateful, make a list anyway. I guarantee that it will help change your mood. When we're grateful, we're in a positive space and if we're feeling positive then the world is a better place. Practice gratitude every day - even on the bad days. Hell, especially on the bad days!

I am a huge believer in positive self-talk. I recite affirmations every morning as part of my daily routine. Yes, I did feel a bit silly at first, but the more I learn about affirmations, the more I understand their power. Research shows that when you repeat them often, you can start to make changes. But here's the catch - you need to BELIEVE them. So make sure you have affirmations that are 100% authentic. Say them like you mean them.

When I was growing up, I didn't need to worry about social media - thank goodness I didn't. My self-worth really didn't need to take a battering from Insta perfect people. I use social media every day now, and if I see a post that makes me feel shit about myself I unfollow the account. I try to only follow people who make me smile or educate and inspire me. I have no time for accounts that make me feel like my life is inadequate. I don't worry about people judging me and I don't compare myself to others - life is way too short for that.

After spending years believing that I'd never earn very much, I now truly believe that the only thing limiting my earning potential is little old me. I have goals and aspirations that I know I can achieve. My past does not determine my future. I will be able to pay the mortgage when the agreement with my ex-husband ends and I will be able to live a life of abundance.

How do I know this?

Because I will take the action I need to get there.

Make sure you surround yourself with good people who love and support you. Don't play small. Always set boundaries and NEVER underestimate yourself. You are SO worth it.

This morning I made a series of Instagram reels for my business account. Yep, me, the wallflower who thought she was too stupid/overweight/common/boring to speak in a work meeting, let alone make a video for Instagram.

I then coached a client who is too scared to be visible on social media in case people judge her. This client has really low self-worth and not much self-belief. I can see that she's bloody awesome and I know that after a few sessions, she will see it too.

I had one of those weird out of body experiences where I was looking down at the scene. Me, Samantha Patel, coaching a woman with a degree and a career on how to change her life. I had to pinch myself. How did I get to this place?

It wasn't easy.

In fact, it was a bit shit sometimes and there were days when I wanted to crawl under the duvet and hide from the world.

But I kept going.

I took action. I read ALL the books, listened to all my coach's advice and started believing in my own abilities.

I made a plan, wrote a strategy and invested in myself. And now, I have the job of my dreams, work the hours that I want, am my own boss and never have to commute into London again (unless I want to). I created freedom and choice in my life by doing the inner work.

I believe that mindset work has helped me in every area of my life. I have a growing business, I'm happy and I'm an awesome single parent. I'm able to help my 11 year old daughter with her own mindset and give her methods and strategies to cope with feelings of overwhelm, low self-worth and lack of confidence. All the things I lacked when growing up. The world has changed so much since I was a teenager and there is so much pressure on our children - I hope my daughter will be able to better deal with that pressure with the tools I am equipping her with.

Mindset work has taught me that the only limits I have are the ones I put up on myself.

I've worked with lots of awesome women since becoming a coach and it's such a privilege to watch them transform their mindset, get visible, find their voice and grow in confidence.

Clients come to me with lots of limiting beliefs including:

Fear of being judged;

Imposter syndrome;

Money mindset;

Lack of self-confidence;

Comparisonitis;

No self-worth.

It's a pretty long list! I work with clients over a number of sessions and we tackle these beliefs, one by one. Often, we uncover beliefs they didn't even know existed! Each and every woman I have worked with has been amazed by what we uncover in the sessions and, more importantly, how they let these beliefs go.

> "I am so grateful for the mindset shift that came through working with you".

These words are from my client Isla, who was being held back by her imposter syndrome and her lack of confidence. Over the course of eight weeks, we worked together to tackle her mindset issues. By the end of her sessions, she was more confident and more visible. She wasn't comparing herself to her peers and had a strategy to help her remain visible and move her life forwards.

Jo was another client who wanted coaching to help her get her business idea into being. She was putting so many blocks in her way and was finding it hard to focus. We worked on the blocks and Jo came away from the sessions with a new positive outlook, tools to help her ensure she stays on track and a new vision for her life.

> "Sam was brilliant. Down to earth, funny and got me motivated and back on track like a demon!"

Seeing the transformation in my client's mindset is a wonderful thing. I know that a lot of you reading this will be thinking "Yeah, yeah, it won't work for me. It's too woo woo."

It WILL work if you put in the effort and it's definitely not woo woo. In fact, there's a ton of research to show that transforming your mindset has a positive impact on your life.

Along with my clients, I'm proof that transforming your mindset can change your life!

And so there you have it. That's my story. It's been a rollercoaster ride, with all the thrills, scares and joy that are part of life. It's been quite a ride in places. Sometimes, I've wanted to get off the rollercoaster because it was too damn scary and other times, I've wanted to ride it fifty times just to get that adrenaline rush over and over again. It's never been dull, that's for sure!

Working on my mindset changed my life. It gave me confidence, self-belief and self-awareness. I don't think I would be where I am today if I hadn't discovered the power of mindset. I certainly wouldn't have written this chapter!

All those limiting beliefs that were holding me back and keeping me small are gone. I'm happier than I have ever been, have a life of freedom and ease and am grateful every single day for all my experiences - good and bad - because they made me the person I am today: Business owner, badass female, divorcee and single mum.

I really hope you can see that if a shy girl from a working class family living on a council estate in North London can do it, then so can you. Go on, take the first step. I promise it will be worth it.

You will live happily ever after.

ABOUT THE AUTHOR
SAMANTHA PATEL

Samantha Patel is a mindset coach and mentor. She works with women who have experienced divorce or a break-up and supports them to transform their lives through mindset work.

Mindset is everything. It affects our confidence, our decision-making, our self-care and can stop us from being visible. When we suffer a trauma, such as a divorce or a relationship breakdown, it can have a massive impact on how we feel about ourselves. We can feel rejected, a failure and our self-worth hits rock bottom. We often have limiting beliefs, which stop us from moving forward, and we get stuck in a place that doesn't serve us.

Sam discovered the power of mindset when she went through a very traumatic period in her life: an unexpected divorce, a stress-related illness and redundancy, which all happened simultaneously. Working on her mindset literally changed her life.

Sam is a graduate coach of the fully accredited Aligned Coaching Academy (ACA MInstLM), and a certified Story Work Coach with Andrea Callanan (ACSWC)

Join my free Facebook Community
https://www.facebook.com/groups/reclaimyourlifeafterdivorce
Website: https://sampatelcoaching.com
Contact me: sam@sampatelcoaching.com

instagram.com/sampatelcoaching

21

SARAH WINTERFLOOD

THE UNIVERSE IS READY AND WAITING FOR YOU TO ASK

I run my own business, which also happens to be my passion. I am a creative person who loves making other women feel good and I get to do that on a regular basis by taking their photographs.

My ambition has been to take away the fear of being in front of the camera. It's such a crucial element to getting visible and yet it is such a barrier. There is always one area that never gets addressed about getting visible and that is the inner fear that holds us back.

My unique approach is to work with my clients, way before the shoot date, within a coaching capacity. I love doing this work as I have been there myself and wish I had had someone holding my hand, guiding and re-assuring me that it was all going to be, not just ok, but fabulous.

Seeing my clients come alive with genuine excitement about getting visible in front of a camera, which only a few weeks/months ago had seemed an impossible barrier, is a truly empowering experience.

Since discovering my niche; empowering women and harnessing the power of the female cycle (our super power), I have been blessed to work with amazing women who are my ideal aligned clients, allowing me to work and earn from my passion with ease and flow.

This is my greatest achievement in business, that through a journey of self-development and self-discovery, I have found my own unique approach to a well populated industry, and, as they say, 'if you build it, they will come'. I believe this is exactly what has happened for me.

My adult life has always been quite fluid. I went to Drama school to pursue my dreams of being a well respected (actually, let's be real and say famous) actor, treading the boards. I also learnt secretarial skills, just in case!

In between the acting jobs, I worked as a temp in offices and those days and weeks sitting behind a desk really used to crush me. The contrast of sitting at one place every day to working in a creative space was a complete juxtaposition and, on reflection, shows how unaligned I was in my life during my twenties.

In general, the plays I was part of were always profit share... and they never made a profit, so nothing to share! My money mindset was not in an abundant or expansive place. I was living a reality that said you had to struggle to be an artist and a creative, which I totally bought into.

My gut instinct has always been that I will be ok, 'I can wing it and whatever I want to achieve will happen'. I have always listened to my gut instinct.

With my acting, I took note of this strong instinct and, along with two other women I was in a play with, we decided to take control of our acting destinies. We formed a theatre company, Another Planet Productions, with the sole purpose of sourcing, producing and performing plays that featured strong female roles. I look back at that with pride, as I feel we were spearheading something that was simmering away which has now come bubbling to the surface, with women demanding equal rights and representation on stage and screen. Of course, only a tiny handful of people knew our mission but with little acorns etc... And we did ok; we worked hard because our passion was fuelling us. We didn't make any money and so that myth that you can't be abundant financially as a creative got fully cemented in my subconscious.

I think what happened to me during my formative adult years was the creation of the belief that I would never be anything great and impressive. I would just coast along and get by.

I fell hard in love when I was at university and we stayed together for a long time. I thought that was my destiny and I was dutifully following what my heart was telling me was the reality. But the reality was that I was stagnating and holding myself back in order to support my partner emotionally. It never dawned on me that I could change the direction I had set my life on until it became a matter of my health either declining or getting better. I chose to get better and to leave. This decision changed my life and took me on the path I have been on ever since. It has been a bumpy one, but I wouldn't change it for anything. This also brought to my attention the strength in trusting my gut instinct and how I had let my heart take over.

It's funny what you take from others and believe it to be the truth. That 'love of my life' I left, used to tease me that I only had an HND and not a degree. I never thought about the damage it was causing me in my subconscious, the myth that, after hearing it enough times, I believed: that I wasn't good enough or clever enough. I let it cast a shadow over me, let it hinder me from my own personal and creative growth.

However, I used that denigration to prove him wrong. Through sheer determination and resourcefulness, I got myself onto the final year of a Drama degree, after an eight-year break from higher education, and graduated with a 2:1. I then decided I would do something that had been on my wish list for years: work a ski season in Europe.

Turns out, the universe was listening. I saw a handwritten ad on a pinboard at my local gym for a chalet girl, I applied and, guess what? I got the job!

The year I turned 30, I had produced and performed in a play on the London Fringe (still didn't earn any profit), completed a degree and worked a ski season, whilst re-discovering the me that had been hidden under layers of societal and emotional conditioning. Oh, and I also got back into my fitness, met my future husband and switched from performer to photographer!

During my twenties and thirties, I adamantly believed that I was going to spend the rest of my days with the 'love of my life', that I would be a Wife and Mother, do the domestic duties and have a perfectly respectable existence doing some acting here and there.

What really happened was the opposite because that wasn't fundamentally who I really was or am. I was forever resisting the narrative that I thought was expected of me, by my own beliefs and those on the outside.

I fought what I was telling myself - how crazy does that sound?!

I was in a state of flux - I needed self-fulfilment and what was interesting was that my parents encouraged it, but couldn't see it through my eyes.

What was it that took me on that journey? I really do believe that growing up in a fairly traditional patriarchal family had a huge effect. I observed how my family interacted and I modelled the same behaviour. That isn't anything ground-breaking at all, but what is interesting is just how long it has taken me to understand that.

As a parent myself, I now understand this on a much deeper level. Whatever we try to do to guide our children, it will always be through our own lens. We will never be able to know how our children will interpret our advice/guidance/support and that is why it takes so long for the one observing and internalising to be able to see it from a perspective of analysis and not judgement.

My father is a very determined person; he will get what he sets out to achieve. We were chatting a few years ago and I complained that I just couldn't find the time or space to knuckle down and focus on what I wanted to achieve. He seemed perplexed and just stated, very matter of factly, that I should outsource parts of the job I didn't enjoy and therefore have the time to be creative!

That was a light bulb moment for me and all of a sudden, I started to review my teenage observations of how my father worked - of course he outsourced what wasn't serving him, he wasn't afraid to say 'I don't want to do that, so you take it off my hands to help me work with my strengths, not weaknesses!'

This was a huge insight because I also realised that as a man, he was perfectly able to say and do that.

It is different for women and I appreciate that I am only focusing on my personal experiences here as a white, privileged, middle-class female!

What prevented me from asking for help was the juxtapose life I was living: loving/caring/selfless girlfriend versus independent creative! I was perfectly discombobulated (I love that word and I think this is the perfect sentence for it) and had no idea!

What happened, over time, was a gradual chipping away of my inner spark and creative flair, because, unbeknownst to me, depression was setting in. It got very exhausting trying to live the dual existence and it felt easier to run away from my family and friends, follow what my heart believed was the best for me and so I made the decision to move abroad to live with my 'love'. This was huge and a decision that felt strange and disconnected but also, as though it was the only choice I had.

Strange now, when I reflect on that because it seems I had such a strong desire to up sticks and move to another country to live out a dream of love and adventure, but the reality was that I was chasing my 'love' because I was in a state of co-dependency and I had created isolation for myself.

I don't even think my partner wanted me there. I think he moved abroad to try to break free but I couldn't accept that and believed we had to be together. Reading that sentence back, I still feel shocked that I was so unaware how intense my actions were. I had lost all sense of my independent, autonomous self.

How did I get to that point of leaving my family, my friends, my work colleagues, to up sticks and move to another country?

There were so many elements to that moment when I got in my little car packed with my life's belongings and made the drive from London to Newcastle to board the overnight ferry to Sweden.

Self-belief had disappeared and co-dependency was my driving force. I had let go of pretty much any self-belief that I could do anything without my partner. We were part of the same whole!!!

So, love, and being heart ruled, was actually very detrimental for me and my health and yet I totally bought into it being the only way to live the rest of my life. As I said before, the behaviours and language that I observed in my formative years really cemented what I thought was how I had to live my own life too.

What I didn't ever know or consider was that every generation is figuring it out too and that whatever I was privy to as I grew up wasn't how life has to be lived. I don't think I was ever explicitly told that I can observe, learn and grow, and then create my own choices from those pre-existing models!

Without realising it, I think I became locked in a cycle of wanting to please and serve, to not offend or cause anyone to pass judgement on me. However, the reality was that the exact opposite was happening and my perceived judgement from others was excruciatingly hard to quieten down and suppress. Those on the outside could have, possibly, thought I was rebelling, being obstinate, being standoffish to cause exactly those reactions: offense, judgement and confusion.

At the time I was sinking deeper and deeper into a depression but had no idea. On the outside it looked like I was fully owning my life but inside, I felt completely adrift. The only stability I could cling to was the metaphysical concept of love, because, who am I kidding, the love we used to have long ago had set sail, so I followed my 'love' to another country!

The reality, once I arrived, was not at all like the romantic fantasy I had created in my mind. I was greeted with a hug a friend would give and I realised in that very moment that it was all a mistake but had no idea how I could get out of it.

Sweden is a beautiful country, and I look back now with a nostalgia of the lush greenery and the little red painted huts dotted along the rocky coastline. However, when I arrived in the dock on the ferry, it was pitch black, freezing cold, sleet falling at an almost horizontal angle and everything about the moment was grim. But I could only keep going forward because this was what my destiny was. I truly believed that.

It took me ten months to re-pack my little car and get on the return ferry back to Newcastle.

On my return, I felt low, confused and sad. I struggled to reach out to friends and family. My belief system at that point was that I was not worth anyone else's time and love. I truly believed no one would even care that I was alive! I struggled to get out of bed, it was hard and I felt like I was trudging through thick mud 24/7.

Something inside me didn't give up though. For whatever reason, I did pick up the phone and made an appointment to see my GP. When I sat down and he asked what was wrong I burst into tears. I said I felt sad. From that moment on, life was going to start to get better. I was kindly informed I was not alone, one in four people have depression.

That one little statistic lifted me up again. I was going to get better. I was going to be ok.

At the time, depression and mental health were still very much stigmatised and not talked about openly. I thank myself now for being kind to me and accepting the help I so needed. I was given a prescription of antidepressants and I can honestly say that after the first dose, the next morning I was up and out of bed with a hint of a smile. I was going to be ok!

I started to take positive action: I signed up to a gym, hired a PT and made my health my number one priority. I had a life ahead of me that I was going to enjoy and live to the fullest. That PT is still a very good friend and she was pivotal in getting me out of bed and becoming my best self; mind you, I had very little alternative as she was knocking at my front door at 7.30am, three days a week!

Four months into my anti-depressant's prescription, I embarked on Cognitive Behavioural Therapy, crossing over with my medication, which I was gradually reducing the dosage of, as recommended by my GP. The therapy continued for six months, the final four months of which were without the aid of the anti depressants as I had successfully and slowly, with supervision, reduced the dosage to zero.

On my final therapy session, my wonderful therapist commented on the broach pinned on my jacket, it was a cute knitted pink flower. He said it represented me now, I was in full bloom and living life to its fullest.

He wasn't wrong. I was back to me, my inner sparkle was lit and I felt fully empowered, ready to face any challenge and achieve whatever I put my mind to.

That year, I turned thirty and it was one of the best years of my life!

Life is a funny old game, isn't it? There is no manual to let you know how to make the choices that will define your life. There is no end game, no final destination of joy and fulfilment. It is all about the journey.

I always think of Robbie Williams and the line of his same titled song 'No regrets, they don't work', it's true they don't. What would life be like if we never faced adversity? I think it would be a life lived very small and inconsequential, with little to look back upon, hardly memorable for that matter.

I couldn't see where my life was heading during my twenties. I gave up quite a large part of myself: my identity, my inner beliefs and settled for what I thought others expected and desired for me. Turns out, I couldn't have been further from the truth and once I was back to myself those closest to me talked of how they were worried about me and were unsure of how to reach out and help me.

Being depressed really warps reality; they wouldn't have been able to help me because I wasn't able to hear them, I wasn't able to see them, I wasn't able to accept them. Thankfully, that inner strength, that gut instinct found me again and brought me up from the depths.

We all have it; it is innate in us; our gut instinct. This is what needs nurturing, because it is what will allow us to soar to our highest desires of fulfilment.

Often, when I work with women, I ask them what is holding them back? More often than not it is the usual suspects of fear, imposter syndrome, perceived judgement of others and insecurity. All of these are created within us and not given to us, believe me when I say that everyone is way too obsessed with themselves to be worrying about anyone else.

Fear is the biggie here and Jen Sincero puts it this way in her book, 'You are a Badass at Making Money':

> 'When you succumb to fear, you are under the illusion that you can predict the future. We waste so much time letting our fears push us around and half the time, our fears and doubts never even freaking pan out!'

So how can we begin to quieten down that loud voice telling us to be fearful of our desires.

It's pretty simple, it's self-care!

I appreciate self-care is a highly overused buzzword these days but it does work. It doesn't have to mean going for a spa day or a huge shopping spree. Self-care starts with allowing yourself space and inner calm. Dedicating time to re-discover you, your loves, your passions, your desires.

The analogy of the aircraft emergency drill, where you need to put the oxygen mask over your own head first before your child, is totally apt for this. If you're not breathing, the ones you love aren't either. Oxygen is essential to life, to ignite your inner spark, to fire you up.

When you are feeling trapped or low, it can seem an impossibility to even think there is any time to dedicate to yourself and your inner needs. But let's not forget that analogy: if you're not functioning, nothing else will either.

There will always be enough time for what matters.

Once I started to consciously include time for self-care into my daily routine, which for me was movement, aka exercise, I soon realised my little world, and all those within it, were not going to suffer because I took out ten minutes for me. In fact, the opposite happened; the endorphins (happy hormones) that were being released by doing exercise allowed me to look forward, not backwards, and see beyond the confines of what my mind used to believe. It released negative thoughts and systems that I had set in place.

Take a moment now to think about how you could incorporate some self-care into your daily routine? Here's some examples of super simple ways to create space that don't have to take longer than ten minutes (although there is no time limit):

Take a walk and listen to nature.

Write in a journal three things you are grateful for every day.

Sit with a cup of something calming, close your eyes and listen to the sounds around you.

The fear that we carry internally can manifest itself as a form of control, from making sure everything is in a certain order, to micro-managing others' lives. This is detrimental to all involved. After all, we are all born with free will and to dampen that is to deny who we really are.

The next step is gratitude. If there is one takeaway from my story, let it be gratitude, gratitude, gratitude!

Gratitude (you're not going to be able to forget it now!) I now know it is the complimentary companion to movement and the endorphin release. Start to look for gratitude in the smallest things and soon, you won't be able to *not* find gratitude everywhere.

So often I am asked 'what can I be grateful for?' and the answer is, start small. Right now, I am hugely grateful for my alarm clock waking me up so that I could get back to writing this chapter before my children wake up. I am grateful for the wi-fi that is helping me to research quotes and I am grateful for spell check!

We are flipping our thought process from negative to positive. Think of gratitude like a muscle, the more you use it the stronger it gets and, in turn, the happier and more fulfilled you will become. It doesn't cost anything and you can do it anywhere! What's not to love?

Ok, so we've got gratitude nailed, now what? Affirmations! Don't panic and think this is all getting a little bit woo, affirmations have been practiced for like, forever, and we have all heard about how looking in the mirror and saying 'I love you' can change your life. But how do you make it something that is going to work for you?

Again, start small. You can find affirmations-a-plenty with a search on the internet or you can make them up. A favourite of mine and perfect for beginners is 'I am enough'. Say it out loud now, how did that make you feel?

Those three words pack a lot of power and just like practising gratitude, this can be done anywhere, anytime and doesn't cost a penny. So, what's stopping you? I would love you to share your favourite affirmations with me - the more we share the more we grow; the more we share the more we have.

Are you ready to ask the universe? The affirmations are a release to ask the universe what you want. If you think, speak and demonstrate in the negative, you will receive more of that back. Switch it to positive and the universe will respond in kind with more positivity. If you don't ask, you don't get. Have you ever noticed that? If you are always looking at the world through a negative lens, what have you always seen?

How can I possibly ask the universe for what I want? I can't make that change happen, can I? Yes, you can - it all comes from you. YOU are the power that makes change happen and it comes from within.

Grab a notebook/journal and start scribbling what you want, what is good, what you love, what you are grateful for and keep going. This is the first day of the new positive, outward viewing you.

And that is pretty much it, see how you can fit these grounding practices into your daily routine (I promise you; it really is totally doable) and then let it go. Do them and then move on, get on with whatever else you need to do. It's like brushing your teeth, you do it every day; it takes a few moments and then you don't think about it till the next time.

Daily practice wasn't something I had ever heard of, back in the day. For me, the only routine I had was to get out of bed, eat, brush my teeth and think, 'how can I get through the day?'.

If I had been privy to the tools that aided creating a positive structure to my thought patterns, I may have navigated through my twenties very differently.

I had such negative, set-in-stone thought patterns that included imposter syndrome, negative money mindset, a sense of lack in my abilities, fear of judgement, not being good enough and so on. It seemed that was always how it had to be because I didn't know any other way.

The diagnosis of depression and the subsequent medication and therapy helped me to get back to a functioning level of living. Perhaps a daily routine would have prevented that slide into depression from happening.

Remember the muscle of gratitude and positivity? Like any other muscle, it has to be worked on regularly to build strength and resilience - which in turn helps to protect from injury.

My life right now is full of abundance. I love what I do and I love seeing how very simple shifts in how we think can make seismic changes in how we live our lives.

Working with women to help them find the clarity that has eluded them in living their best life is a huge privilege. It is my passion driver. I am living what I am teaching.

I am deeply grateful for the journey I have been on because without those lived experiences, I wouldn't have discovered what I deeply love doing - empowering women to be themselves with ease and flow.

You don't have to take my word for it. The women I have worked with have seen huge shifts in their businesses and their personal lives. Positive daily routines create positive change within all aspects of your life.

'Sarah helped me slow my mind, so I could focus on the individual tasks, rather than constantly viewing it as a whole. She would ask me to set tasks each week and I found that being accountable to her really helped keep me motivated.

I really looked forward to our weekly sessions and cannot thank Sarah enough for helping me reframe the way I think and view my business.' C P, Coaching Client.

'I was in a bit of a bad place mentally when I started, and actually, the coaching was a bit like counselling. Talking through everything really helped clear out the mess and start to work out how to move forward.' F M, Coaching Client.

'Sarah's style of coaching is informal, friendly, relaxing and unintrusive. I found myself opening up to her within the sessions, whilst still feeling very comfortable. Her advice and perspective was insightful and incredibly helpful. I did make progress in some key areas within quite a short amount of time following the coaching sessions I had.' E S, Coaching Client.

In a pretty short period of time, my life has changed from hanging up the washing and thinking there was nothing much to be hopeful about to living my best life on my terms.

I wouldn't have got to this point had I not been on a journey of discovery, so, no regrets, but what changed things was allowing myself to ask for help. I made a choice that was for me and no one else

That simple act, which can feel so mammoth and hard, is the first step to becoming empowered. If you feel stuck and don't know which way to turn; are lost, in overwhelm, then please know you don't have to stay this way.

There is an abundance of help out there waiting for you to receive it. If it helps, let me offer you permission to ask for help right now, to take the action to fully embrace your amazing self and live the abundant life you know you are meant to live.

You know that well used acronym: K.I.S.S. - Keep it simple stupid. It's well used because it's true. We can choose to over complicate or we can choose to simplify. Please choose the latter, it will give you space to gain clarity, which in turn, will allow you to re-discover your inner spark and what your dreams and desires for your life are.

I want to thank you for reading my chapter. I am full of gratitude that you have taken the time to learn about my life (a small part of it anyway - perhaps that means there is a book in me waiting to be written!) and the positive conclusion it has created for me.

My wish is that you can take away the most simple, yet highly effective tools to make your life even more empowering and positive. So here is the re-cap:

You are enough.

Get started with that essential self-care, move your body, write down three things you are grateful for (this list will get longer and longer with every day you do it), say out loud (and proud) your affirmation, ask the universe what you want. Then, let it all go, ready to live life on your terms.

With love and keep shining bright,

Sarah x

ABOUT THE AUTHOR
SARAH WINTERFLOOD

Sarah Winterflood is a female empowerment coach and photographer who helps women break down their fears and embrace being visible, which in turn, allows them to shine bright and work with truly aligned clients.

Before starting her coaching practice, Sarah was an actor, working the London Fringe scene for five years. With a change in creative direction, Sarah has been a freelance photographer for the past fifteen years, working with many businesses and individuals. Sarah now uses her performance knowledge, combined with her photography skills, to empower women to feel confident in front of the lens.

Sarah is an avid reader with a passion for dystopian fiction and also loves skiing, especially the challenging red and black runs!

If you would like to know more about how Sarah can help you gain clarity and stand in your power, you can find her here:

Email - sarah@sarahwinterflood.com
Website - www.sarahwinterflood.com

instagram.com/sarahwinterfloodphoto

22

AFTERWORD
STEP ASIDE & RISE

Thank you so much for investing time in yourself to read these inspiring stories. I hope you've laughed, cried and had some significant food for thought.

And, now what?

What do you want to do now?

You now have an opportunity, a choice, right now today, to do something with this information.

I'd like to invite you to think about what *you* want to create in your life personally and professionally.

What do you want, *or need* to change?

What do you want more, or less of?

What's your heart's desire?

And what's in your way?

Once you've explored this, the next question is, **how do you want to *feel*** in your life and business?

Reflect on the women you've just read about. Their courage, determination and desire to be, have and experience more – stories of adversity, triumph and everything in between.

Here's the thing...they're just like you.

If you want to change something about your life, business or work, perhaps this book will be the catalyst for you to lean into what you really want.

The first step is to give yourself permission to Step Aside & Rise in whichever area of your life you feel you want to level up. The next is reverse engineering from your end goal and plotting out your master plan for how you're going to achieve what you want.

To help motivate you to step into your future self, I've provided a 7-step strategy to get your creative juices flowing and inspire some hands-on action-taking.

Have a look at my 7 essential steps for success to get you on your way. Then, see if you can work through them. Maybe give yourself 6 weeks to implement what resonates with you.

1) You're worth it. **Give yourself permission** to go for it and honour your desires (whatever they are). Commit to achieving what you want as if you were self-parenting yourself. That is, if you were talking to one of your children, follow the advice you would give them, and be as committed to yourself as you would be to them.

2) **Get some support**. Perhaps with a coach, a success community or both – you are the sum of the 5 people you invest your time with daily. If you know you need to switch this up, so you have the right mindset and encouragement around you – do it.

3) Don't give up. **Be tenacious**. You can do hard things and you can go the distance.

Afterword

4) **Create a visual representation** of what you want in your life and put it somewhere you can see it every day. Be it a vision board, video or Pinterest board. If you can see it, you can be it.

Top tip! Whatever you create needs to make you *feel something* when you look at it - ideally, excitement and inspiration of some kind. So, make sure you include visual elements that spark high-frequency emotions within you, like excitement, love, gratitude, happiness and pleasure.

5) **Get grateful**, truly grateful. Gratitude is THE gamechanger. Cultivate daily gratitude where you emotionally connect to what you've got in your life rather than what you haven't. Leaning into appreciation will change so much for you. It's an incredible positive psychology discipline that yields excellent results.

When you are in a state of gratitude, there's no room for fear, and you will have removed the blocks that might keep you stuck so you can move forward. It's scientifically proven that when we are in a state of appreciation, we are happier, more productive and likely to achieve our goals.

6) **Be on purpose**. Work out why you want this change so badly. Is it for more flexibility? Time or financial freedom? Maybe you want a different lifestyle for your health? Perhaps you want to leave a legacy for your children so they can have whatever they want in their lives too.......and you're going to show them the way. Whatever it is, get super intentional about why you're doing what you're doing, feel into it and allow it to propel you forward.

7) Finally, allow yourself to *feel the feelings* of how you would feel, behave and operate if you had what you wanted.

How would your daily life differ from now?

How would you show up?

How would your experience differ from today?

Would you be calmer, happier, healthier, wealthier, more in control, freer? How would this impact your life and the decisions and choices you make? Feel those feelings as often as you can, and switch up your behaviours to match that version of yourself. These two actions are possibly the fastest way you'll bring your vision into being and thrive. Aligning yourself emotionally with what you want in your life and career is the key to breathing life into your heart's desire and unfolding the next chapter in your story.

If you want some support with a gorgeous, aligned group of women, including the badasses you've met in this book, please come and join my free Facebook Success community – <u>Women Who Choose Higher</u>. Come and access some free resources to help you bring into life what you want and get you on the path to your success, whatever that looks like for you. You are most welcome.

If you're serious about making a change in your business, head over to <u>www.andreacallanan.com/successbundle</u> for a set of free resources to get you kick started.

And don't forget. Ultimately, you're the only one responsible for your behaviour, happiness, and success in your life and career.

You *have* got this. Get intentional, get on purpose and allow yourself to Step Aside & Rise.

We'll be waiting!

ABOUT THE CURATOR

Entrepreneur, Voice, Mindset & Business Coach, Andrea Callanan is passionate about helping people and businesses find their confidence and their voice.

Over nearly 3 decades, she has helped tens of thousands start and grow businesses, become singers, speakers, leaders and find their self-worth.

Hailing from Barry in South Wales, married to Matt Callanan and mother to two boys, a singer by trade, and later a Music Industry Voice Coach and record Label owner, Andrea now speaks, coaches, writes and helps others succeed in their professional lives.

A certified Positive Psychology Coach, Andrea has worked in the workplace happiness space with many global brands over the past decade, specializing in culture, workplace engagement and leadership.

She supports high achieving women and entrepreneurs internationally with their mindset, aligned business growth, visibility and speaking skills with multiple online offerings and 121 coaching.

These include her Institute of Leadership accredited Aligned Coaching Academy and her gold standard mindset and business course, The Unapologetic Self Mastery Accelerator, which is part of her Unapologetic Business Accelerator.

She is co-founder of the Real Women's Business Mastermind and also provides the Aligned Performance Business membership which includes a range of product offerings to support female entrepreneurs with their mindset and wellbeing, including a monthly subscription membership box and beautiful card decks.

As a musician-turned-entrepreneur with a top 4 charting business podcast, Creating Superstars at Work, and quoted in international press alongside influencers such as Gary Veynerchuk and Tai Lopez, Andrea is a vibrant motivational speaker worldwide. She has shared the stage with the likes of Simon Sinek, Sara Blakely, Niyc Pidgeon and Natalie Ellis to name a few.

She has been personally invited along with 40 other international female entrepreneurs to attend Necker Island to mastermind with Sir Richard Branson.

Named as a top 25 inspirational Welsh woman. Andrea is a small business Guardian Leader of the year. Great British Entrepreneur of the Year finalist and an Insider Magazine Rising Star. She is also a contributing member of the esteemed Forbes Coaches Council. She's a co- author of the number 1 International Business Best Seller "You Are Meant For More".

Forbes Entrepreneur CNBC BBC YAHOO! FINANCE Money
BUSINESS INSIDER THRIVE GLOBAL HUFFPOST BOSSBABE GOOD MORNING LALALAND

ANDREA CALLANAN
realise your true voice

Andreacallanan.com

facebook.com/AndreaCallananVoice
twitter.com/Andrea_Callanan
instagram.com/AndreaCallananVoice
pinterest.com/AndreaCallananVoice
youtube.com/AndreaCallananTV

Printed in Great Britain
by Amazon